WITHDRAWN

DANA LAFUENTE

C.S. PACAT

FENCE ™

RIVALS

Published by

BOOM! BOX™

BOOM! BOX™

FENCE: RIVALS, October 2021. Published by BOOM! Box, a division of Boom Entertainment, Inc. Fence is ™ & © 2021 C.S. Pacat. All rights reserved. BOOM! Box™ and the BOOM! Box logo are trademarks of Boom Entertainment, Inc., registered in various countries and categories. All characters, events, and institutions depicted herein are fictional. Any similarity between any of the names, characters, persons, events, and/or institutions in this publication to actual names, characters, and persons, whether living or dead, events, and/or institutions is unintended and purely coincidental. BOOM! Studios does not read or accept unsolicited submissions of ideas, stories, or artwork.

BOOM! Studios, 5670 Wilshire Boulevard, Suite 400, Los Angeles, CA 90036-5679. Printed in China. Second Printing.

ISBN: 978-1-68415-538-5, eISBN: 978-1-64144-704-1

MIRABILE VINCULUM

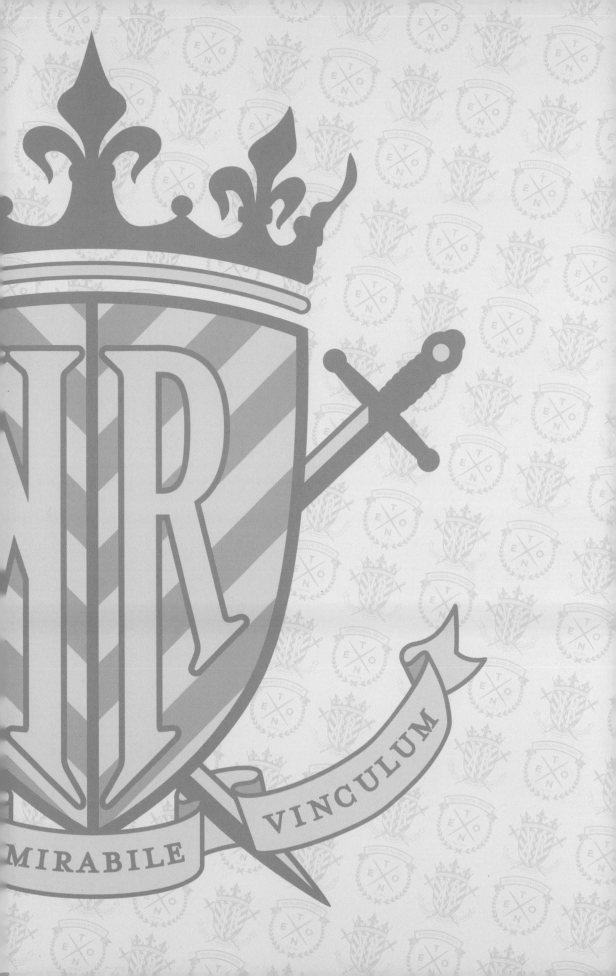

EXCELLENTIA VI

T

E

N

EST. 1874

WRITTEN BY
C.S. PACAT

ILLUSTRATED BY
JOHANNA THE MAD

COLORS BY
JOANA LAFUENTE

LETTERS BY
JIM CAMPBELL
WITH TAYLOR ESPOSITO

TECHNICAL CONSULTANT
PIETER LEEUWENBURGH

SCHOOL LOGO DESIGNS
FAWN LAU

COVER BY
JOHANNA THE MAD

DESIGNERS
JILLIAN CRAB & CHELSEA ROBERTS

ASSOCIATE EDITOR
SOPHIE PHILIPS-ROBERTS

EDITOR
SHANNON WATTERS

CREATED BY
C.S. PACAT & JOHANNA THE MAD

UNITATIS MIRABILE VINCULUM

CHAPTER THIRTEEN

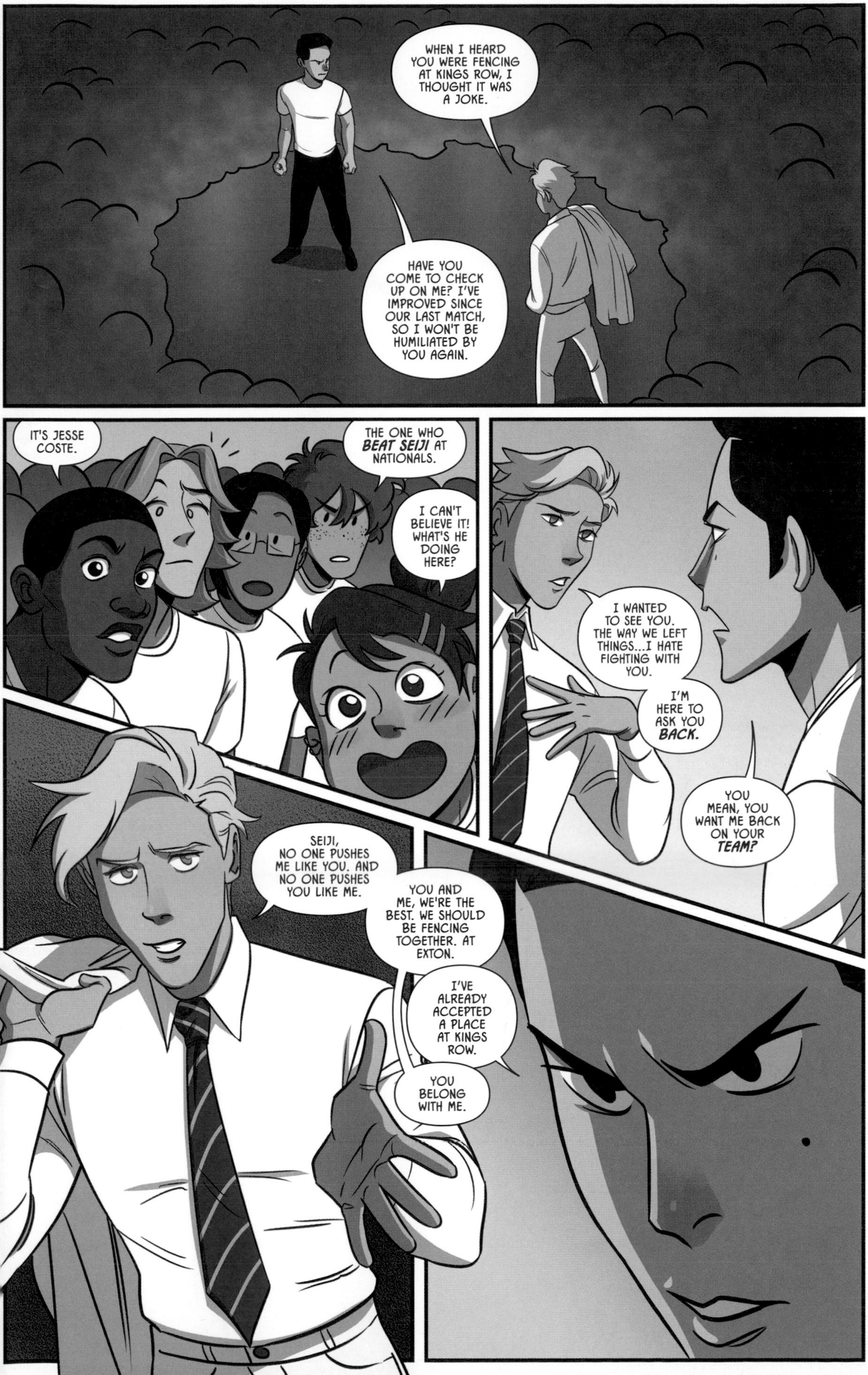
WHEN I HEARD YOU WERE FENCING AT KINGS ROW, I THOUGHT IT WAS A JOKE.
HAVE YOU COME TO CHECK UP ON ME? I'VE IMPROVED SINCE OUR LAST MATCH, SO I WON'T BE HUMILIATED BY YOU AGAIN.
IT'S JESSE COSTE.
THE ONE WHO ***BEAT SEIJI*** AT NATIONALS.
I CAN'T BELIEVE IT! WHAT'S HE DOING HERE?
I WANTED TO SEE YOU. THE WAY WE LEFT THINGS...I HATE FIGHTING WITH YOU.
I'M HERE TO ASK YOU ***BACK.***
YOU MEAN, YOU WANT ME BACK ON YOUR ***TEAM?***
SEIJI, NO ONE PUSHES ME LIKE YOU. AND NO ONE PUSHES YOU LIKE ME.
YOU AND ME, WE'RE THE BEST. WE SHOULD BE FENCING TOGETHER. AT EXTON.
I'VE ALREADY ACCEPTED A PLACE AT KINGS ROW.
YOU BELONG WITH ME.

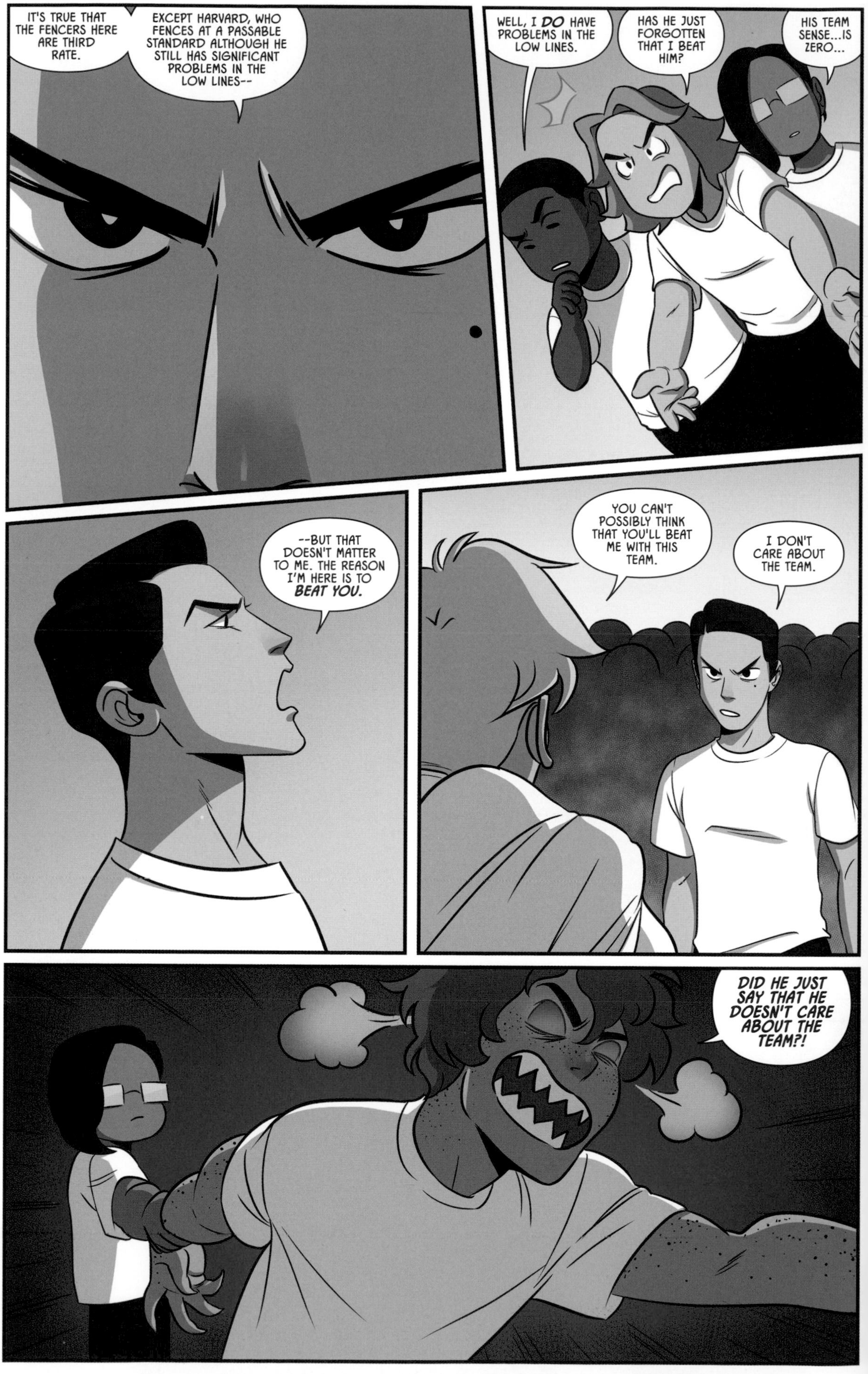
IT'S TRUE THAT THE FENCERS HERE ARE THIRD RATE.
EXCEPT HARVARD, WHO FENCES AT A PASSABLE STANDARD ALTHOUGH HE STILL HAS SIGNIFICANT PROBLEMS IN THE LOW LINES--
WELL, I DO HAVE PROBLEMS IN THE LOW LINES.
HAS HE JUST FORGOTTEN THAT I BEAT HIM?
HIS TEAM SENSE...IS ZERO...
--BUT THAT DOESN'T MATTER TO ME. THE REASON I'M HERE IS TO BEAT YOU.
YOU CAN'T POSSIBLY THINK THAT YOU'LL BEAT ME WITH THIS TEAM.
I DON'T CARE ABOUT THE TEAM.
DID HE JUST SAY THAT HE DOESN'T CARE ABOUT THE TEAM?!

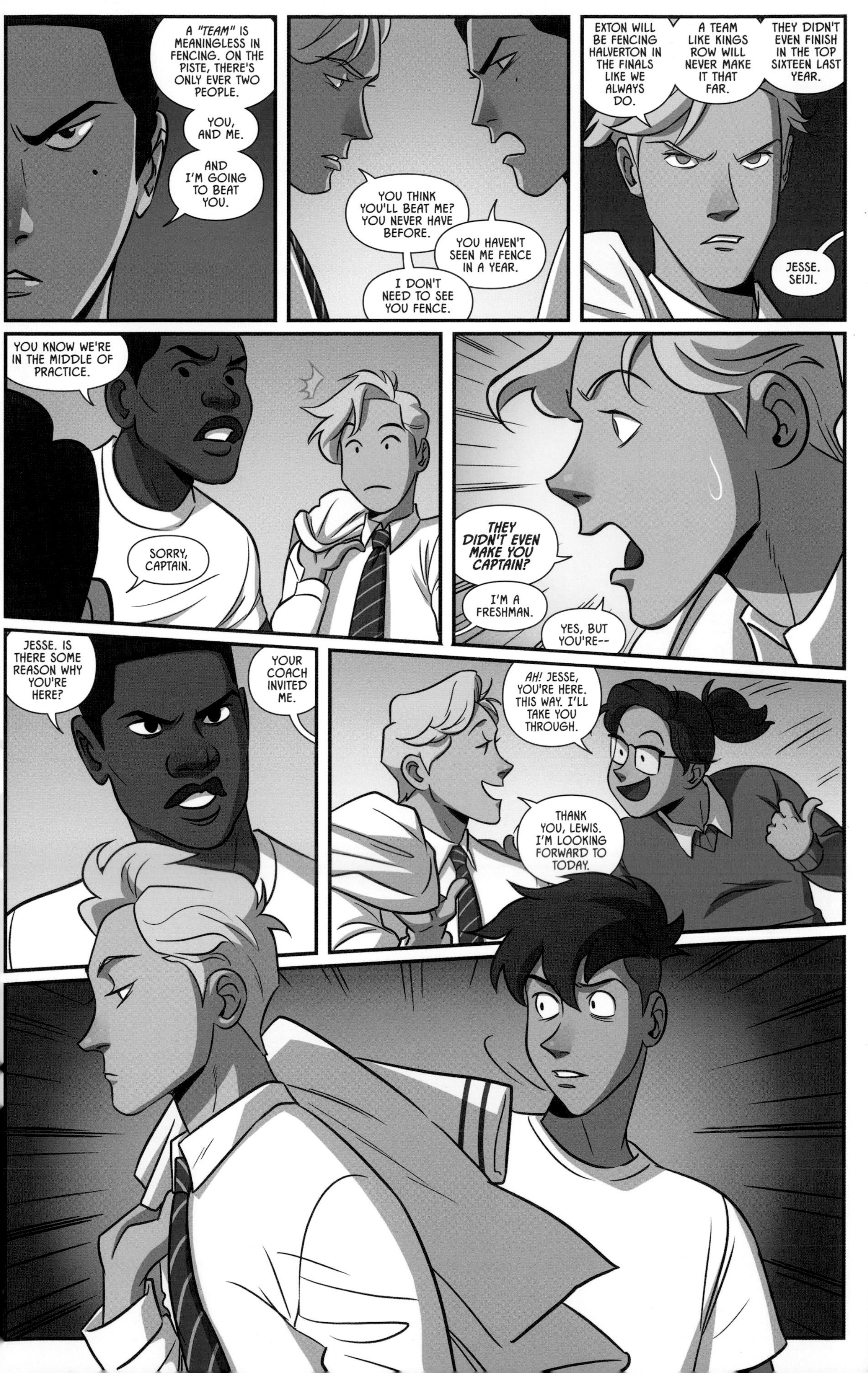
A "TEAM" IS MEANINGLESS IN FENCING. ON THE PISTE, THERE'S ONLY EVER TWO PEOPLE.
YOU, AND ME.
AND I'M GOING TO BEAT YOU.
YOU THINK YOU'LL BEAT ME? YOU NEVER HAVE BEFORE.
YOU HAVEN'T SEEN ME FENCE IN A YEAR.
I DON'T NEED TO SEE YOU FENCE.
EXTON WILL BE FENCING HALVERTON IN THE FINALS LIKE WE ALWAYS DO.
A TEAM LIKE KINGS ROW WILL NEVER MAKE IT THAT FAR.
THEY DIDN'T EVEN FINISH IN THE TOP SIXTEEN LAST YEAR.
JESSE. SEIJI.
YOU KNOW WE'RE IN THE MIDDLE OF PRACTICE.
SORRY, CAPTAIN.
THEY DIDN'T EVEN MAKE YOU CAPTAIN?
I'M A FRESHMAN.
YES, BUT YOU'RE--
JESSE. IS THERE SOME REASON WHY YOU'RE HERE?
YOUR COACH INVITED ME.
AH! JESSE, YOU'RE HERE. THIS WAY. I'LL TAKE YOU THROUGH.
THANK YOU, LEWIS. I'M LOOKING FORWARD TO TODAY.

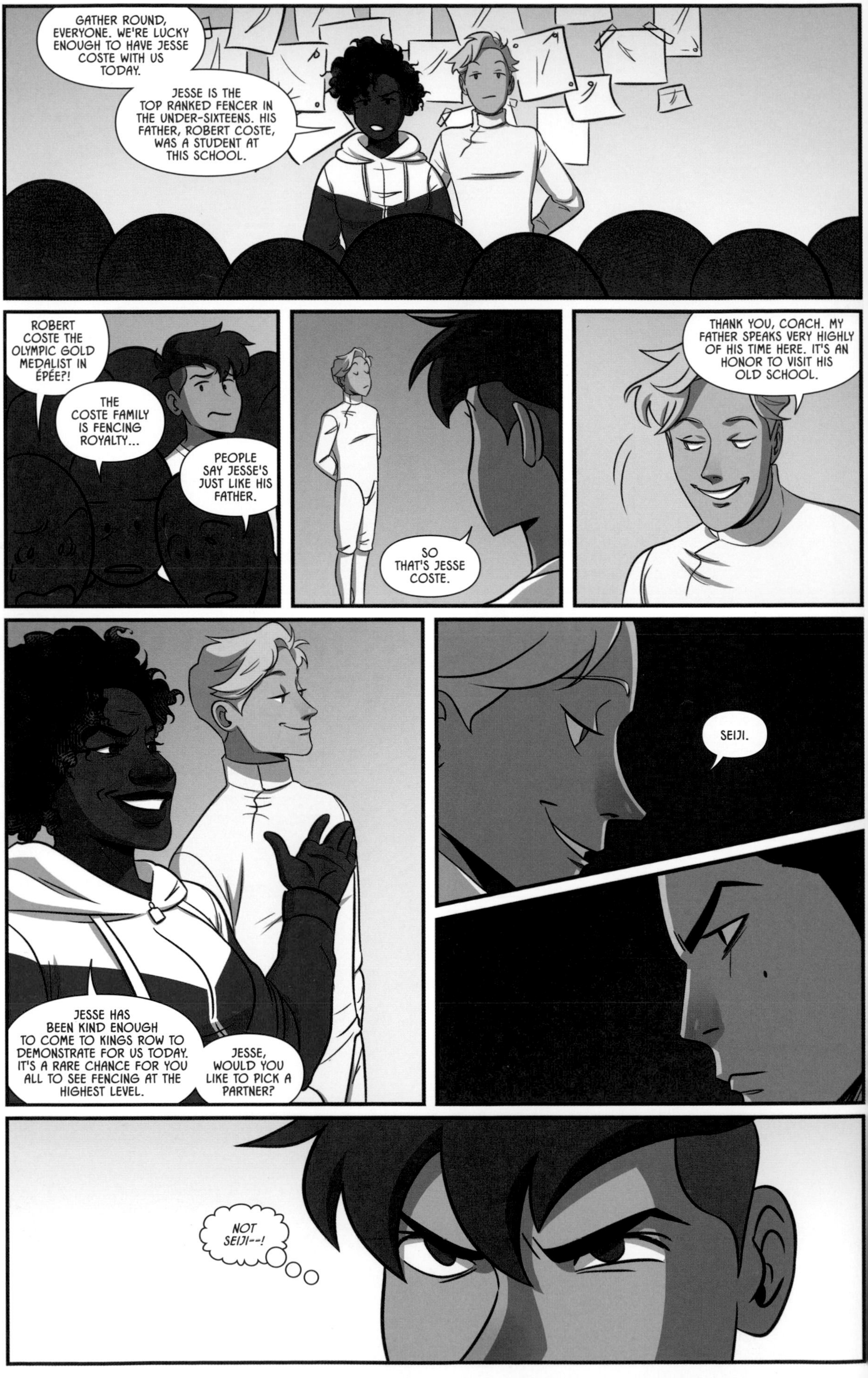
GATHER ROUND, EVERYONE. WE'RE LUCKY ENOUGH TO HAVE JESSE COSTE WITH US TODAY.
JESSE IS THE TOP RANKED FENCER IN THE UNDER-SIXTEENS. HIS FATHER, ROBERT COSTE, WAS A STUDENT AT THIS SCHOOL.
ROBERT COSTE THE OLYMPIC GOLD MEDALIST IN ÉPÉE?!
THE COSTE FAMILY IS FENCING ROYALTY...
PEOPLE SAY JESSE'S JUST LIKE HIS FATHER.
SO THAT'S JESSE COSTE.
THANK YOU, COACH. MY FATHER SPEAKS VERY HIGHLY OF HIS TIME HERE. IT'S AN HONOR TO VISIT HIS OLD SCHOOL.
JESSE HAS BEEN KIND ENOUGH TO COME TO KINGS ROW TO DEMONSTRATE FOR US TODAY. IT'S A RARE CHANCE FOR YOU ALL TO SEE FENCING AT THE HIGHEST LEVEL.
JESSE, WOULD YOU LIKE TO PICK A PARTNER?
SEIJI.
NOT SEIJI--!

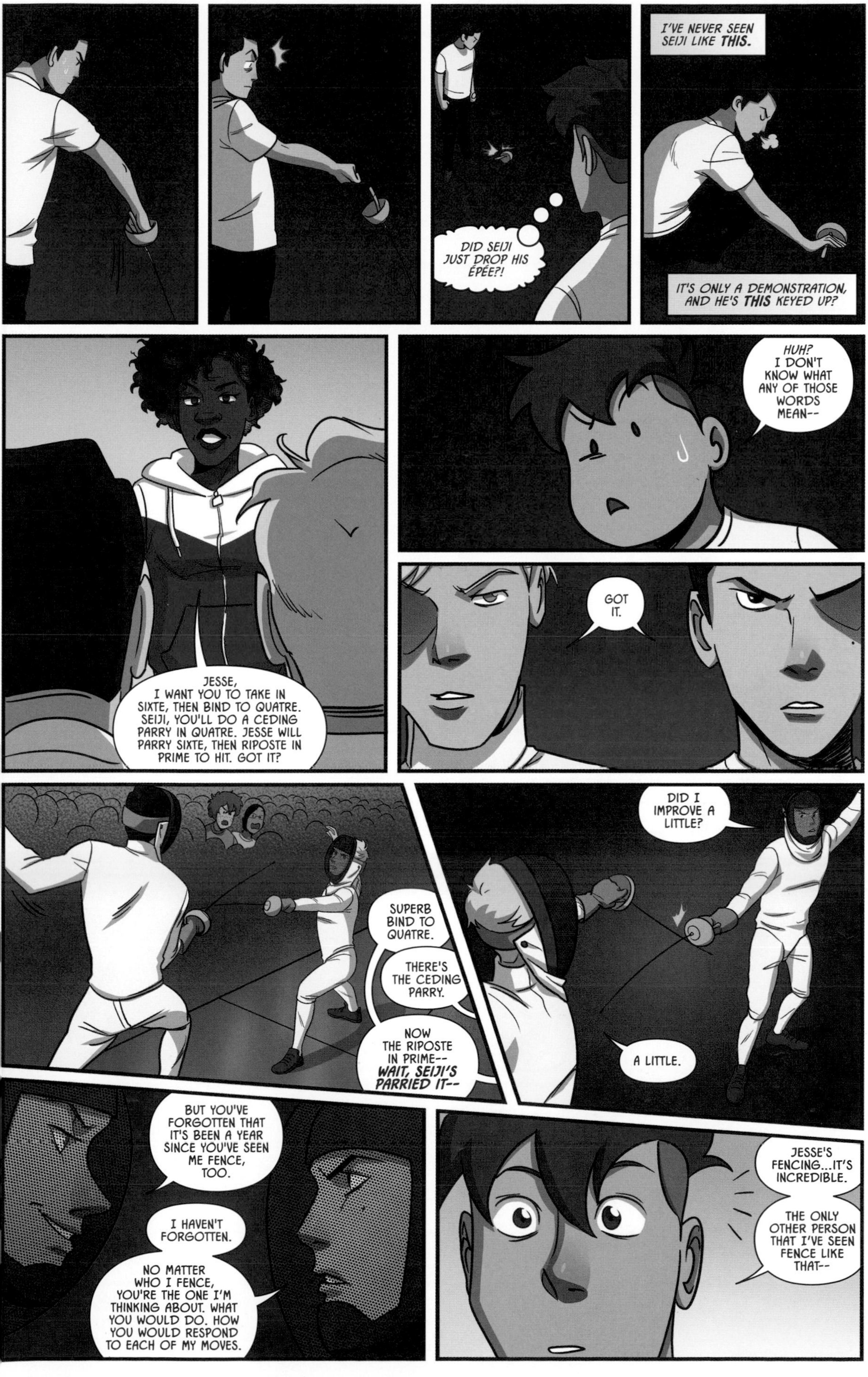
DID SEIJI JUST DROP HIS ÉPÉE?!
I'VE NEVER SEEN SEIJI LIKE THIS.
IT'S ONLY A DEMONSTRATION, AND HE'S THIS KEYED UP?
JESSE, I WANT YOU TO TAKE IN SIXTE, THEN BIND TO QUATRE. SEIJI, YOU'LL DO A CEDING PARRY IN QUATRE. JESSE WILL PARRY SIXTE, THEN RIPOSTE IN PRIME TO HIT. GOT IT?
HUH? I DON'T KNOW WHAT ANY OF THOSE WORDS MEAN--
GOT IT.
SUPERB BIND TO QUATRE.
THERE'S THE CEDING PARRY.
NOW THE RIPOSTE IN PRIME-- WAIT, SEIJI'S PARRIED IT--
DID I IMPROVE A LITTLE?
A LITTLE.
BUT YOU'VE FORGOTTEN THAT IT'S BEEN A YEAR SINCE YOU'VE SEEN ME FENCE, TOO.
I HAVEN'T FORGOTTEN.
NO MATTER WHO I FENCE, YOU'RE THE ONE I'M THINKING ABOUT. WHAT YOU WOULD DO. HOW YOU WOULD RESPOND TO EACH OF MY MOVES.
JESSE'S FENCING...IT'S INCREDIBLE.
THE ONLY OTHER PERSON THAT I'VE SEEN FENCE LIKE THAT--

--IS SEIJI.

ALL RIGHT, NOW LET'S TRY IT WITH YOUR POSITIONS REVERSED--

EVEN THOUGH IT'S JUST A DEMONSTRATION... THERE'S NO DOUBT THAT THEY'RE TESTING EACH OTHER.

IS THAT WHAT THEY'RE DOING?

PARRY!

SORRY, COACH!

JESSE...YOU WERE SUPPOSED TO LET THAT LAST HIT THROUGH.

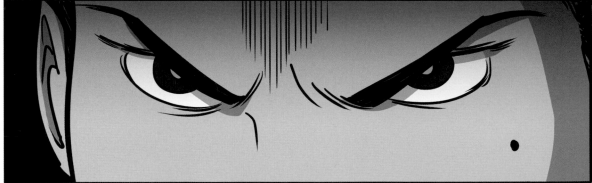

WOW, THOSE TWO ARE ON A TOTALLY DIFFERENT LEVEL.

SO, THIS IS WHAT IT MEANS TO BE THE TWO BEST FENCERS IN THE COUNTRY.

RIGHT? THERE'S NO ONE ELSE EVEN CLOSE TO THEM.

NO ONE ELSE EVEN CLOSE...

NICHOLAS? ARE YOU OKAY?

YEAH, I JUST... I NEVER SAW THEM FENCE TOGETHER BEFORE.

AREN'T THEY AMAZING?! THEY'RE LIGHT-YEARS AHEAD OF EVERYONE ELSE IN THEIR AGE BRACKET.

I GUESS THAT'S WHAT A LIFETIME OF TRAINING LOOKS LIKE.

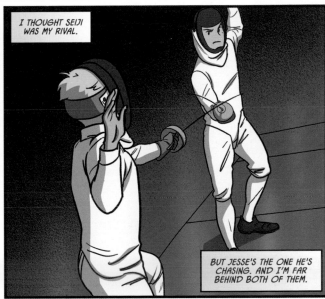

I THOUGHT SEIJI WAS MY RIVAL.

BUT JESSE'S THE ONE HE'S CHASING. AND I'M FAR BEHIND BOTH OF THEM.

I'M SO FAR AHEAD OF YOU I'M SURPRISED YOU CAN SEE ME AT ALL.

SEIJI WAS RIGHT. BACK THEN, I COULDN'T SEE HIM CLEARLY.

BACK THEN, I DIDN'T UNDERSTAND--

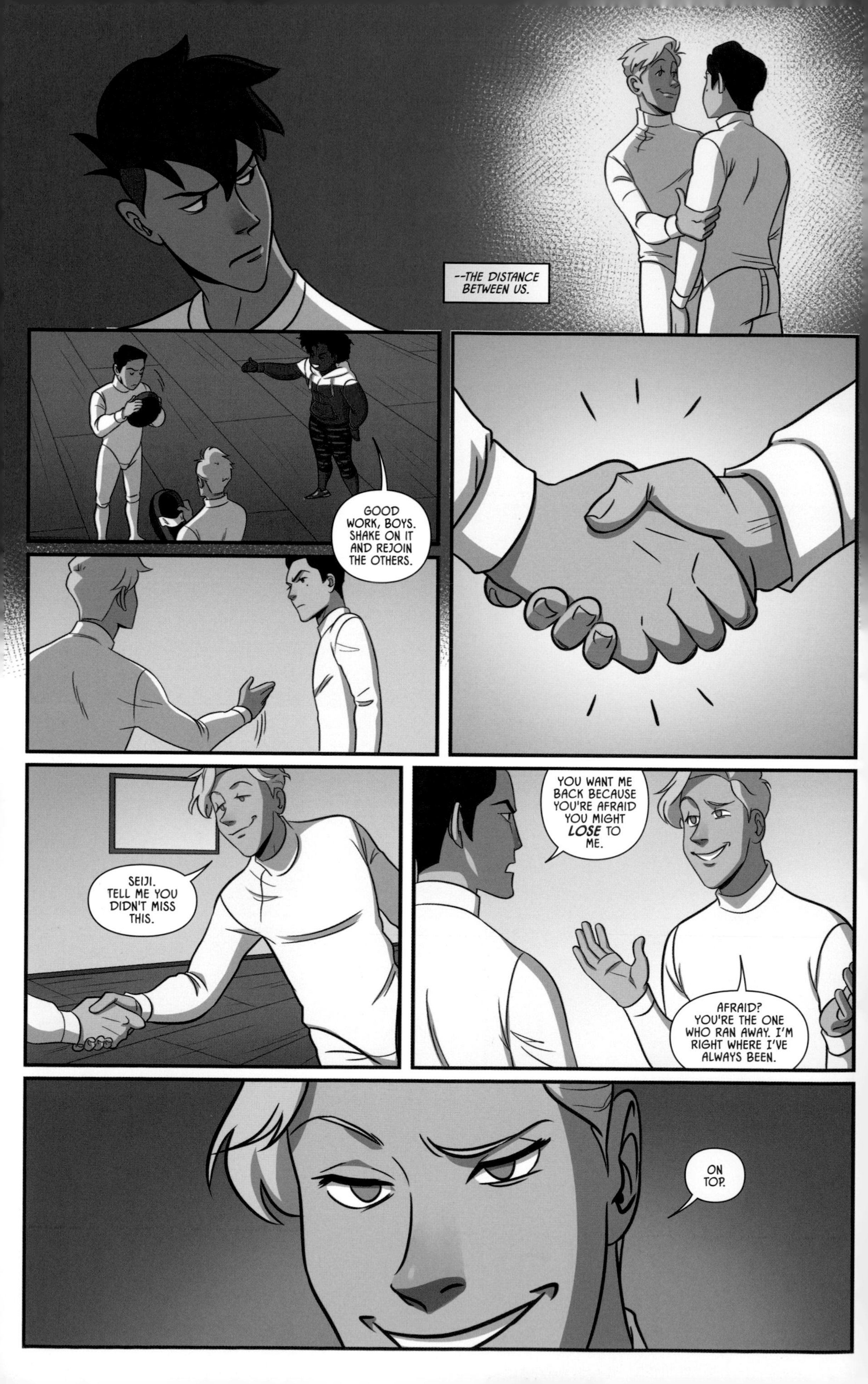
--THE DISTANCE BETWEEN US.
GOOD WORK, BOYS. SHAKE ON IT AND REJOIN THE OTHERS.
SEIJI. TELL ME YOU DIDN'T MISS THIS.
YOU WANT ME BACK BECAUSE YOU'RE AFRAID YOU MIGHT LOSE TO ME.
AFRAID? YOU'RE THE ONE WHO RAN AWAY. I'M RIGHT WHERE I'VE ALWAYS BEEN.
ON TOP.

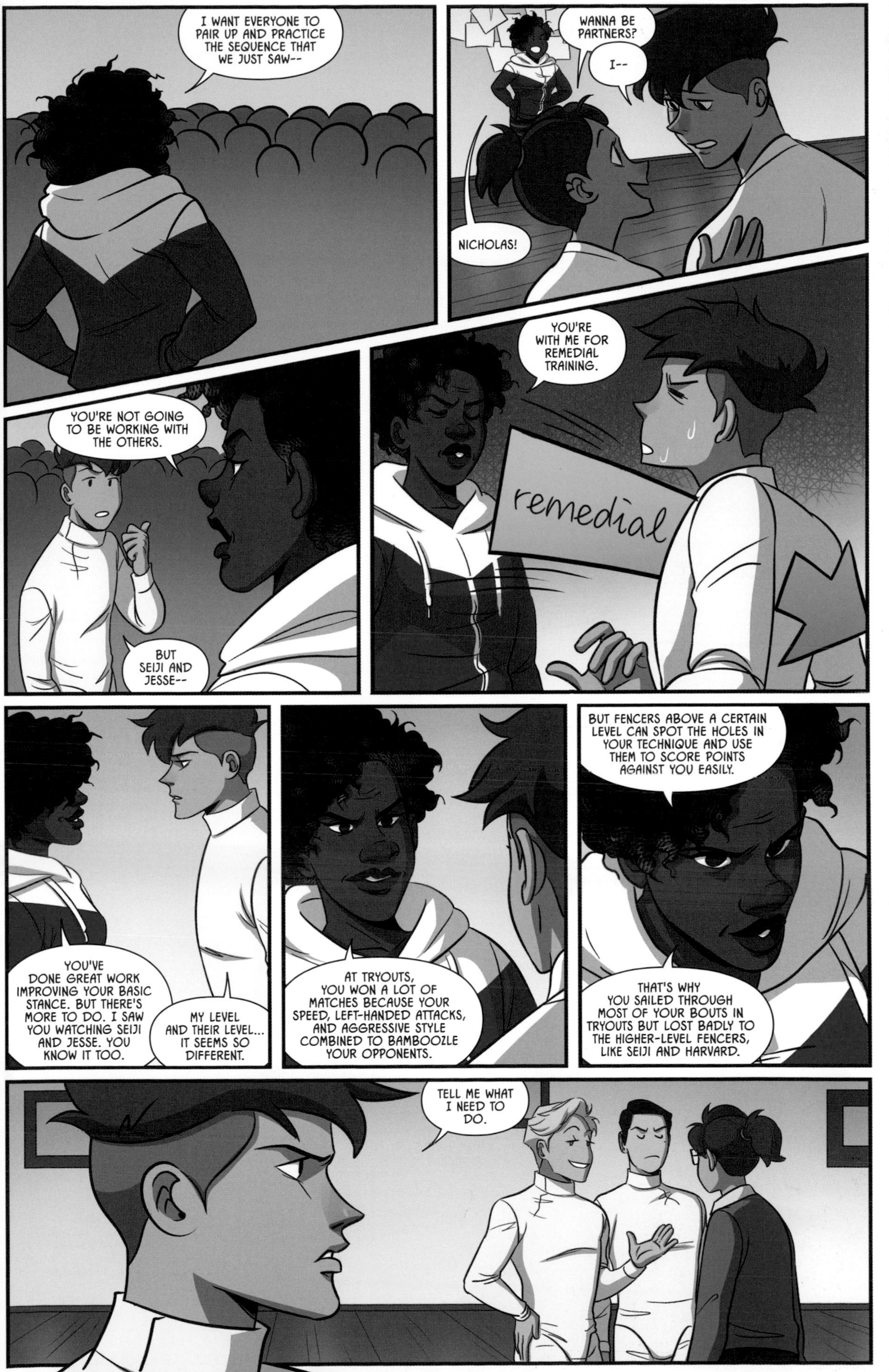
I WANT EVERYONE TO PAIR UP AND PRACTICE THE SEQUENCE THAT WE JUST SAW--
WANNA BE PARTNERS?
I--
NICHOLAS!
YOU'RE NOT GOING TO BE WORKING WITH THE OTHERS.
BUT SEIJI AND JESSE--
YOU'RE WITH ME FOR REMEDIAL TRAINING.
remedial
YOU'VE DONE GREAT WORK IMPROVING YOUR BASIC STANCE. BUT THERE'S MORE TO DO. I SAW YOU WATCHING SEIJI AND JESSE. YOU KNOW IT TOO.
MY LEVEL AND THEIR LEVEL... IT SEEMS SO DIFFERENT.
AT TRYOUTS, YOU WON A LOT OF MATCHES BECAUSE YOUR SPEED, LEFT-HANDED ATTACKS, AND AGGRESSIVE STYLE COMBINED TO BAMBOOZLE YOUR OPPONENTS.
BUT FENCERS ABOVE A CERTAIN LEVEL CAN SPOT THE HOLES IN YOUR TECHNIQUE AND USE THEM TO SCORE POINTS AGAINST YOU EASILY.
THAT'S WHY YOU SAILED THROUGH MOST OF YOUR BOUTS IN TRYOUTS BUT LOST BADLY TO THE HIGHER-LEVEL FENCERS, LIKE SEIJI AND HARVARD.
TELL ME WHAT I NEED TO DO.

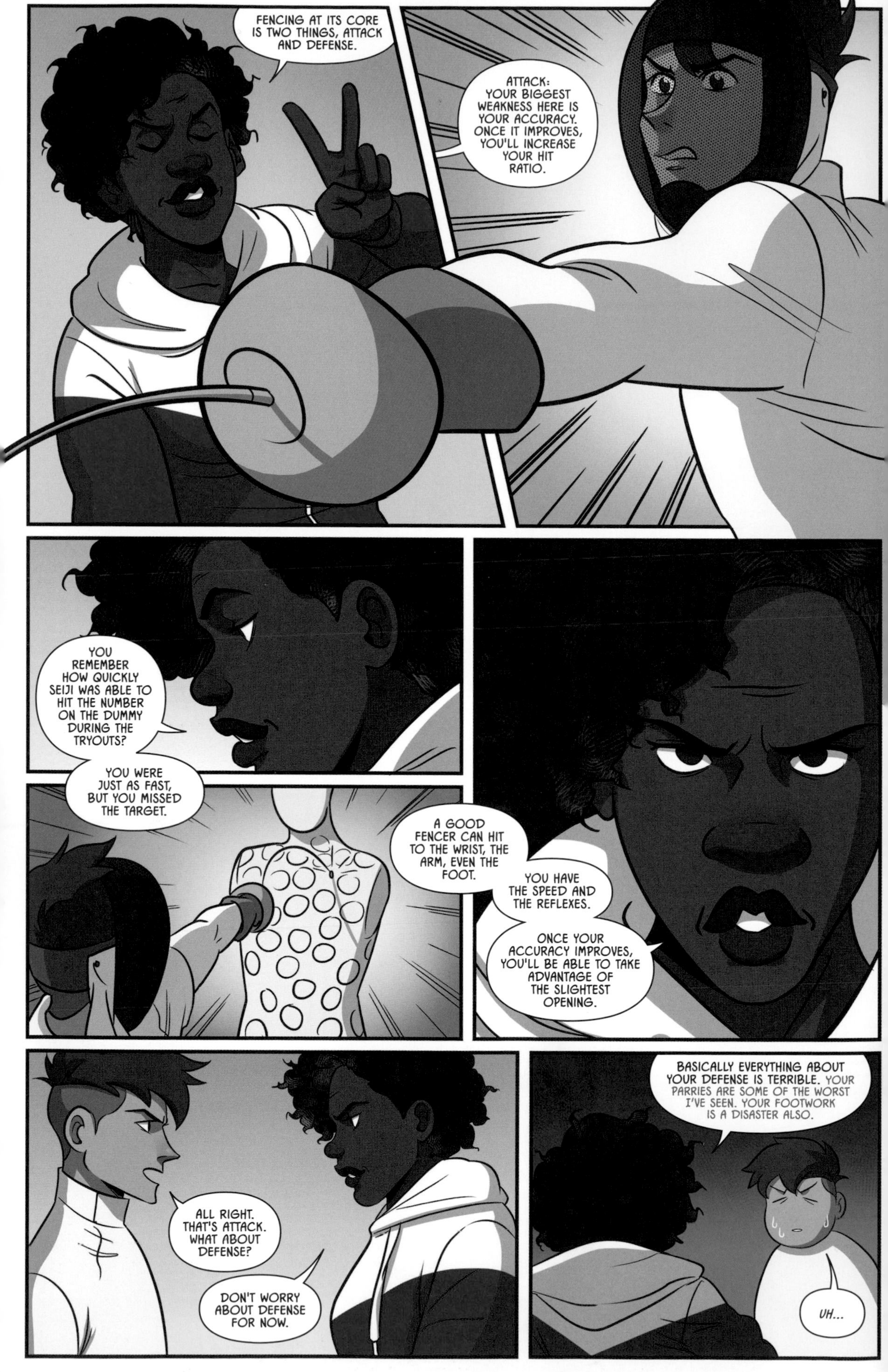

FENCING AT ITS CORE IS TWO THINGS, ATTACK AND DEFENSE.
ATTACK: YOUR BIGGEST WEAKNESS HERE IS YOUR ACCURACY. ONCE IT IMPROVES, YOU'LL INCREASE YOUR HIT RATIO.
YOU REMEMBER HOW QUICKLY SEIJI WAS ABLE TO HIT THE NUMBER ON THE DUMMY DURING THE TRYOUTS?
YOU WERE JUST AS FAST, BUT YOU MISSED THE TARGET.
A GOOD FENCER CAN HIT TO THE WRIST, THE ARM, EVEN THE FOOT.
YOU HAVE THE SPEED AND THE REFLEXES.
ONCE YOUR ACCURACY IMPROVES, YOU'LL BE ABLE TO TAKE ADVANTAGE OF THE SLIGHTEST OPENING.
ALL RIGHT. THAT'S ATTACK. WHAT ABOUT DEFENSE?
DON'T WORRY ABOUT DEFENSE FOR NOW.
BASICALLY EVERYTHING ABOUT YOUR DEFENSE IS TERRIBLE. YOUR PARRIES ARE SOME OF THE WORST I'VE SEEN. YOUR FOOTWORK IS A DISASTER ALSO.
UH...

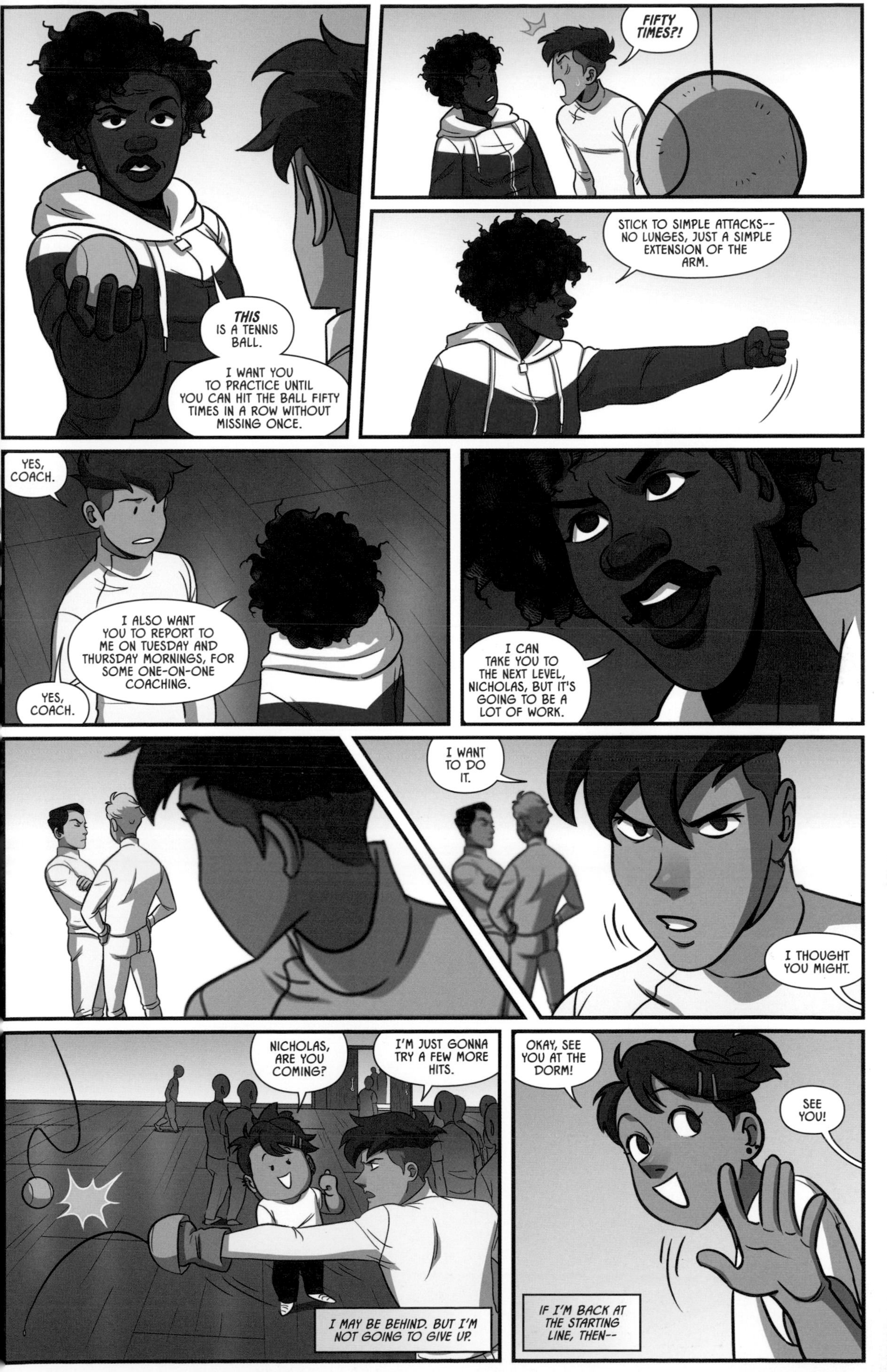
THIS IS A TENNIS BALL.
I WANT YOU TO PRACTICE UNTIL YOU CAN HIT THE BALL FIFTY TIMES IN A ROW WITHOUT MISSING ONCE.
FIFTY TIMES?!
STICK TO SIMPLE ATTACKS-- NO LUNGES, JUST A SIMPLE EXTENSION OF THE ARM.
YES, COACH.
I ALSO WANT YOU TO REPORT TO ME ON TUESDAY AND THURSDAY MORNINGS, FOR SOME ONE-ON-ONE COACHING.
YES, COACH.
I CAN TAKE YOU TO THE NEXT LEVEL, NICHOLAS, BUT IT'S GOING TO BE A LOT OF WORK.
I WANT TO DO IT.
I THOUGHT YOU MIGHT.
NICHOLAS, ARE YOU COMING?
I'M JUST GONNA TRY A FEW MORE HITS.
I MAY BE BEHIND. BUT I'M NOT GOING TO GIVE UP.
OKAY, SEE YOU AT THE DORM!
SEE YOU!
IF I'M BACK AT THE STARTING LINE, THEN--

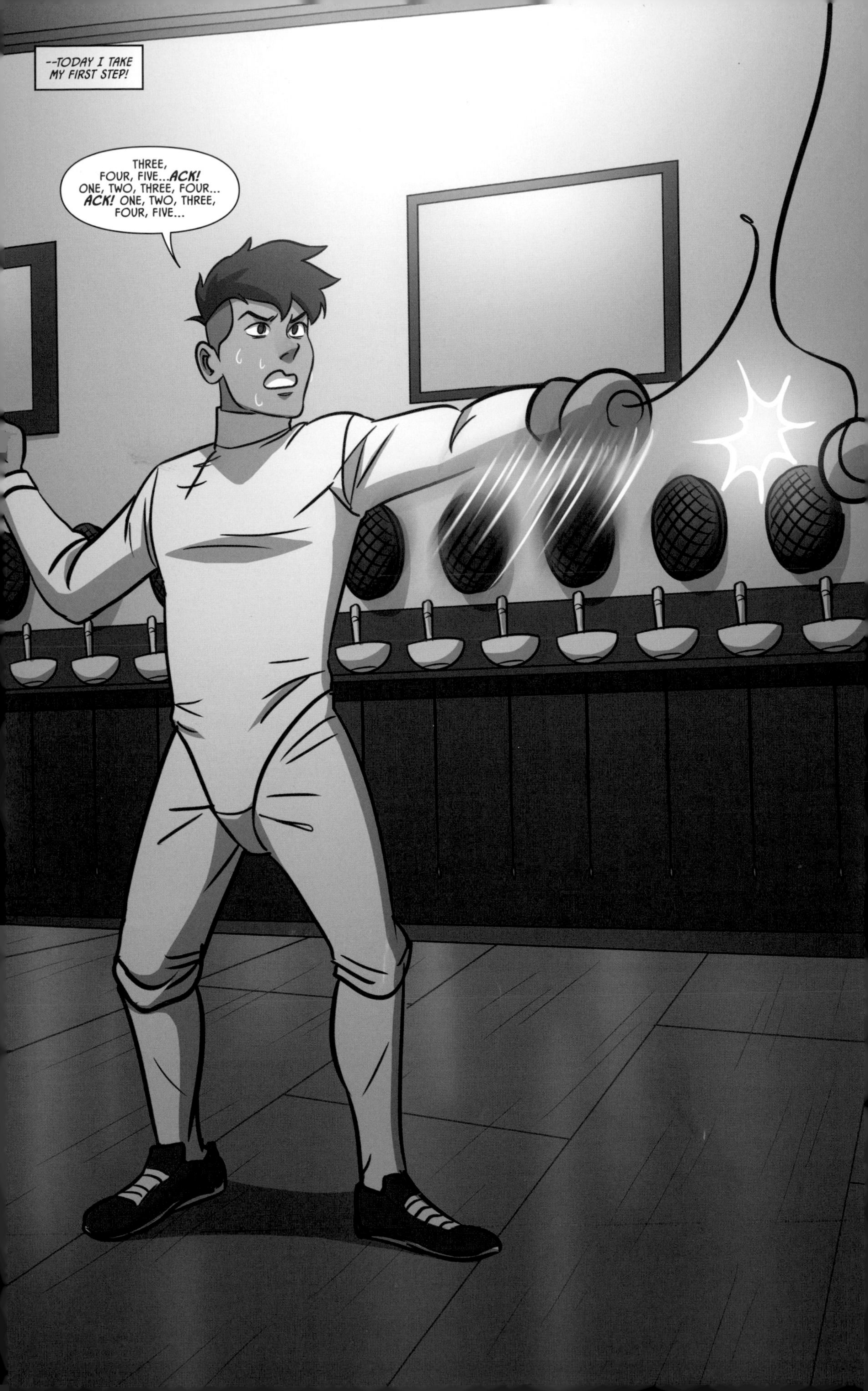
--TODAY I TAKE MY FIRST STEP!
THREE, FOUR, FIVE...ACK! ONE, TWO, THREE, FOUR... ACK! ONE, TWO, THREE, FOUR, FIVE...

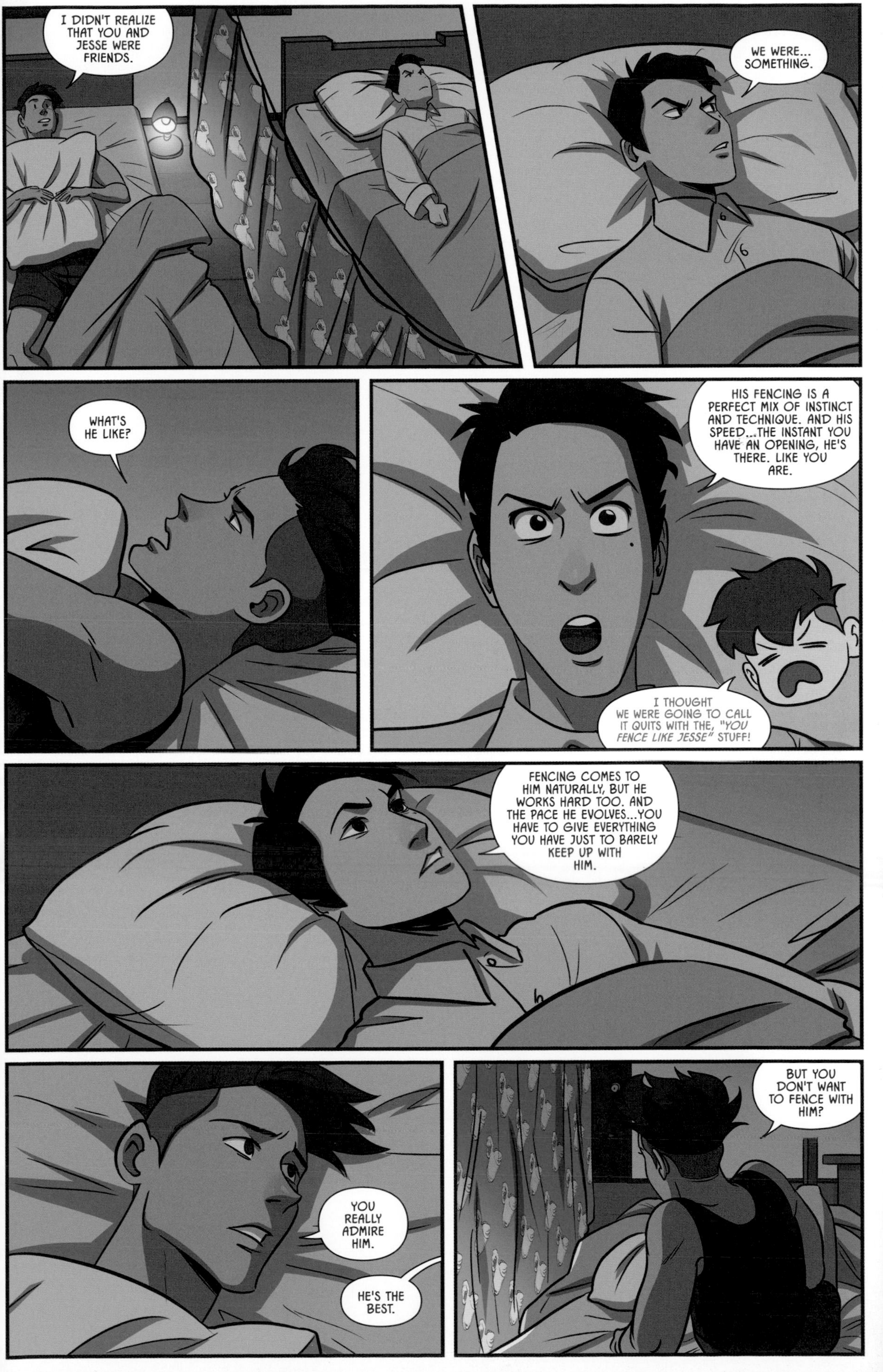
I DIDN'T REALIZE THAT YOU AND JESSE WERE FRIENDS.
WE WERE... SOMETHING.
WHAT'S HE LIKE?
HIS FENCING IS A PERFECT MIX OF INSTINCT AND TECHNIQUE. AND HIS SPEED...THE INSTANT YOU HAVE AN OPENING, HE'S THERE. LIKE YOU ARE.
I THOUGHT WE WERE GOING TO CALL IT QUITS WITH THE, *"YOU FENCE LIKE JESSE"* STUFF!
FENCING COMES TO HIM NATURALLY, BUT HE WORKS HARD TOO. AND THE PACE HE EVOLVES...YOU HAVE TO GIVE EVERYTHING YOU HAVE JUST TO BARELY KEEP UP WITH HIM.
YOU REALLY ADMIRE HIM.
HE'S THE BEST.
BUT YOU DON'T WANT TO FENCE WITH HIM?

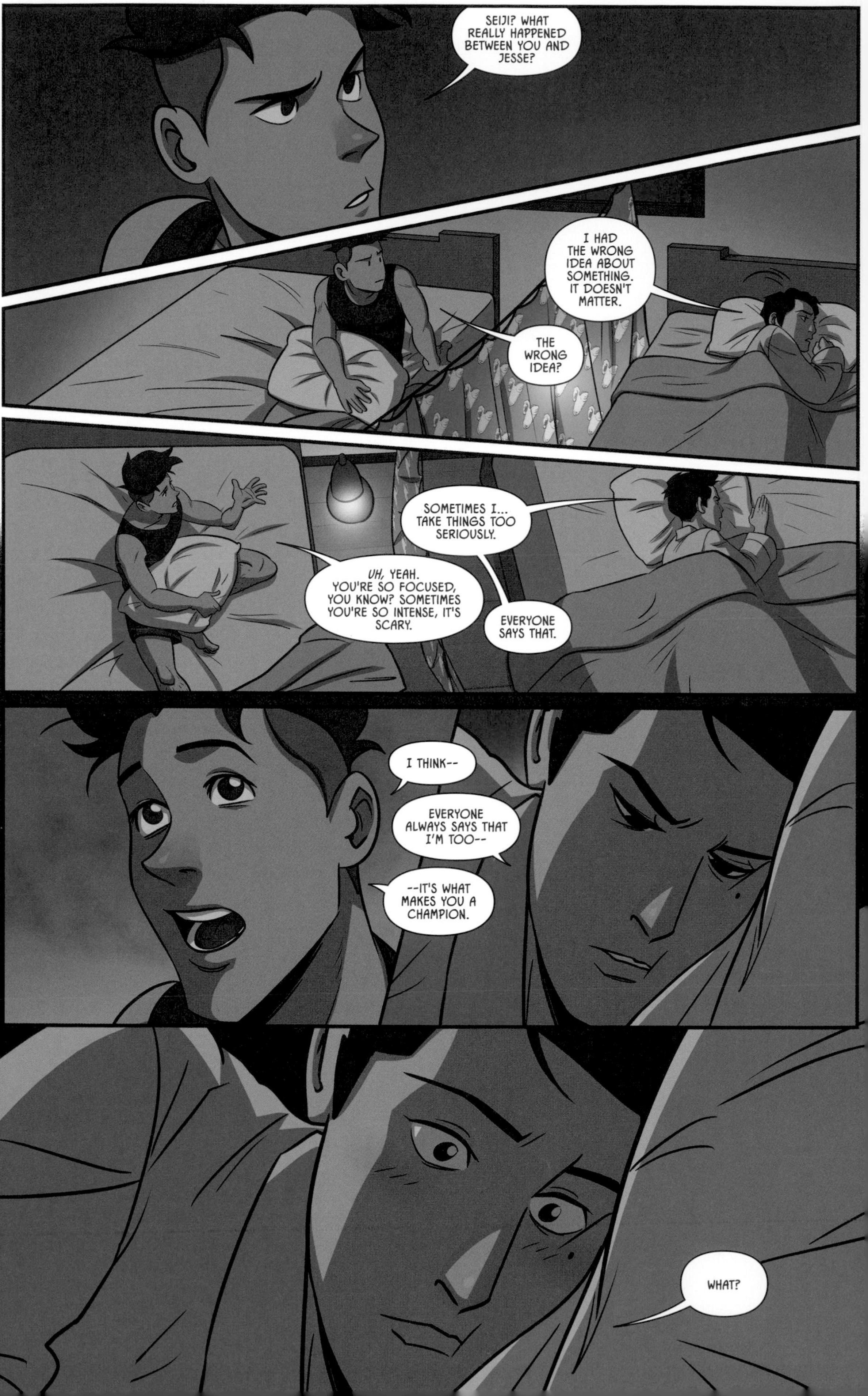
SEIJI? WHAT REALLY HAPPENED BETWEEN YOU AND JESSE?
I HAD THE WRONG IDEA ABOUT SOMETHING. IT DOESN'T MATTER.
THE WRONG IDEA?
SOMETIMES I... TAKE THINGS TOO SERIOUSLY.
UH, YEAH. YOU'RE SO FOCUSED, YOU KNOW? SOMETIMES YOU'RE SO INTENSE, IT'S SCARY.
EVERYONE SAYS THAT.
I THINK--
EVERYONE ALWAYS SAYS THAT I'M TOO--
--IT'S WHAT MAKES YOU A CHAMPION.
WHAT?

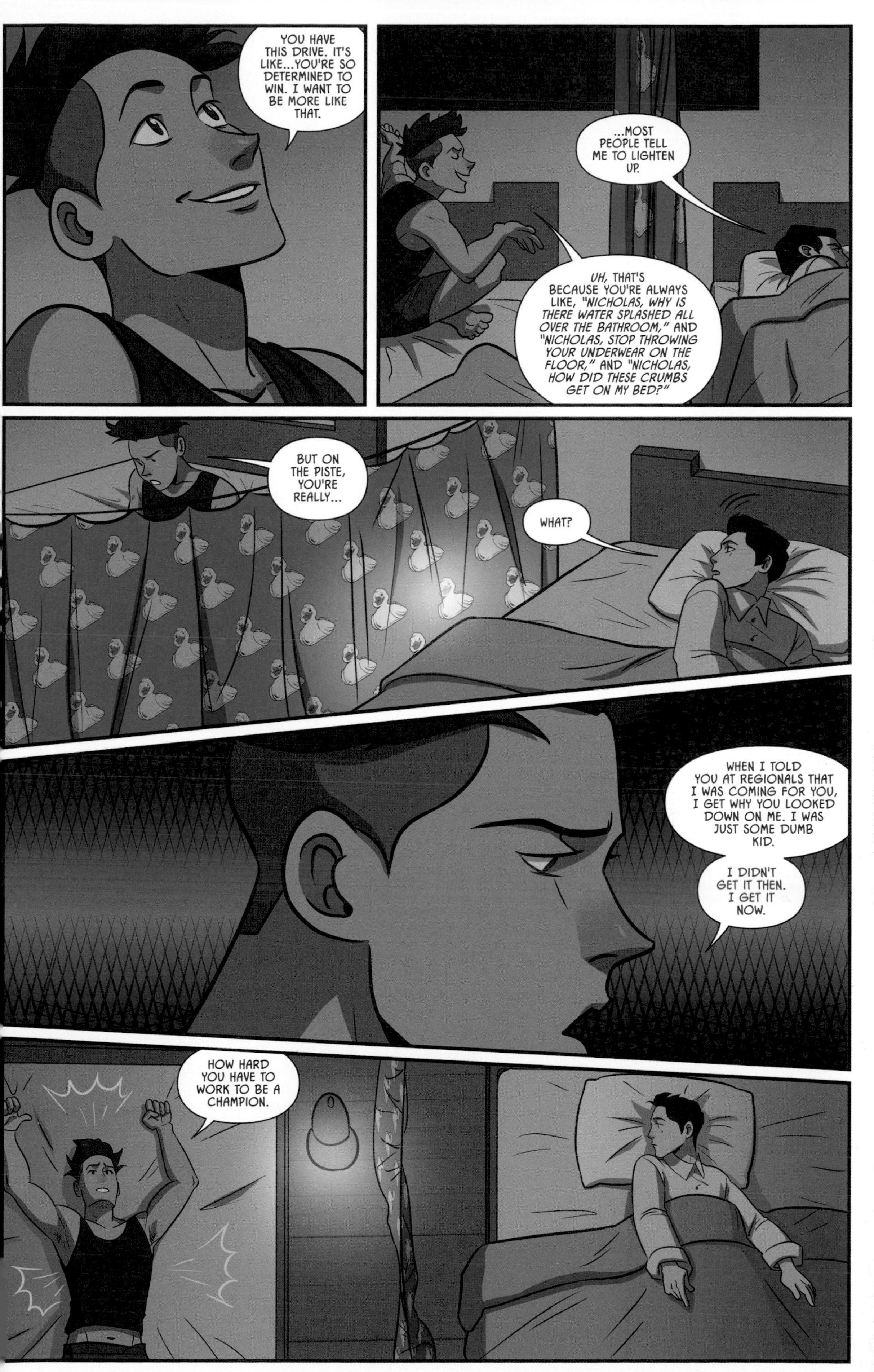
YOU HAVE THIS DRIVE. IT'S LIKE...YOU'RE SO DETERMINED TO WIN. I WANT TO BE MORE LIKE THAT.
...MOST PEOPLE TELL ME TO LIGHTEN UP.
UH, THAT'S BECAUSE YOU'RE ALWAYS LIKE, "NICHOLAS, WHY IS THERE WATER SPLASHED ALL OVER THE BATHROOM," AND "NICHOLAS, STOP THROWING YOUR UNDERWEAR ON THE FLOOR," AND "NICHOLAS, HOW DID THESE CRUMBS GET ON MY BED?"
BUT ON THE PISTE, YOU'RE REALLY...
WHAT?
WHEN I TOLD YOU AT REGIONALS THAT I WAS COMING FOR YOU, I GET WHY YOU LOOKED DOWN ON ME. I WAS JUST SOME DUMB KID.
I DIDN'T GET IT THEN. I GET IT NOW.
HOW HARD YOU HAVE TO WORK TO BE A CHAMPION.

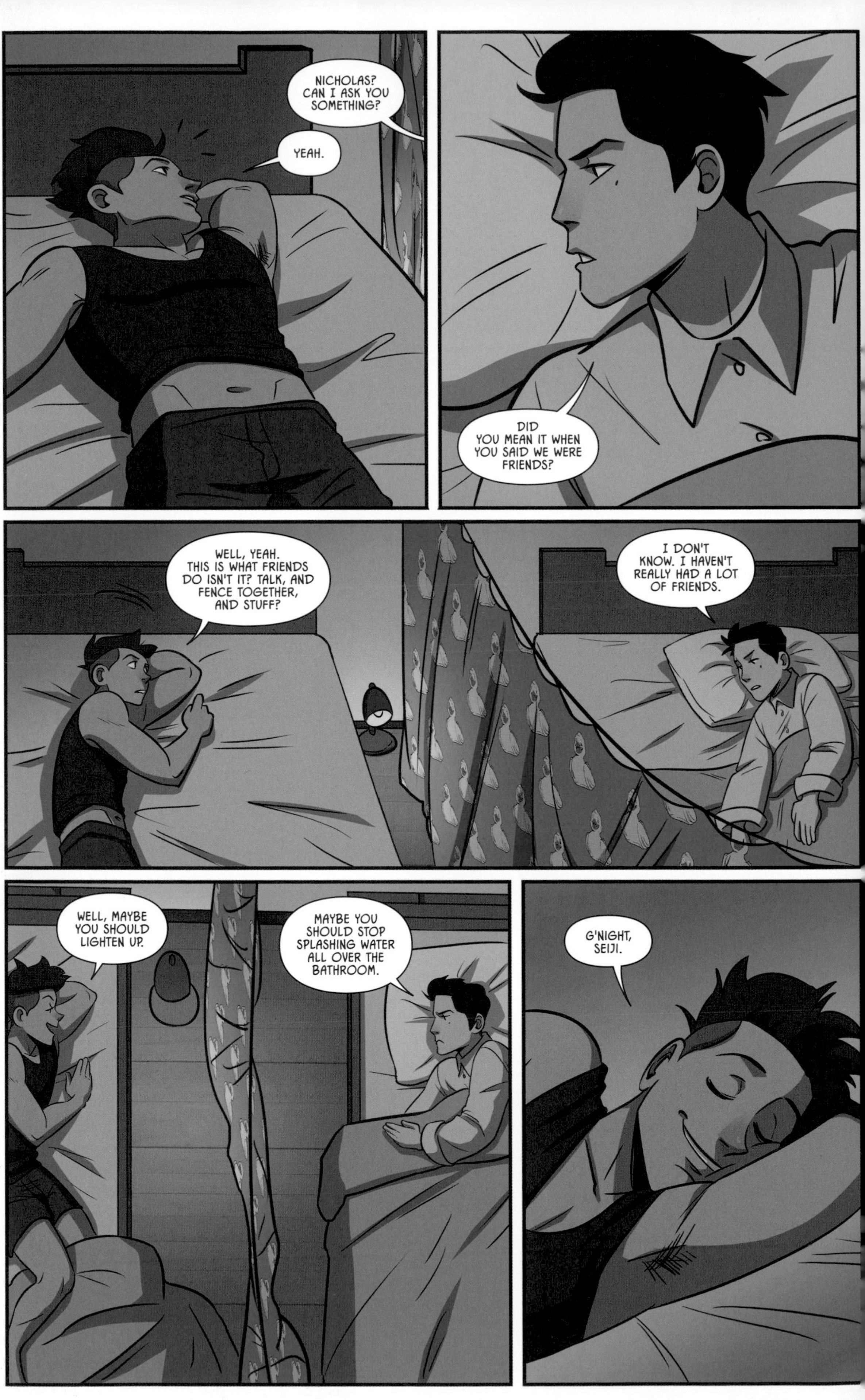
NICHOLAS? CAN I ASK YOU SOMETHING?
YEAH.
DID YOU MEAN IT WHEN YOU SAID WE WERE FRIENDS?
WELL, YEAH. THIS IS WHAT FRIENDS DO ISN'T IT? TALK, AND FENCE TOGETHER, AND STUFF?
I DON'T KNOW. I HAVEN'T REALLY HAD A LOT OF FRIENDS.
WELL, MAYBE YOU SHOULD LIGHTEN UP.
MAYBE YOU SHOULD STOP SPLASHING WATER ALL OVER THE BATHROOM.
G'NIGHT, SEIJI.

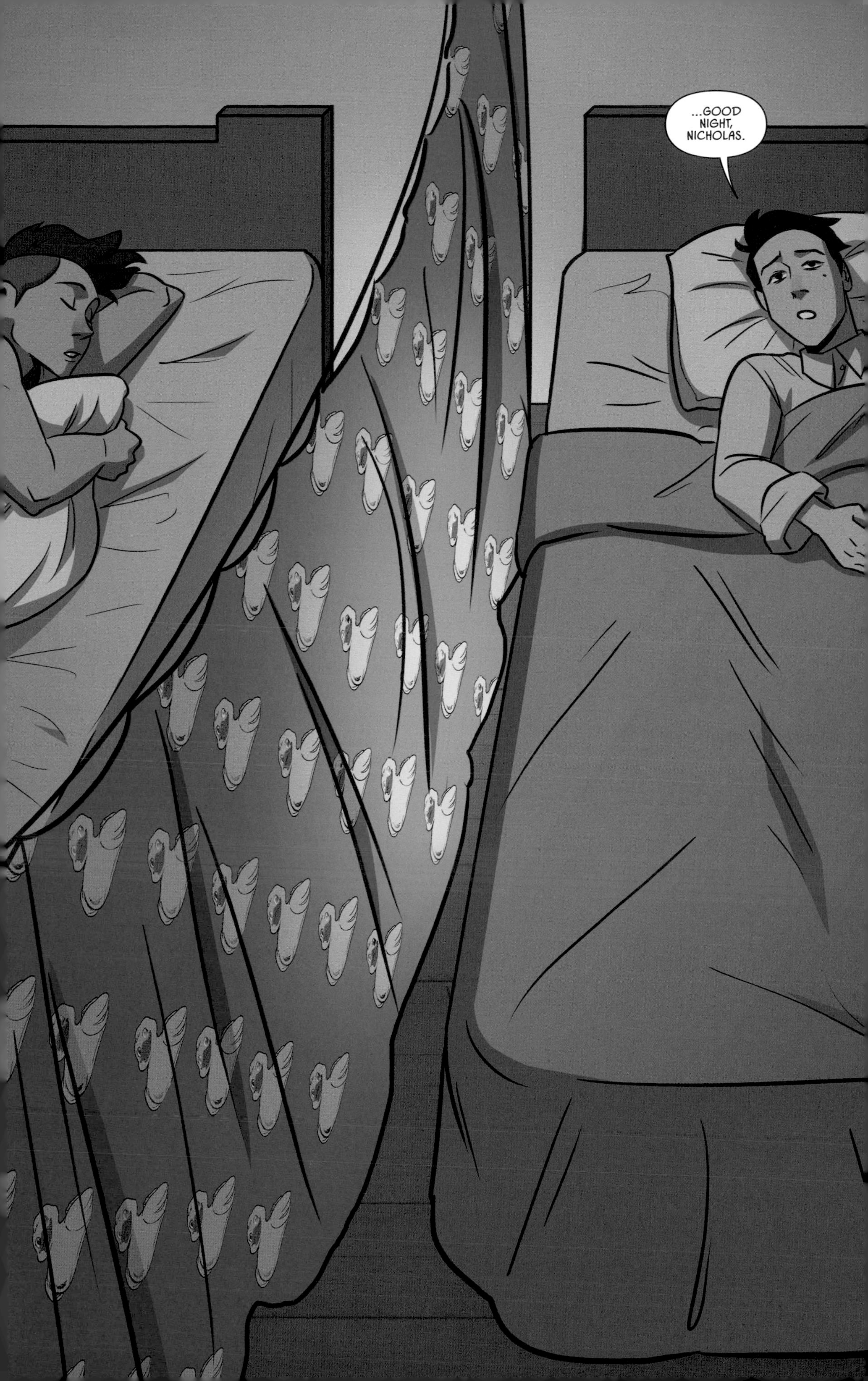
...GOOD NIGHT, NICHOLAS.

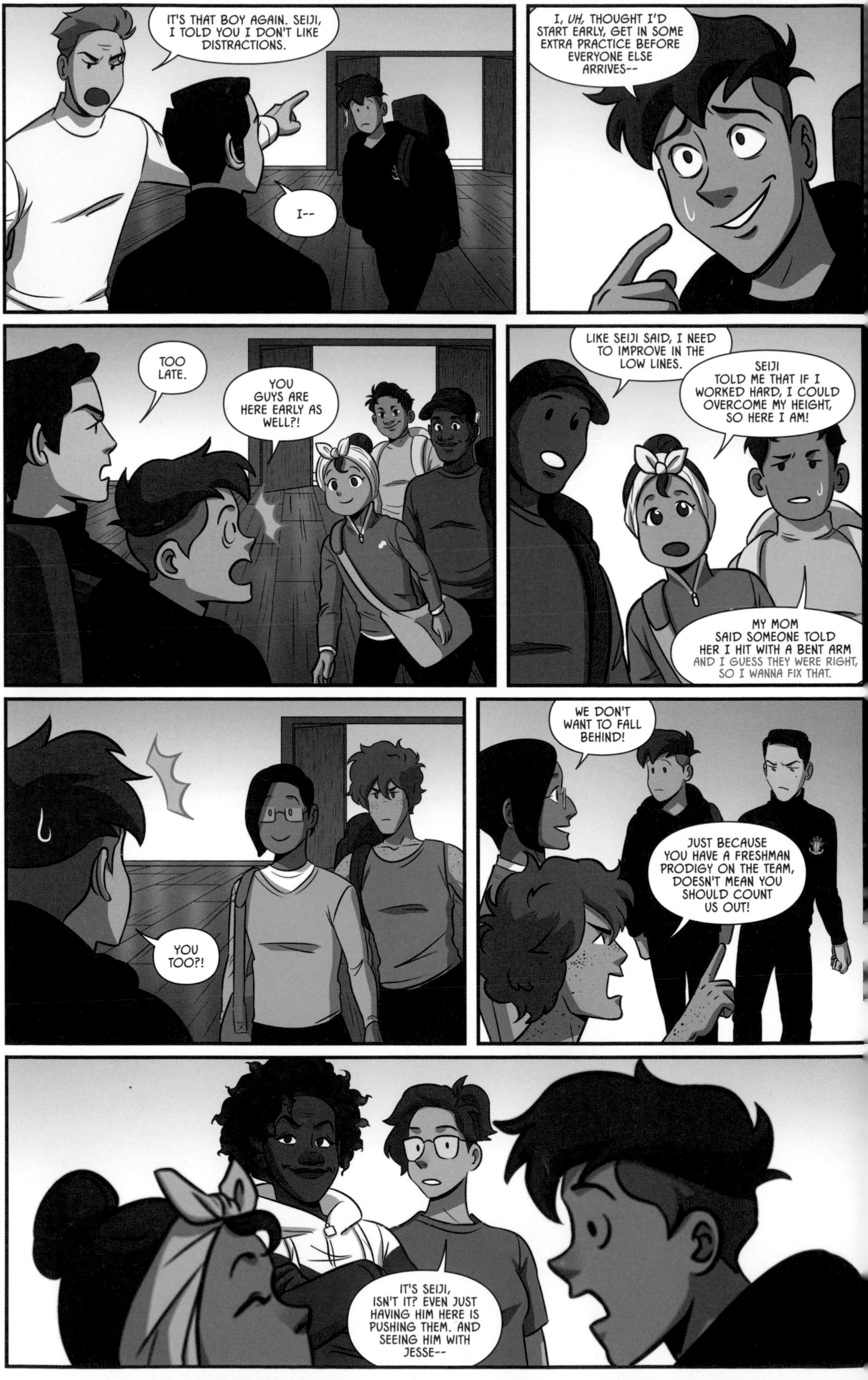
IT'S THAT BOY AGAIN. SEIJI, I TOLD YOU I DON'T LIKE DISTRACTIONS.
I--
I, UH, THOUGHT I'D START EARLY, GET IN SOME EXTRA PRACTICE BEFORE EVERYONE ELSE ARRIVES--
TOO LATE.
YOU GUYS ARE HERE EARLY AS WELL?!
LIKE SEIJI SAID, I NEED TO IMPROVE IN THE LOW LINES.
SEIJI TOLD ME THAT IF I WORKED HARD, I COULD OVERCOME MY HEIGHT, SO HERE I AM!
MY MOM SAID SOMEONE TOLD HER I HIT WITH A BENT ARM AND I GUESS THEY WERE RIGHT, SO I WANNA FIX THAT.
YOU TOO?!
WE DON'T WANT TO FALL BEHIND!
JUST BECAUSE YOU HAVE A FRESHMAN PRODIGY ON THE TEAM, DOESN'T MEAN YOU SHOULD COUNT US OUT!
IT'S SEIJI, ISN'T IT? EVEN JUST HAVING HIM HERE IS PUSHING THEM. AND SEEING HIM WITH JESSE--

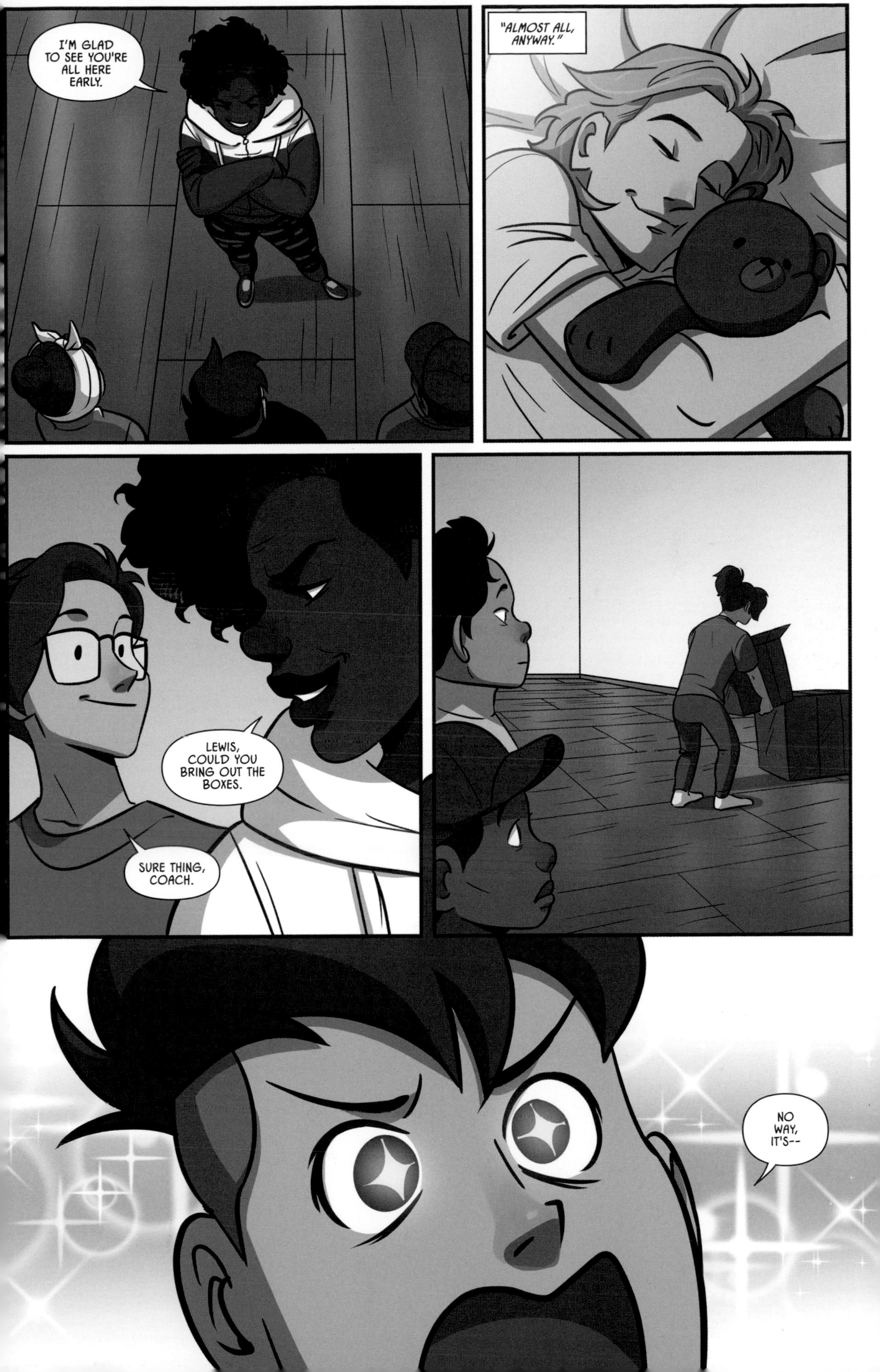
I'M GLAD TO SEE YOU'RE ALL HERE EARLY.
"ALMOST ALL, ANYWAY."
LEWIS, COULD YOU BRING OUT THE BOXES.
SURE THING, COACH.
NO WAY, IT'S--

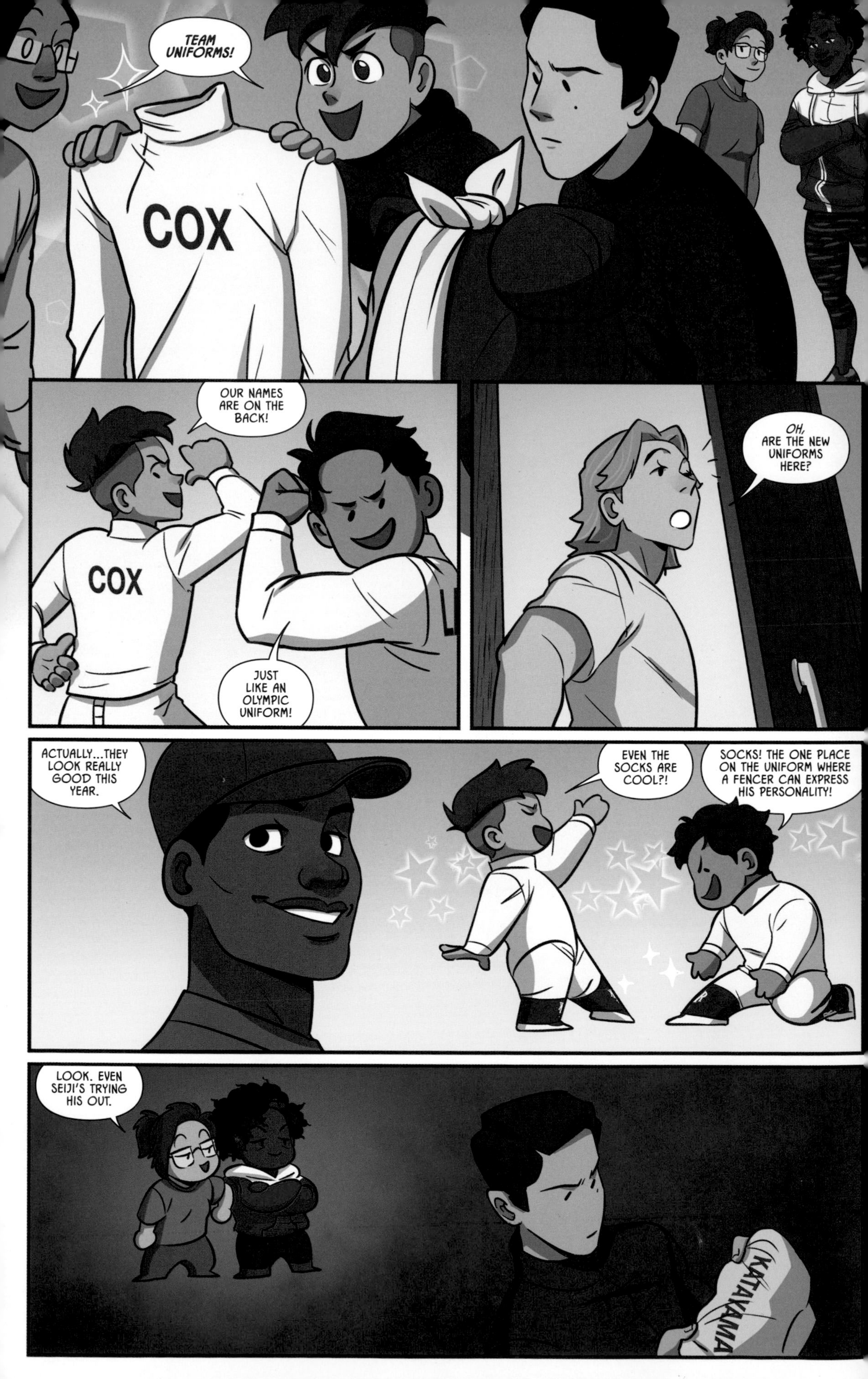
TEAM UNIFORMS!
COX
OUR NAMES ARE ON THE BACK!
COX
JUST LIKE AN OLYMPIC UNIFORM!
OH, ARE THE NEW UNIFORMS HERE?
ACTUALLY...THEY LOOK REALLY GOOD THIS YEAR.
EVEN THE SOCKS ARE COOL?!
SOCKS! THE ONE PLACE ON THE UNIFORM WHERE A FENCER CAN EXPRESS HIS PERSONALITY!
LOOK. EVEN SEIJI'S TRYING HIS OUT.
KATAYAMA

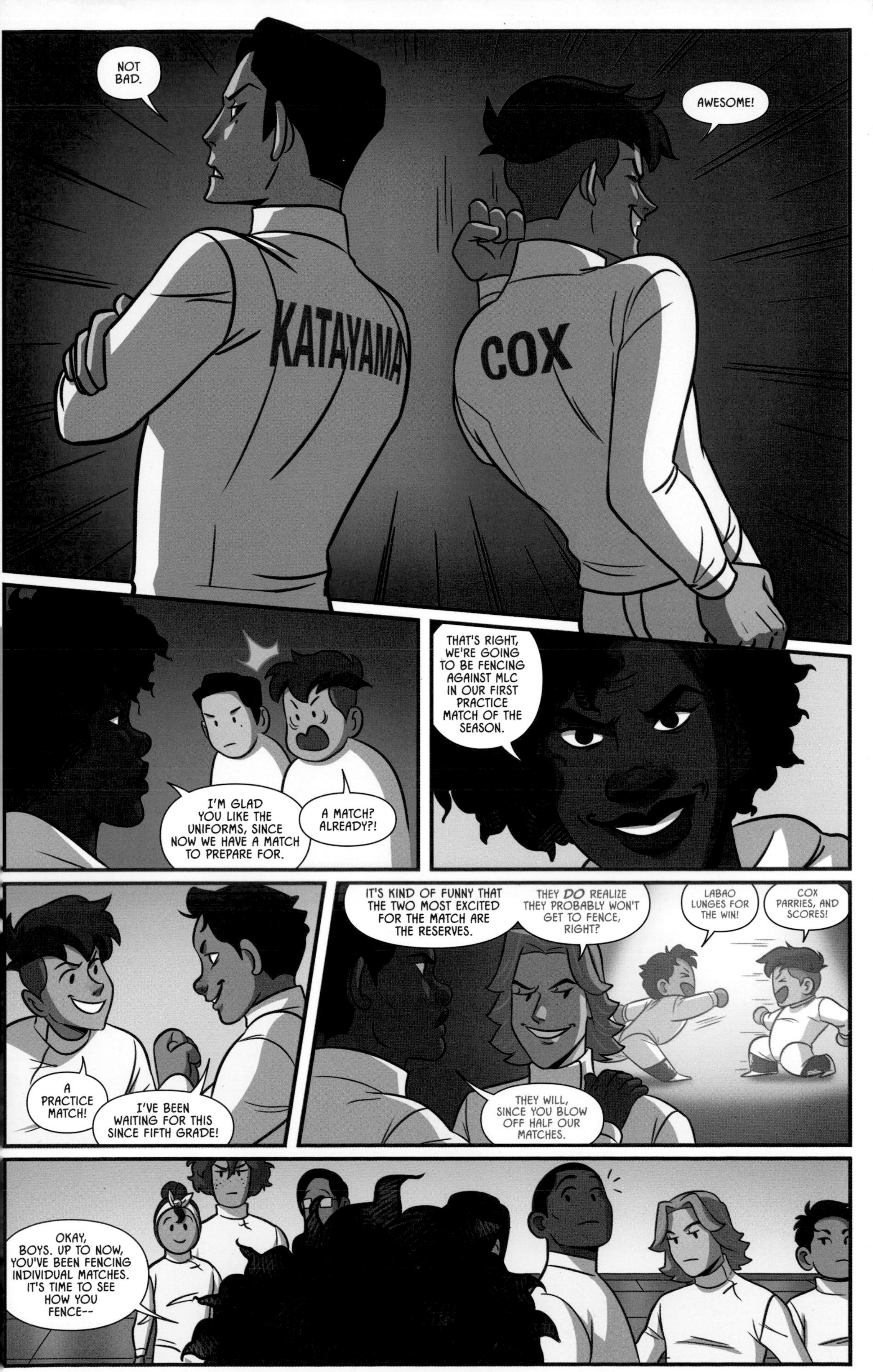
NOT BAD.
AWESOME!
KATAYAMA
COX
I'M GLAD YOU LIKE THE UNIFORMS, SINCE NOW WE HAVE A MATCH TO PREPARE FOR.
A MATCH? ALREADY?!
THAT'S RIGHT, WE'RE GOING TO BE FENCING AGAINST MLC IN OUR FIRST PRACTICE MATCH OF THE SEASON.
A PRACTICE MATCH!
I'VE BEEN WAITING FOR THIS SINCE FIFTH GRADE!
IT'S KIND OF FUNNY THAT THE TWO MOST EXCITED FOR THE MATCH ARE THE RESERVES.
THEY *DO* REALIZE THEY PROBABLY WON'T GET TO FENCE, RIGHT?
LABAO LUNGES FOR THE WIN!
COX PARRIES, AND SCORES!
THEY WILL, SINCE YOU BLOW OFF HALF OUR MATCHES.
OKAY, BOYS. UP TO NOW, YOU'VE BEEN FENCING INDIVIDUAL MATCHES. IT'S TIME TO SEE HOW YOU FENCE--

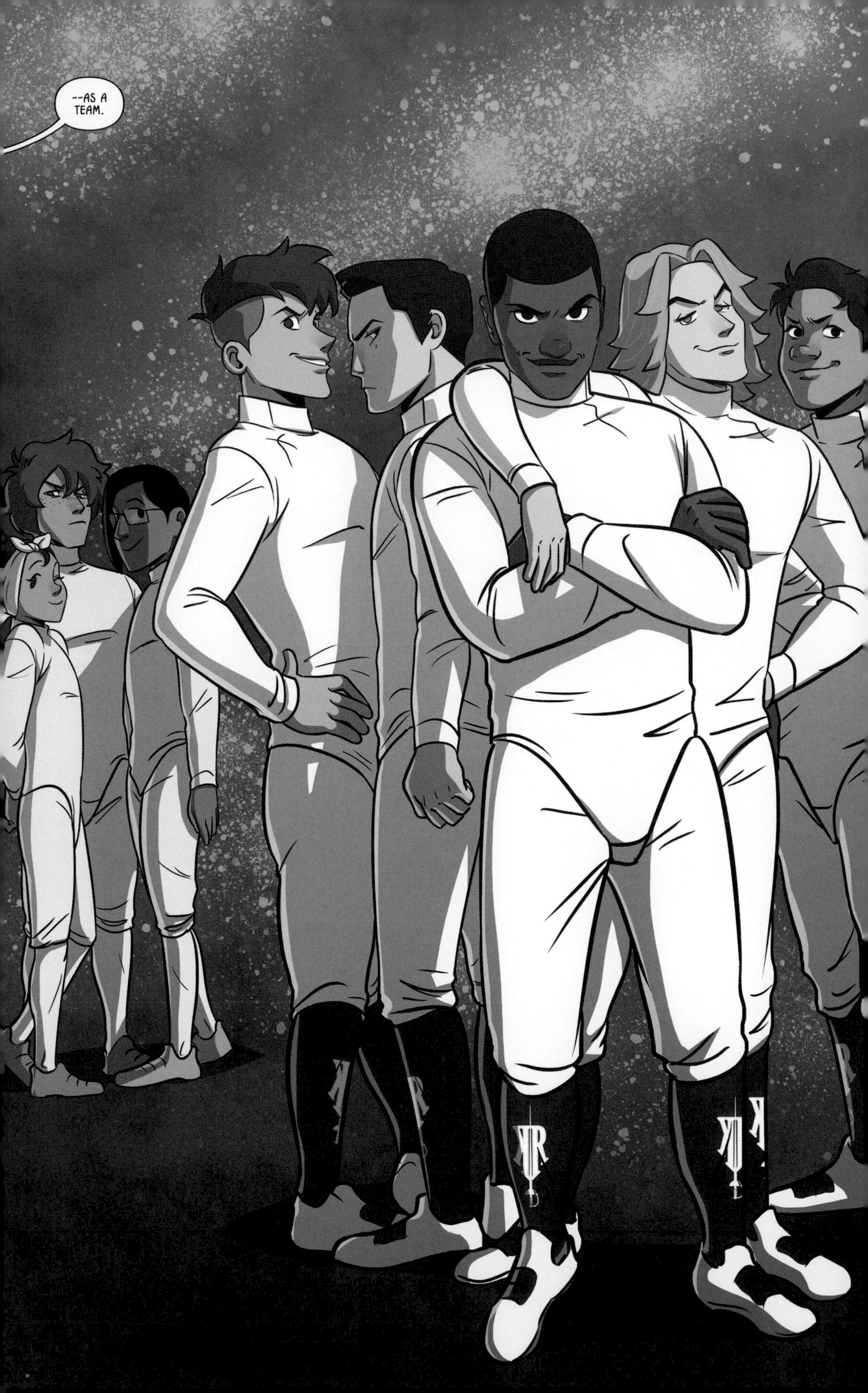
--AS A TEAM.

CHAPTER
FOURTEEN

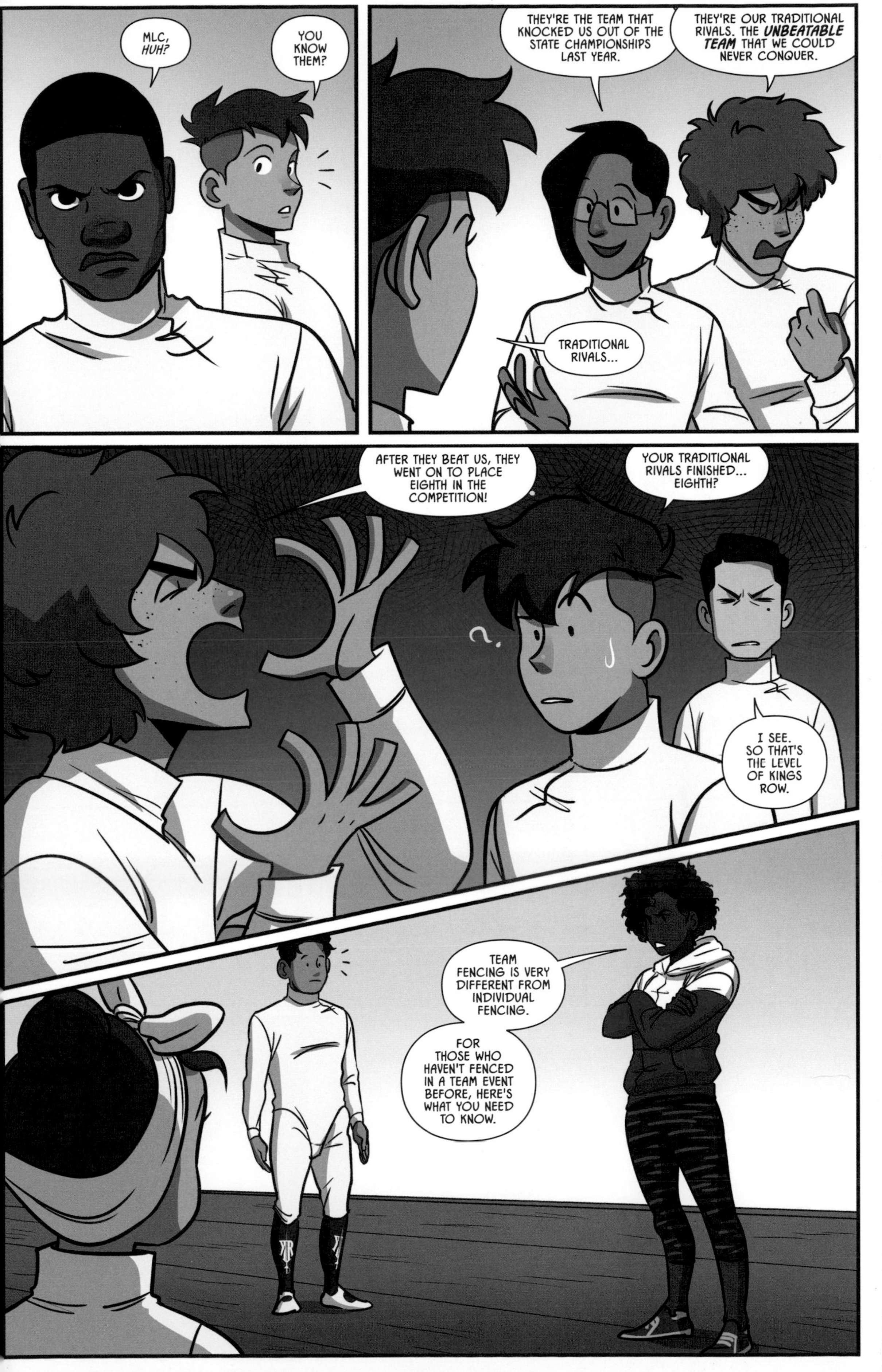
MLC, HUH?
YOU KNOW THEM?
THEY'RE THE TEAM THAT KNOCKED US OUT OF THE STATE CHAMPIONSHIPS LAST YEAR.
THEY'RE OUR TRADITIONAL RIVALS. THE UNBEATABLE TEAM THAT WE COULD NEVER CONQUER.
TRADITIONAL RIVALS...
AFTER THEY BEAT US, THEY WENT ON TO PLACE EIGHTH IN THE COMPETITION!
YOUR TRADITIONAL RIVALS FINISHED... EIGHTH?
?
I SEE. SO THAT'S THE LEVEL OF KINGS ROW.
TEAM FENCING IS VERY DIFFERENT FROM INDIVIDUAL FENCING.
FOR THOSE WHO HAVEN'T FENCED IN A TEAM EVENT BEFORE, HERE'S WHAT YOU NEED TO KNOW.

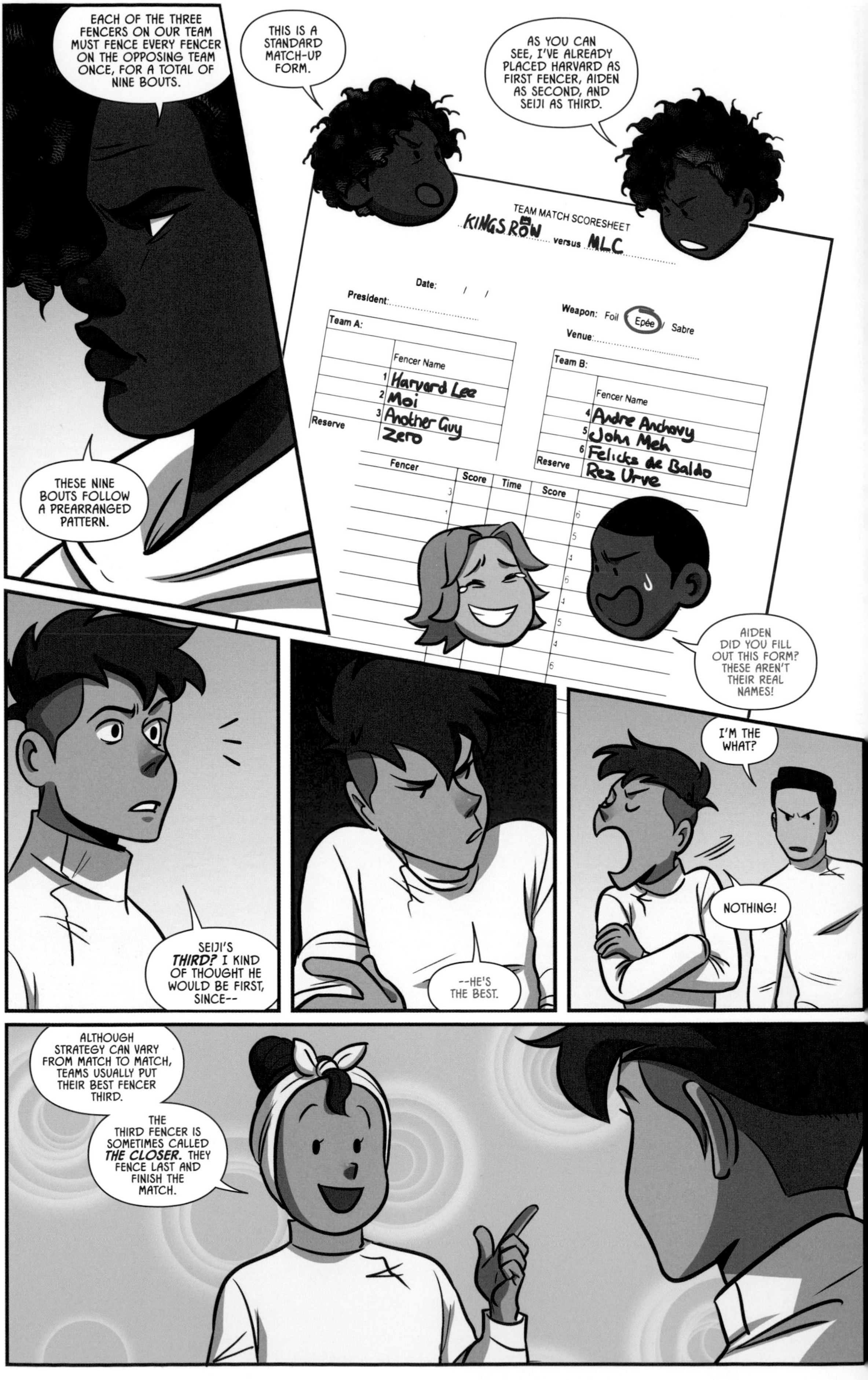
EACH OF THE THREE FENCERS ON OUR TEAM MUST FENCE EVERY FENCER ON THE OPPOSING TEAM ONCE, FOR A TOTAL OF NINE BOUTS.
THESE NINE BOUTS FOLLOW A PREARRANGED PATTERN.
THIS IS A STANDARD MATCH-UP FORM.
AS YOU CAN SEE, I'VE ALREADY PLACED HARVARD AS FIRST FENCER, AIDEN AS SECOND, AND SEIJI AS THIRD.
TEAM MATCH SCORESHEET
KINGS ROW versus MLC
Date: / /
President:
Weapon: Foil Epée / Sabre
Venue:
Team A:
Fencer Name
1 Harvard Lee
2 Moi
3 Another Guy
Reserve Zero
Team B:
Fencer Name
4 Andre Anchovy
5 John Meh
6 Felicks de Baldo
Reserve Rez Urve
Fencer
Score
Time
Score
AIDEN DID YOU FILL OUT THIS FORM? THESE AREN'T THEIR REAL NAMES!
SEIJI'S THIRD? I KIND OF THOUGHT HE WOULD BE FIRST, SINCE--
--HE'S THE BEST.
I'M THE WHAT?
NOTHING!
ALTHOUGH STRATEGY CAN VARY FROM MATCH TO MATCH, TEAMS USUALLY PUT THEIR BEST FENCER THIRD.
THE THIRD FENCER IS SOMETIMES CALLED THE CLOSER. THEY FENCE LAST AND FINISH THE MATCH.

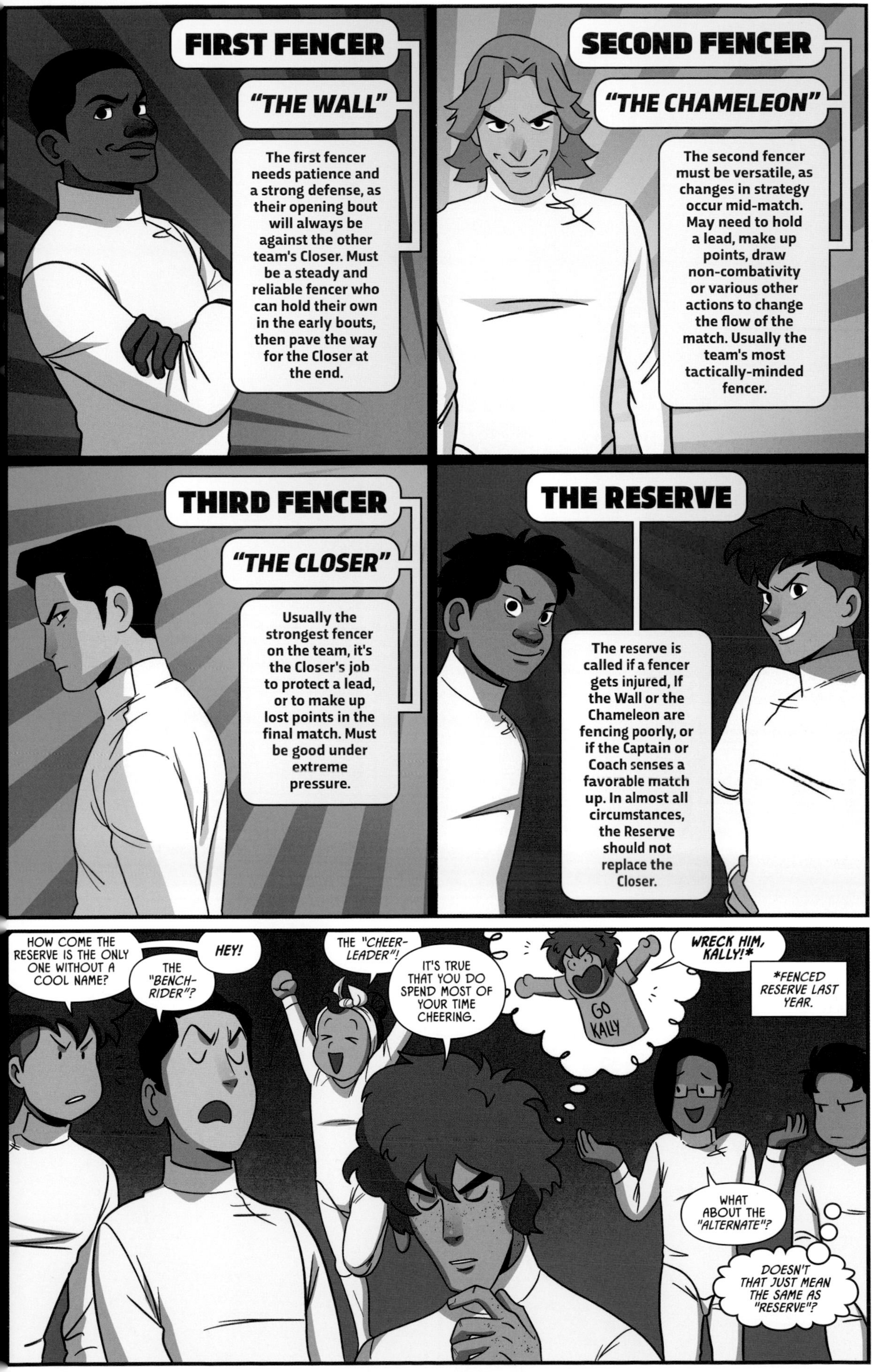

FIRST FENCER
"THE WALL"
The first fencer needs patience and a strong defense, as their opening bout will always be against the other team's Closer. Must be a steady and reliable fencer who can hold their own in the early bouts, then pave the way for the Closer at the end.
SECOND FENCER
"THE CHAMELEON"
The second fencer must be versatile, as changes in strategy occur mid-match. May need to hold a lead, make up points, draw non-combativity or various other actions to change the flow of the match. Usually the team's most tactically-minded fencer.
THIRD FENCER
"THE CLOSER"
Usually the strongest fencer on the team, it's the Closer's job to protect a lead, or to make up lost points in the final match. Must be good under extreme pressure.
THE RESERVE
The reserve is called if a fencer gets injured, If the Wall or the Chameleon are fencing poorly, or if the Captain or Coach senses a favorable match up. In almost all circumstances, the Reserve should not replace the Closer.
HOW COME THE RESERVE IS THE ONLY ONE WITHOUT A COOL NAME?
THE "BENCH-RIDER"?
HEY!
THE "CHEER-LEADER"!
IT'S TRUE THAT YOU DO SPEND MOST OF YOUR TIME CHEERING.
GO KALLY
WRECK HIM, KALLY!*
*FENCED RESERVE LAST YEAR.
WHAT ABOUT THE "ALTERNATE"?
DOESN'T THAT JUST MEAN THE SAME AS "RESERVE"?

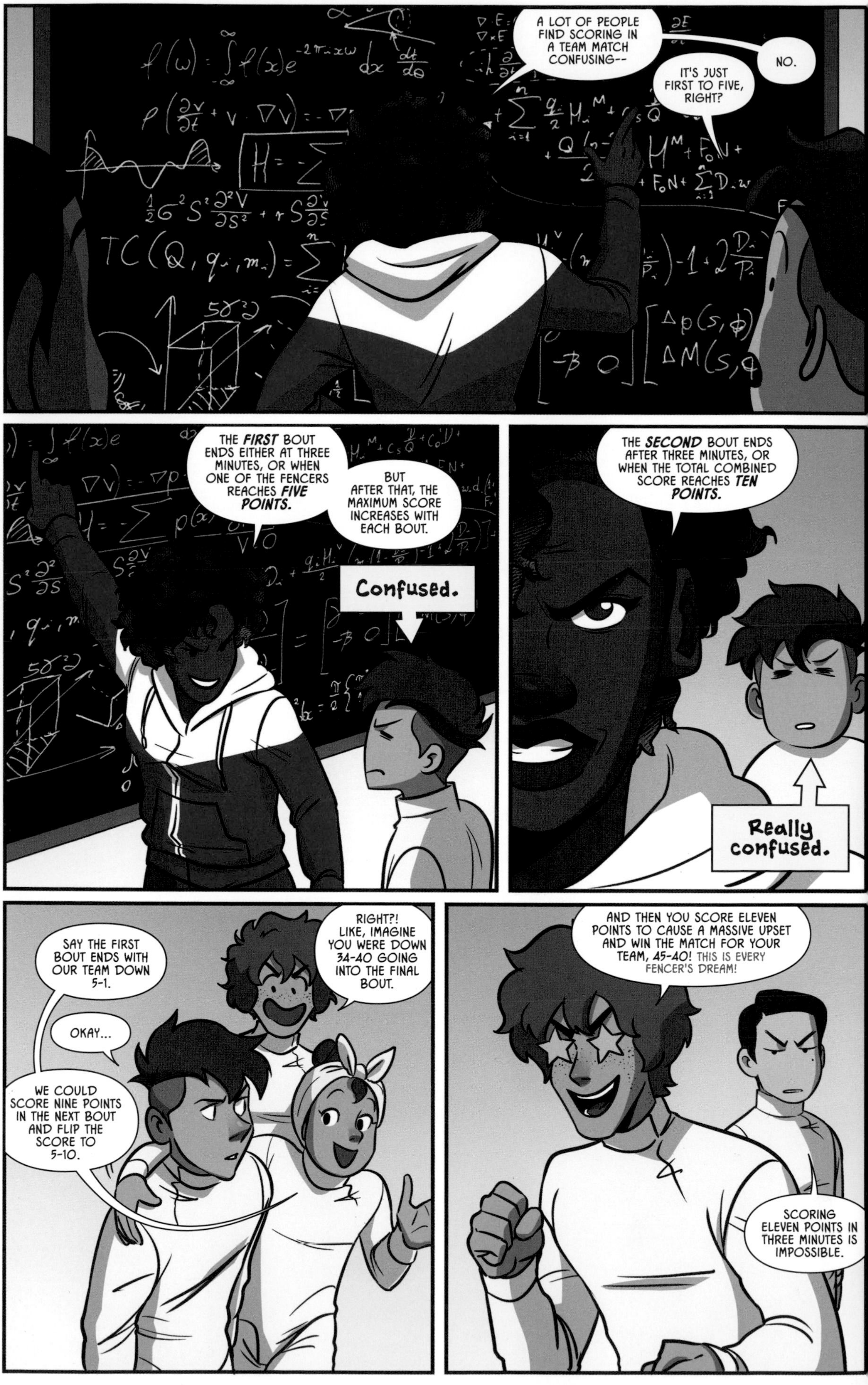
A LOT OF PEOPLE FIND SCORING IN A TEAM MATCH CONFUSING--
IT'S JUST FIRST TO FIVE, RIGHT?
NO.
THE *FIRST* BOUT ENDS EITHER AT THREE MINUTES, OR WHEN ONE OF THE FENCERS REACHES *FIVE POINTS.*
BUT AFTER THAT, THE MAXIMUM SCORE INCREASES WITH EACH BOUT.
Confused.
THE *SECOND* BOUT ENDS AFTER THREE MINUTES, OR WHEN THE TOTAL COMBINED SCORE REACHES *TEN POINTS.*
Really confused.
SAY THE FIRST BOUT ENDS WITH OUR TEAM DOWN 5-1.
OKAY...
WE COULD SCORE NINE POINTS IN THE NEXT BOUT AND FLIP THE SCORE TO 5-10.
RIGHT?! LIKE, IMAGINE YOU WERE DOWN 34-40 GOING INTO THE FINAL BOUT.
AND THEN YOU SCORE ELEVEN POINTS TO CAUSE A MASSIVE UPSET AND WIN THE MATCH FOR YOUR TEAM, 45-40! THIS IS EVERY FENCER'S DREAM!
SCORING ELEVEN POINTS IN THREE MINUTES IS IMPOSSIBLE.

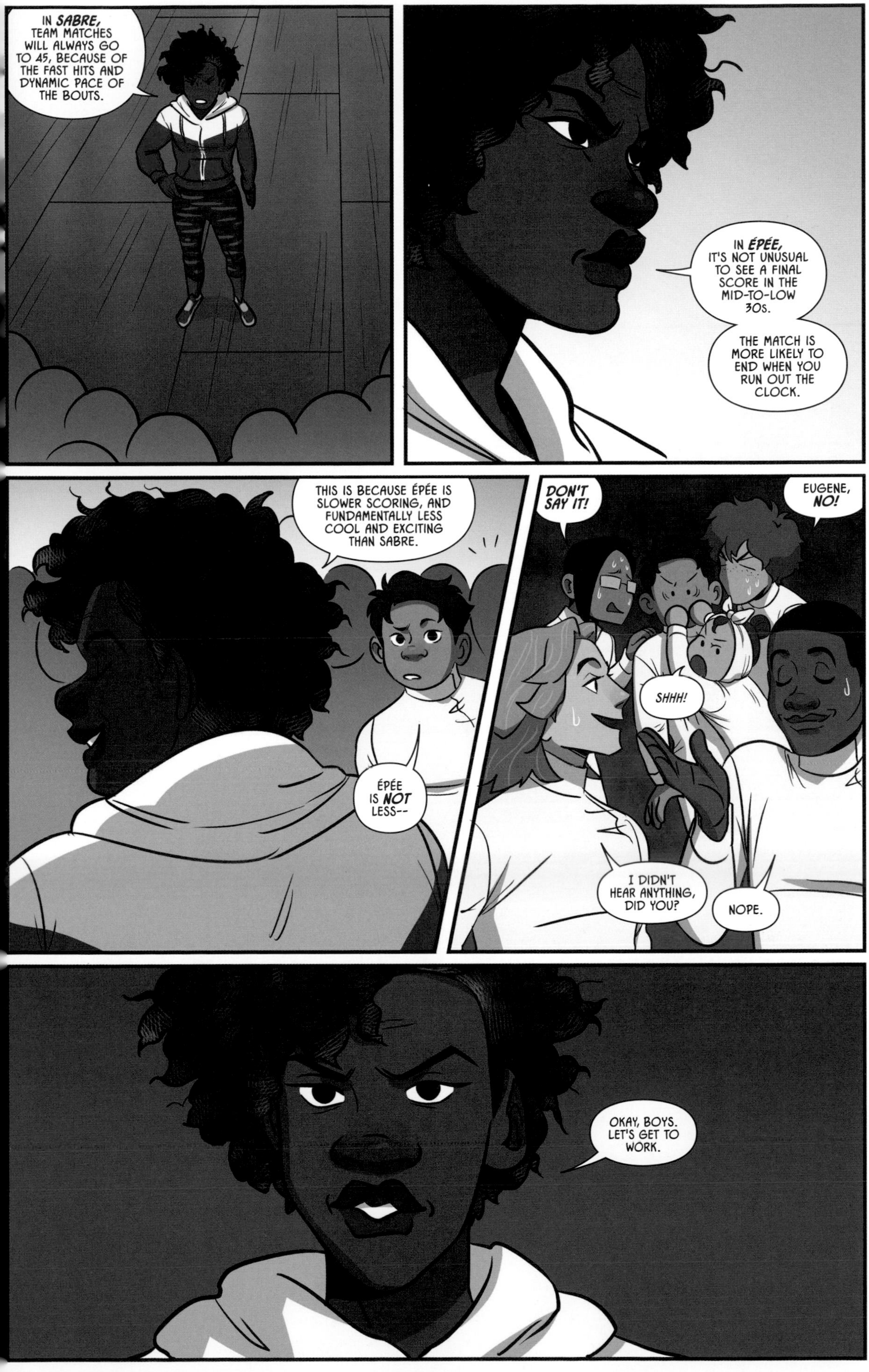
IN SABRE, TEAM MATCHES WILL ALWAYS GO TO 45, BECAUSE OF THE FAST HITS AND DYNAMIC PACE OF THE BOUTS.
IN ÉPÉE, IT'S NOT UNUSUAL TO SEE A FINAL SCORE IN THE MID-TO-LOW 30s.
THE MATCH IS MORE LIKELY TO END WHEN YOU RUN OUT THE CLOCK.
THIS IS BECAUSE ÉPÉE IS SLOWER SCORING, AND FUNDAMENTALLY LESS COOL AND EXCITING THAN SABRE.
ÉPÉE IS NOT LESS--
DON'T SAY IT!
EUGENE, NO!
SHHH!
I DIDN'T HEAR ANYTHING, DID YOU?
NOPE.
OKAY, BOYS. LET'S GET TO WORK.

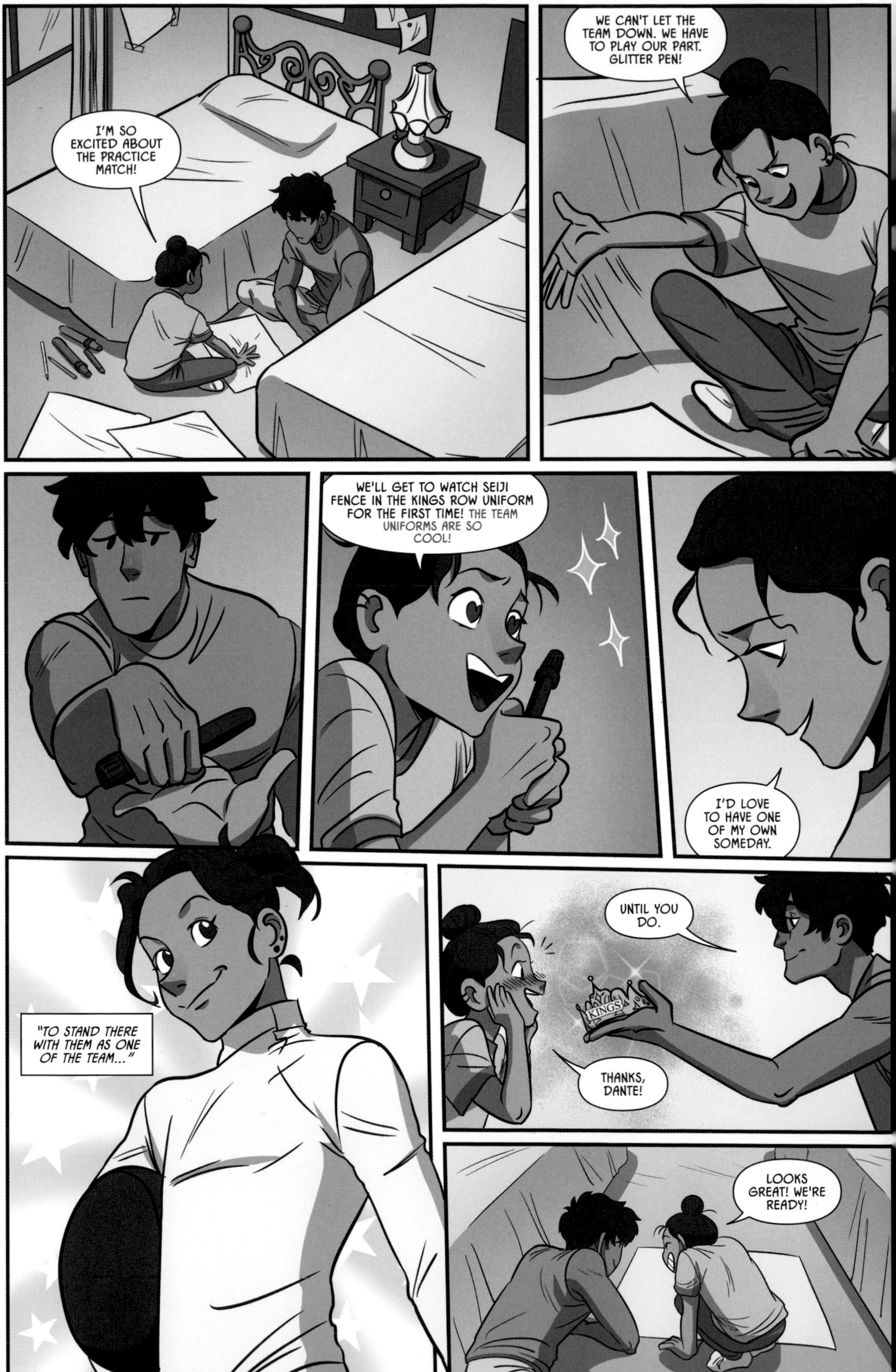
I'M SO EXCITED ABOUT THE PRACTICE MATCH!
WE CAN'T LET THE TEAM DOWN. WE HAVE TO PLAY OUR PART. GLITTER PEN!
WE'LL GET TO WATCH SEIJI FENCE IN THE KINGS ROW UNIFORM FOR THE FIRST TIME! THE TEAM UNIFORMS ARE SO COOL!
I'D LOVE TO HAVE ONE OF MY OWN SOMEDAY.
"TO STAND THERE WITH THEM AS ONE OF THE TEAM..."
UNTIL YOU DO.
KINGS
THANKS, DANTE!
LOOKS GREAT! WE'RE READY!

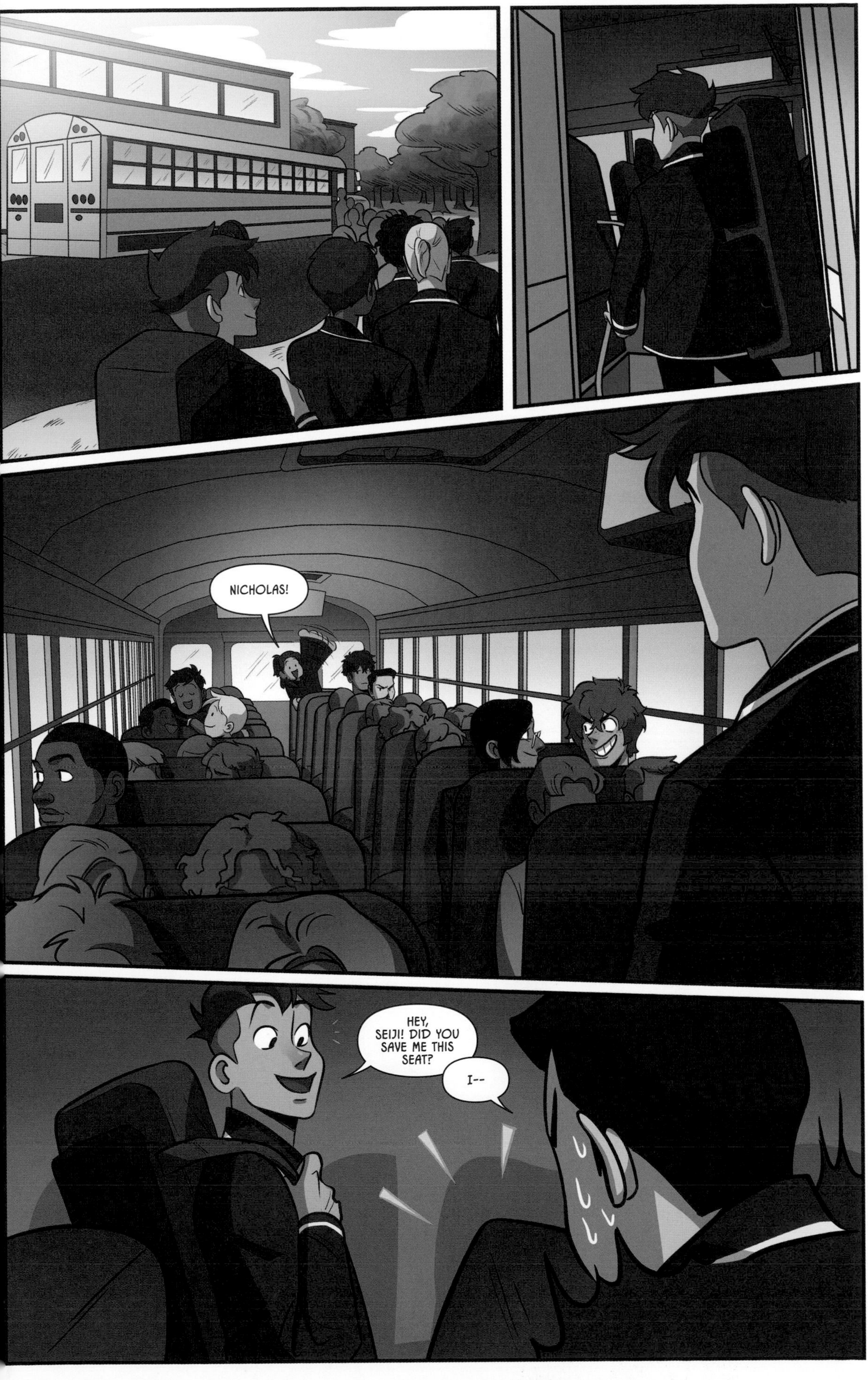
NICHOLAS!
HEY, SEIJI! DID YOU SAVE ME THIS SEAT?
I--

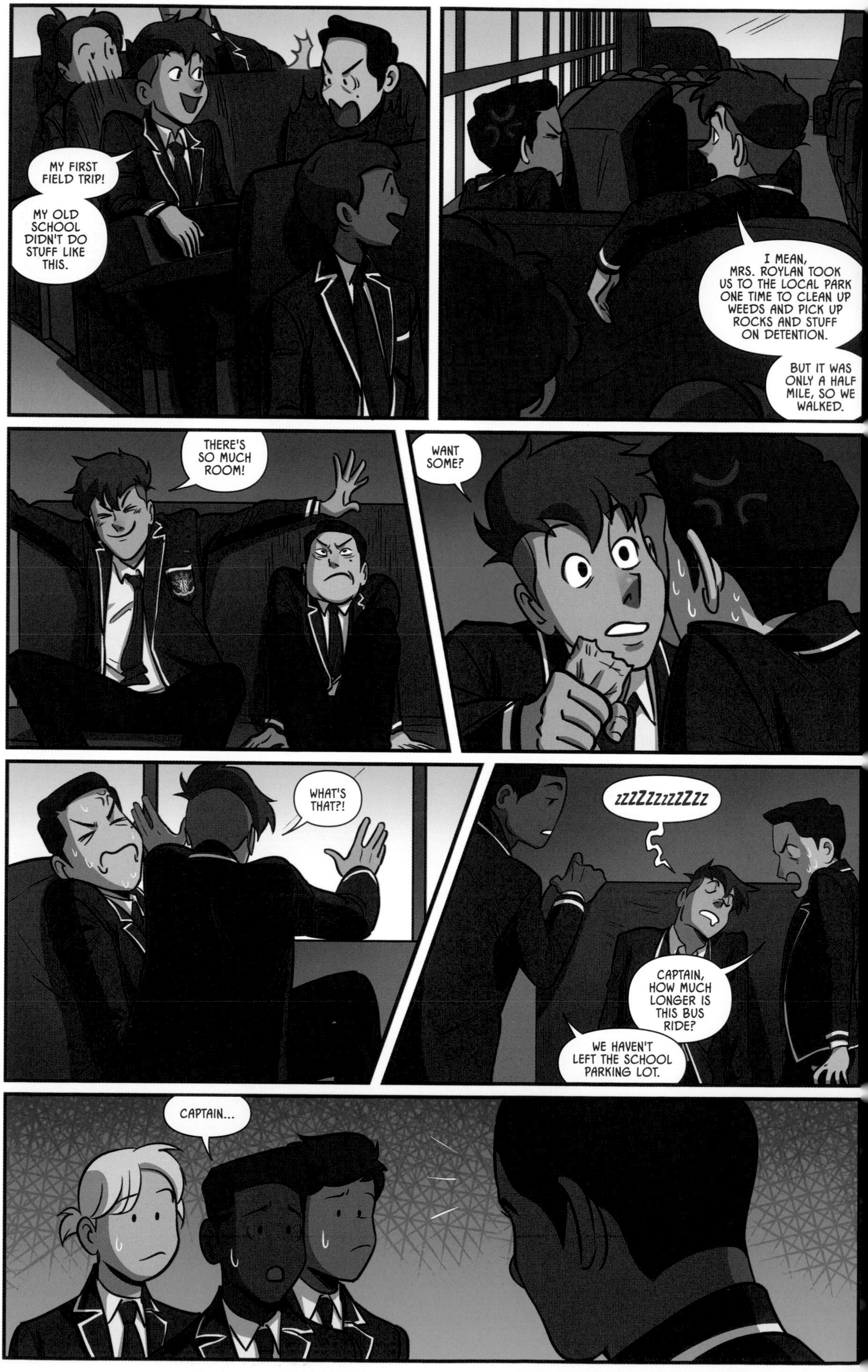
MY FIRST FIELD TRIP!
MY OLD SCHOOL DIDN'T DO STUFF LIKE THIS.
I MEAN, MRS. ROYLAN TOOK US TO THE LOCAL PARK ONE TIME TO CLEAN UP WEEDS AND PICK UP ROCKS AND STUFF ON DETENTION.
BUT IT WAS ONLY A HALF MILE, SO WE WALKED.
THERE'S SO MUCH ROOM!
WANT SOME?
WHAT'S THAT?!
zzZZZzzzZZzz
CAPTAIN, HOW MUCH LONGER IS THIS BUS RIDE?
WE HAVEN'T LEFT THE SCHOOL PARKING LOT.
CAPTAIN...

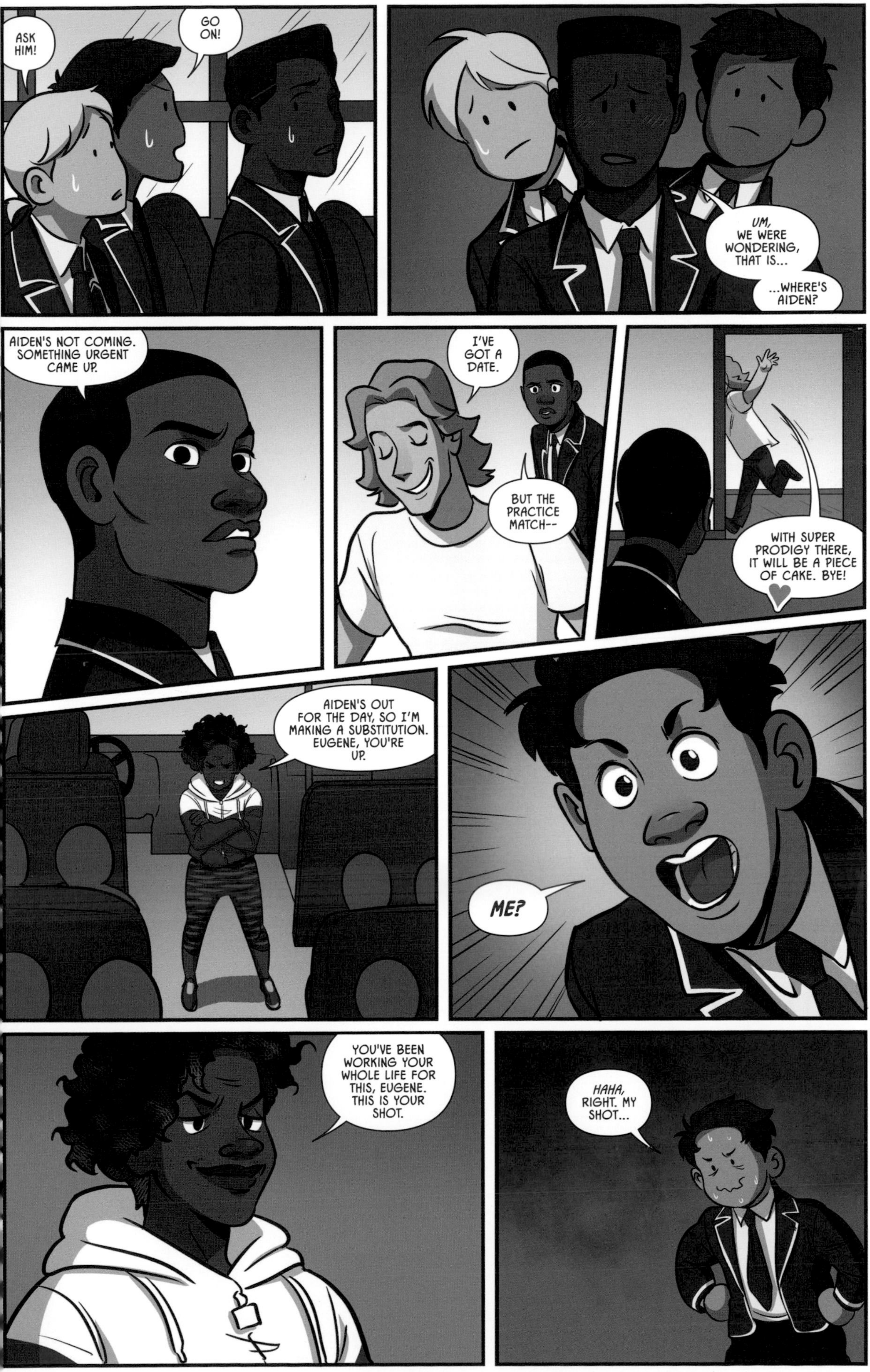
ASK HIM!
GO ON!
UM, WE WERE WONDERING, THAT IS...
...WHERE'S AIDEN?
AIDEN'S NOT COMING. SOMETHING URGENT CAME UP.
I'VE GOT A DATE.
BUT THE PRACTICE MATCH--
WITH SUPER PRODIGY THERE, IT WILL BE A PIECE OF CAKE. BYE!
AIDEN'S OUT FOR THE DAY, SO I'M MAKING A SUBSTITUTION. EUGENE, YOU'RE UP.
ME?
YOU'VE BEEN WORKING YOUR WHOLE LIFE FOR THIS, EUGENE. THIS IS YOUR SHOT.
HAHA, RIGHT. MY SHOT...

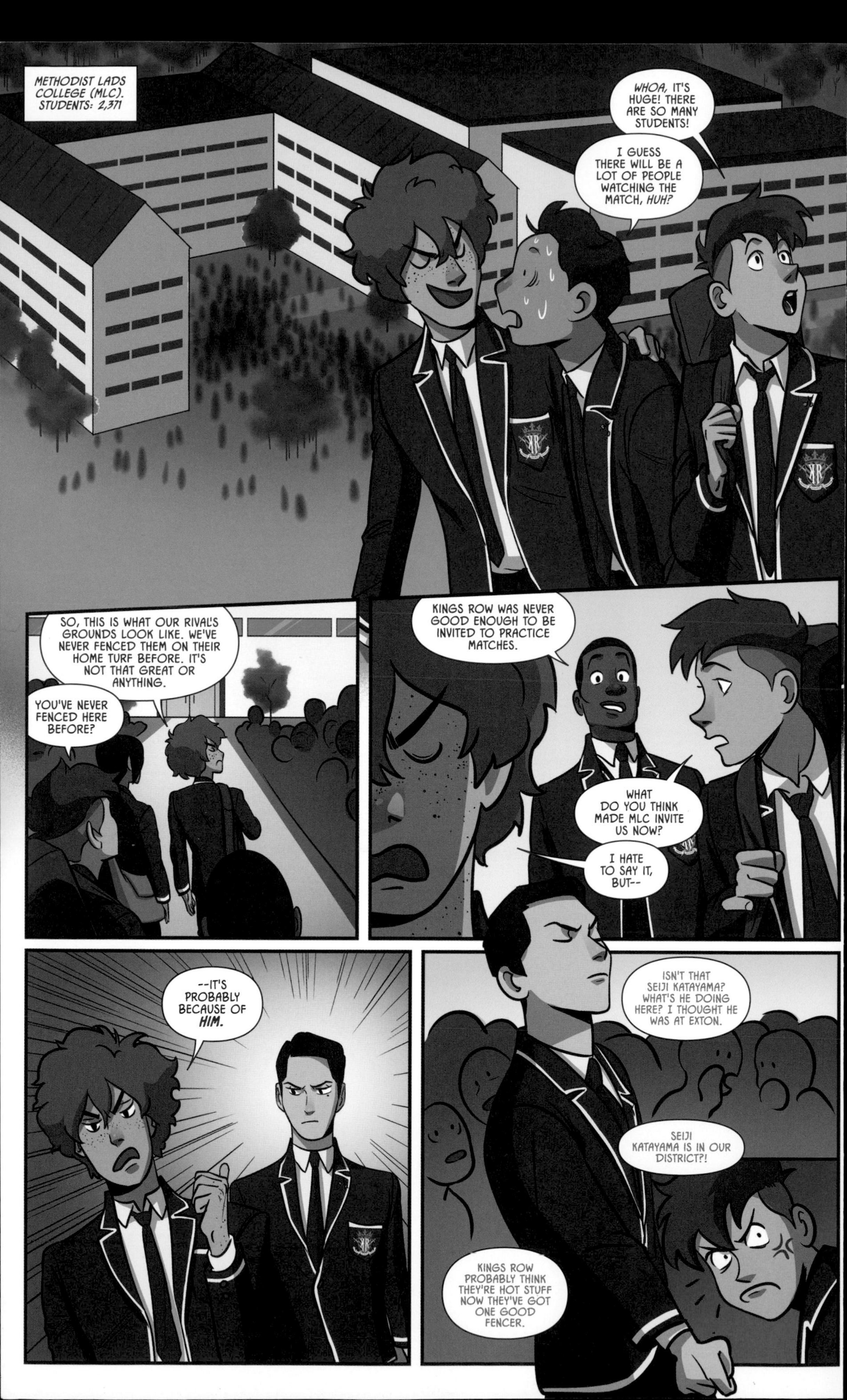
METHODIST LADS COLLEGE (MLC). STUDENTS: 2,371
WHOA, IT'S HUGE! THERE ARE SO MANY STUDENTS!
I GUESS THERE WILL BE A LOT OF PEOPLE WATCHING THE MATCH, HUH?
SO, THIS IS WHAT OUR RIVAL'S GROUNDS LOOK LIKE. WE'VE NEVER FENCED THEM ON THEIR HOME TURF BEFORE. IT'S NOT THAT GREAT OR ANYTHING.
YOU'VE NEVER FENCED HERE BEFORE?
KINGS ROW WAS NEVER GOOD ENOUGH TO BE INVITED TO PRACTICE MATCHES.
WHAT DO YOU THINK MADE MLC INVITE US NOW?
I HATE TO SAY IT, BUT--
--IT'S PROBABLY BECAUSE OF HIM.
ISN'T THAT SEIJI KATAYAMA? WHAT'S HE DOING HERE? I THOUGHT HE WAS AT EXTON.
SEIJI KATAYAMA IS IN OUR DISTRICT?!
KINGS ROW PROBABLY THINK THEY'RE HOT STUFF NOW THEY'VE GOT ONE GOOD FENCER.

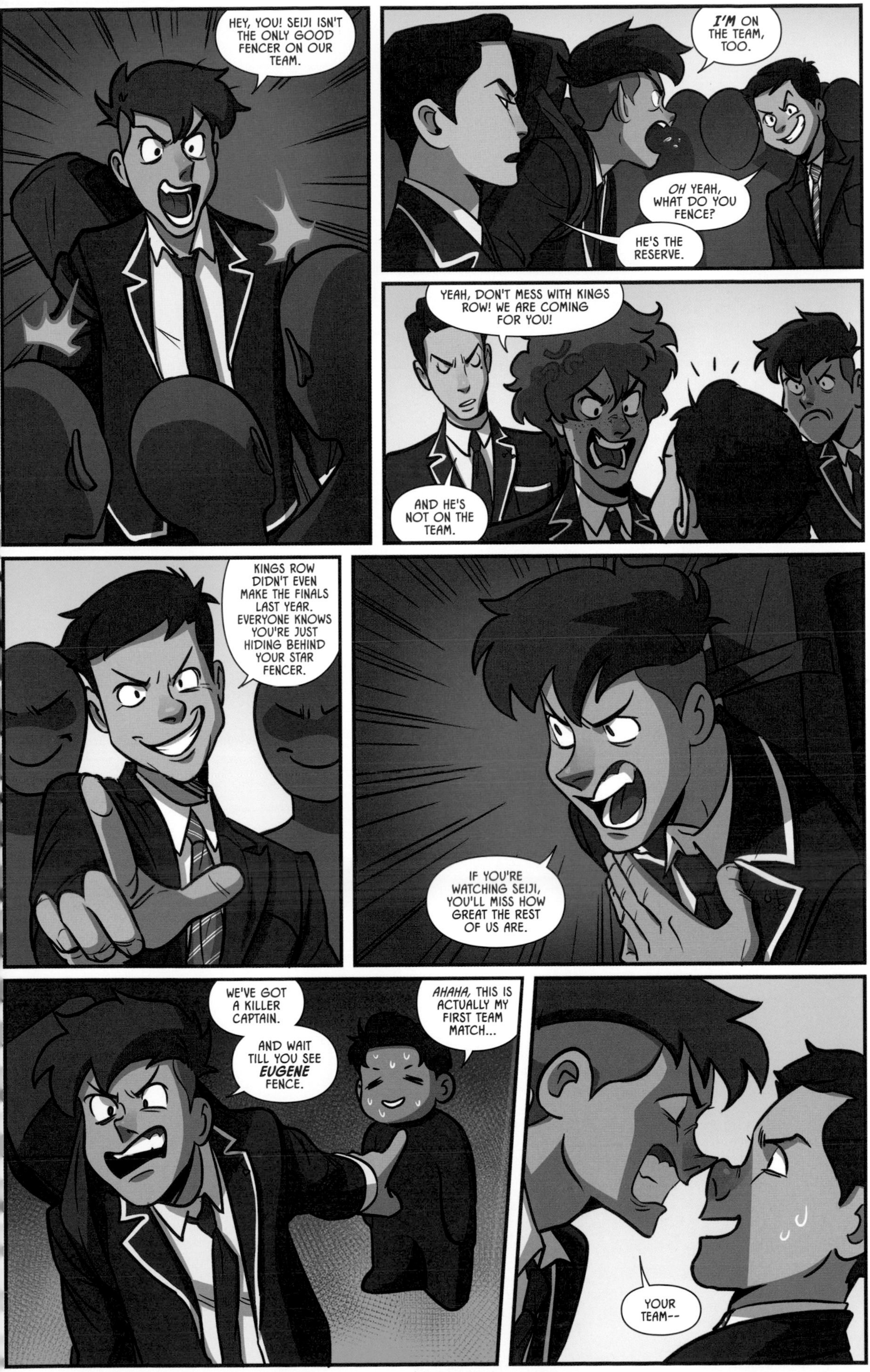
HEY, YOU! SEIJI ISN'T THE ONLY GOOD FENCER ON OUR TEAM.
I'M ON THE TEAM, TOO.
OH YEAH, WHAT DO YOU FENCE?
HE'S THE RESERVE.
YEAH, DON'T MESS WITH KINGS ROW! WE ARE COMING FOR YOU!
AND HE'S NOT ON THE TEAM.
KINGS ROW DIDN'T EVEN MAKE THE FINALS LAST YEAR. EVERYONE KNOWS YOU'RE JUST HIDING BEHIND YOUR STAR FENCER.
IF YOU'RE WATCHING SEIJI, YOU'LL MISS HOW GREAT THE REST OF US ARE.
WE'VE GOT A KILLER CAPTAIN.
AND WAIT TILL YOU SEE EUGENE FENCE.
AHAHA, THIS IS ACTUALLY MY FIRST TEAM MATCH...
YOUR TEAM--

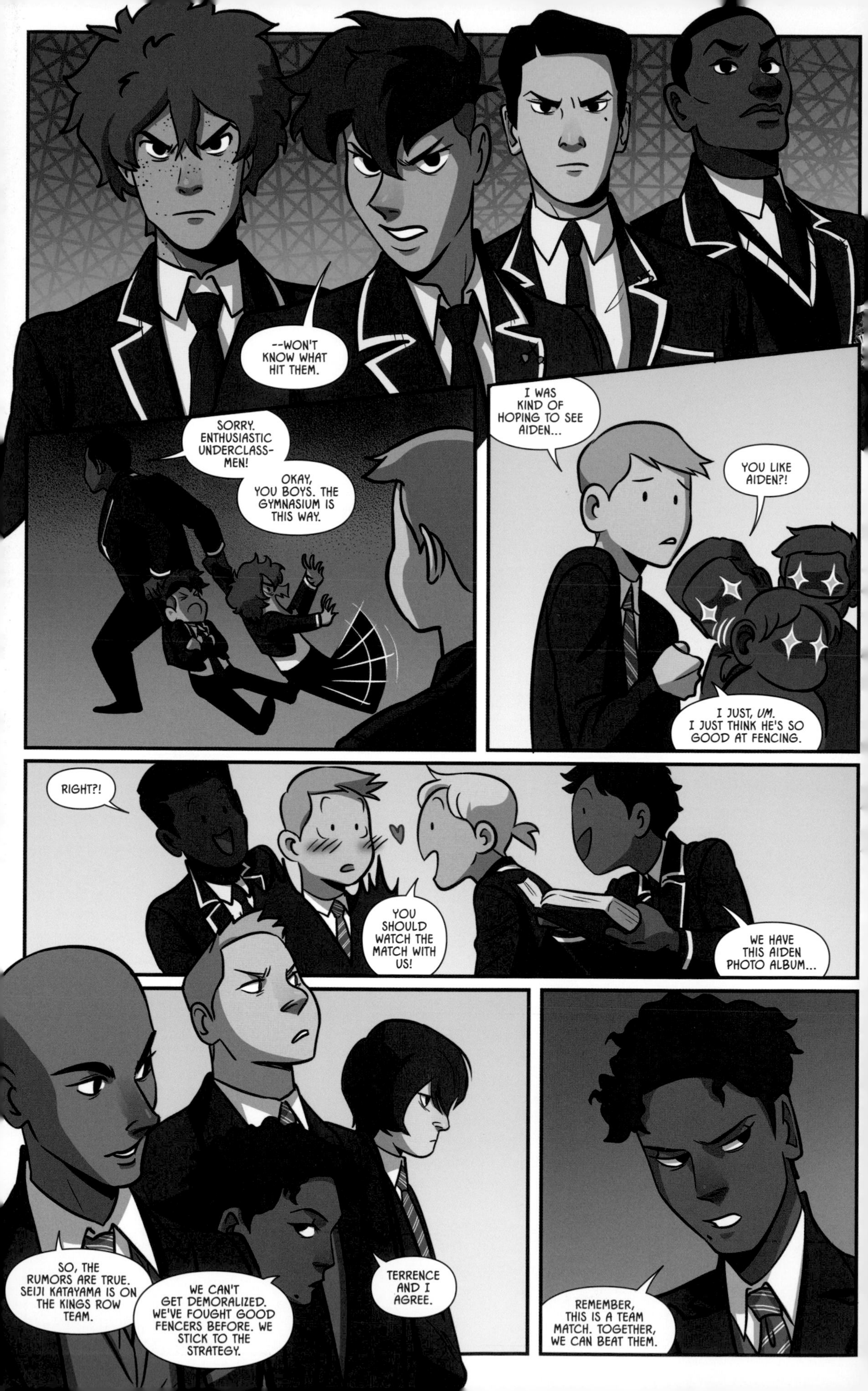
--WON'T KNOW WHAT HIT THEM.
SORRY. ENTHUSIASTIC UNDERCLASS-MEN!
OKAY, YOU BOYS. THE GYMNASIUM IS THIS WAY.
I WAS KIND OF HOPING TO SEE AIDEN...
YOU LIKE AIDEN?!
I JUST, *UM*. I JUST THINK HE'S SO GOOD AT FENCING.
RIGHT?!
YOU SHOULD WATCH THE MATCH WITH US!
WE HAVE THIS AIDEN PHOTO ALBUM...
SO, THE RUMORS ARE TRUE. SEIJI KATAYAMA IS ON THE KINGS ROW TEAM.
WE CAN'T GET DEMORALIZED. WE'VE FOUGHT GOOD FENCERS BEFORE. WE STICK TO THE STRATEGY.
TERRENCE AND I AGREE.
REMEMBER, THIS IS A TEAM MATCH. TOGETHER, WE CAN BEAT THEM.

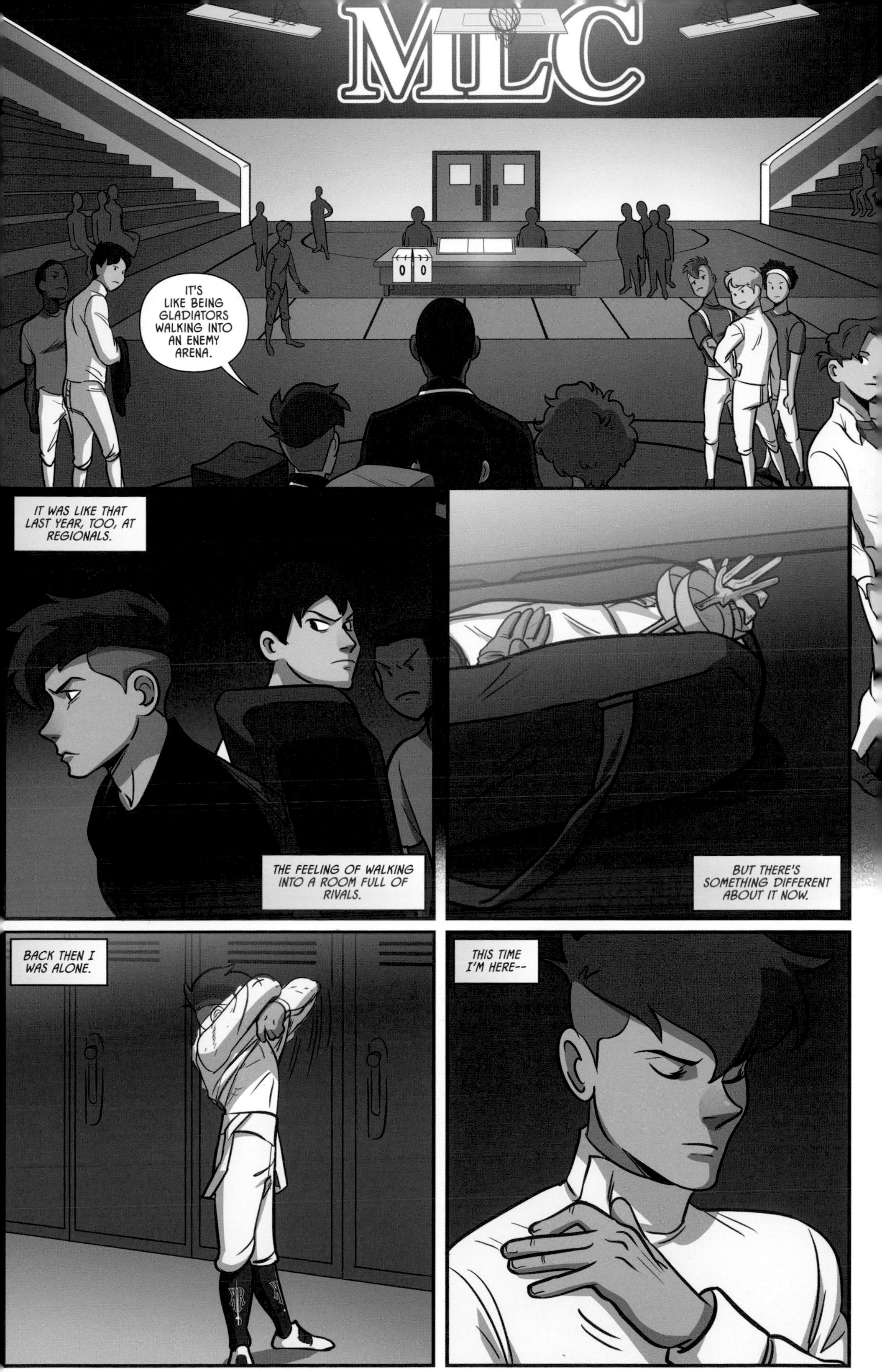
MLC
IT'S LIKE BEING GLADIATORS WALKING INTO AN ENEMY ARENA.
IT WAS LIKE THAT LAST YEAR, TOO, AT REGIONALS.
THE FEELING OF WALKING INTO A ROOM FULL OF RIVALS.
BUT THERE'S SOMETHING DIFFERENT ABOUT IT NOW.
BACK THEN I WAS ALONE.
THIS TIME I'M HERE--

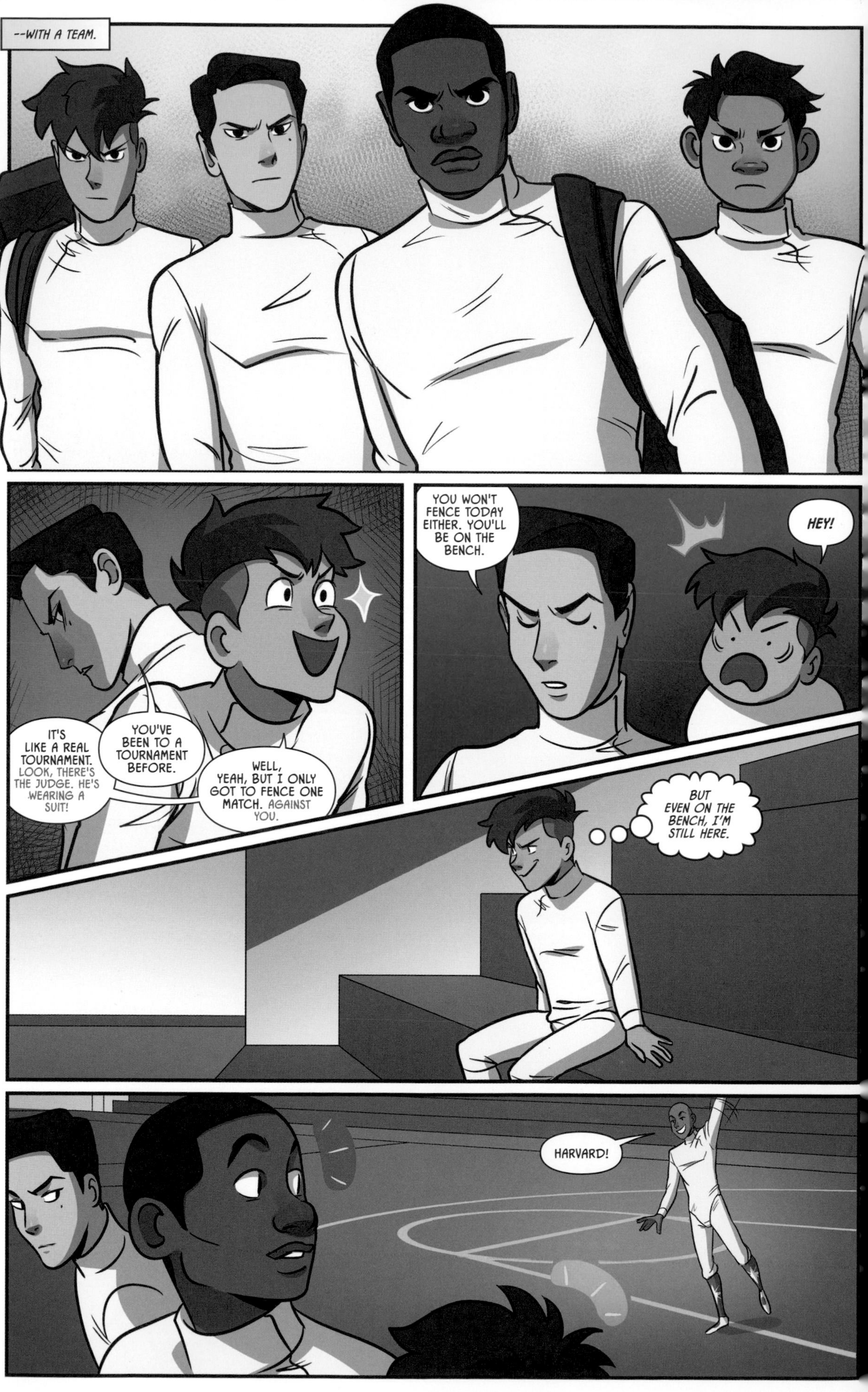
--WITH A TEAM.
IT'S LIKE A REAL TOURNAMENT. LOOK, THERE'S THE JUDGE. HE'S WEARING A SUIT!
YOU'VE BEEN TO A TOURNAMENT BEFORE.
WELL, YEAH, BUT I ONLY GOT TO FENCE ONE MATCH. AGAINST YOU.
YOU WON'T FENCE TODAY EITHER. YOU'LL BE ON THE BENCH.
HEY!
BUT EVEN ON THE BENCH, I'M STILL HERE.
HARVARD!

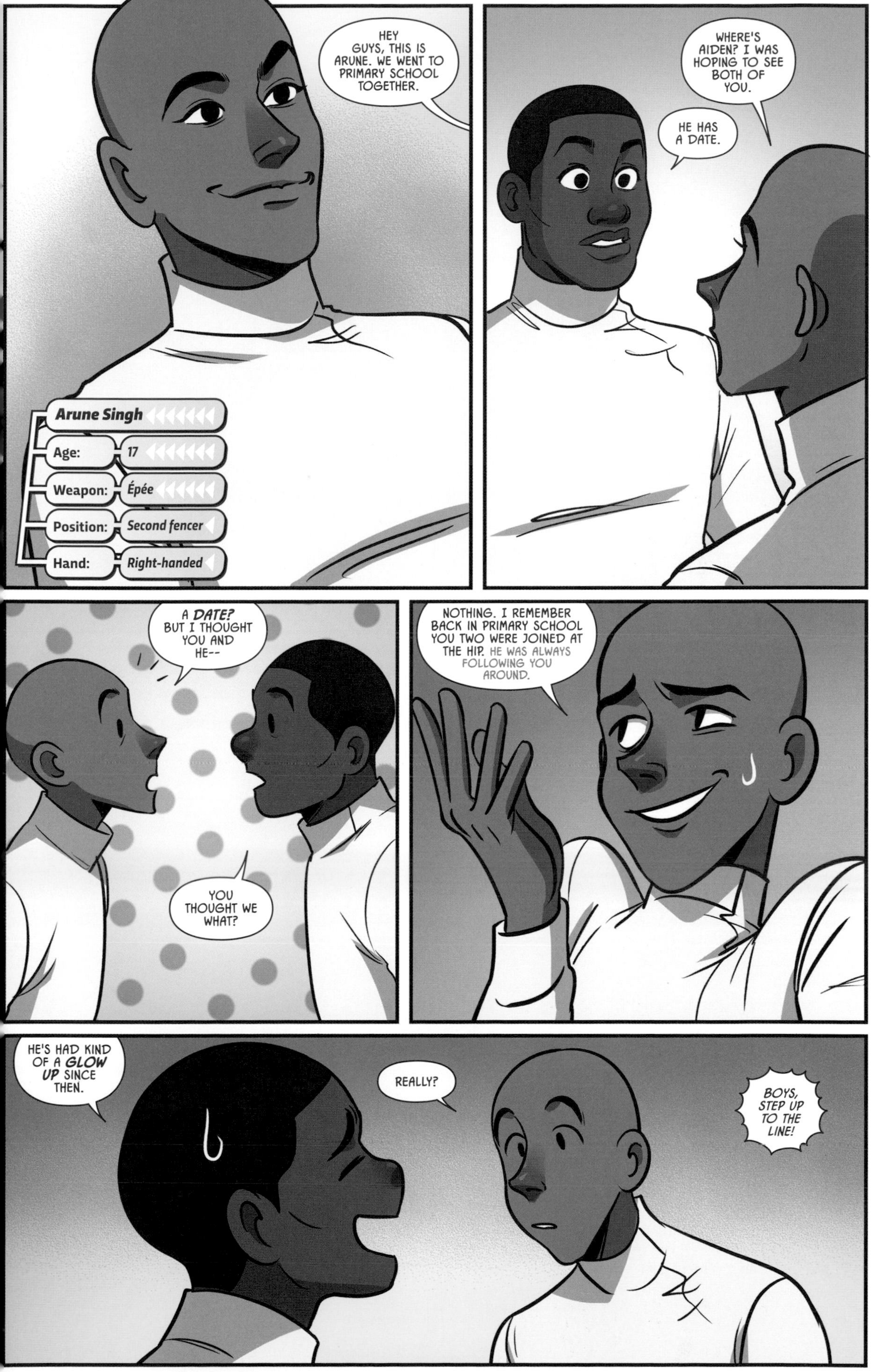
HEY GUYS, THIS IS ARUNE. WE WENT TO PRIMARY SCHOOL TOGETHER.
Arune Singh
Age: 17
Weapon: Épée
Position: Second fencer
Hand: Right-handed
WHERE'S AIDEN? I WAS HOPING TO SEE BOTH OF YOU.
HE HAS A DATE.
A DATE? BUT I THOUGHT YOU AND HE--
YOU THOUGHT WE WHAT?
NOTHING. I REMEMBER BACK IN PRIMARY SCHOOL YOU TWO WERE JOINED AT THE HIP. HE WAS ALWAYS FOLLOWING YOU AROUND.
HE'S HAD KIND OF A GLOW UP SINCE THEN.
REALLY?
BOYS, STEP UP TO THE LINE!

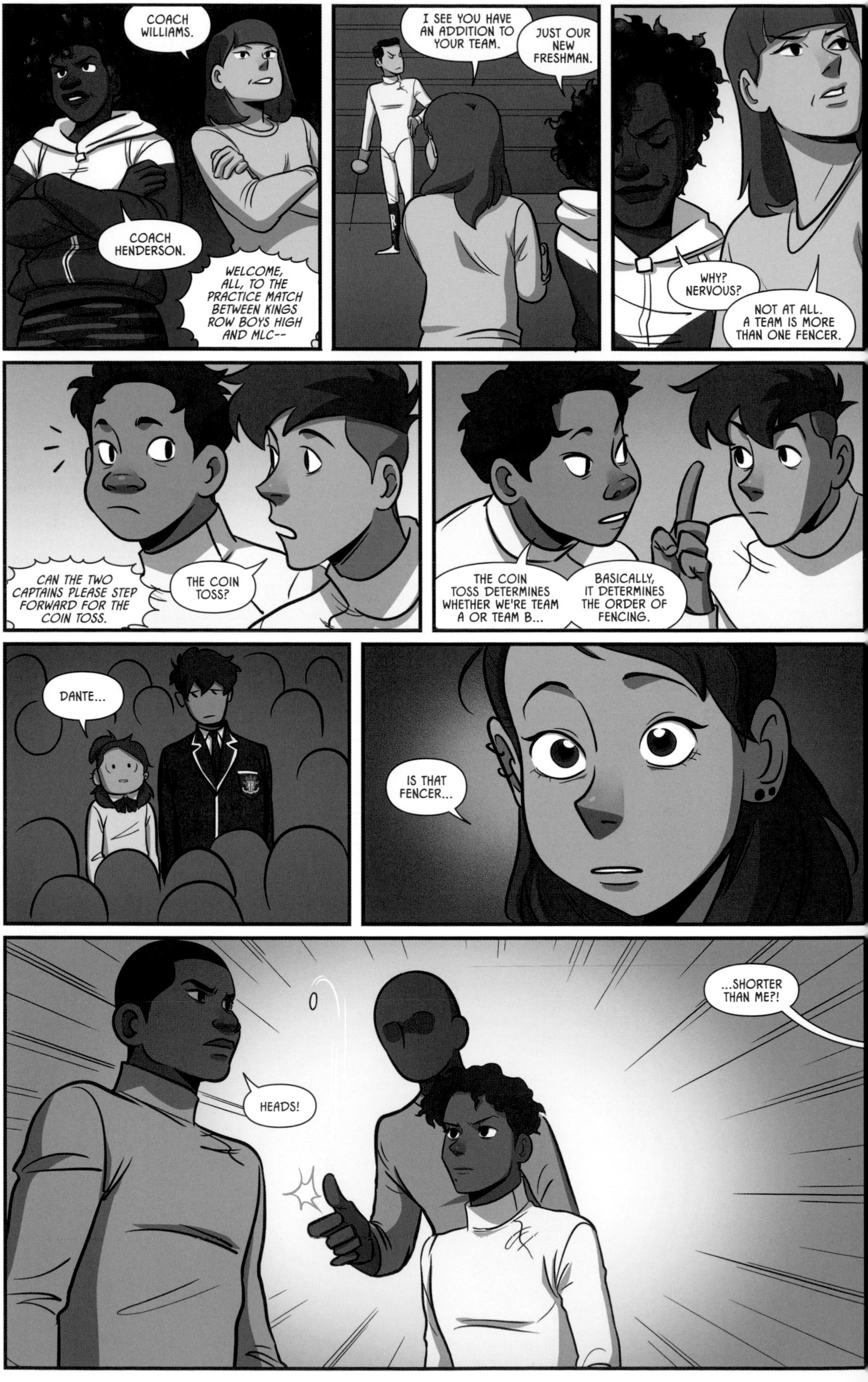
COACH WILLIAMS.
COACH HENDERSON.
WELCOME, ALL, TO THE PRACTICE MATCH BETWEEN KINGS ROW BOYS HIGH AND MLC--
I SEE YOU HAVE AN ADDITION TO YOUR TEAM.
JUST OUR NEW FRESHMAN.
WHY? NERVOUS?
NOT AT ALL. A TEAM IS MORE THAN ONE FENCER.
CAN THE TWO CAPTAINS PLEASE STEP FORWARD FOR THE COIN TOSS.
THE COIN TOSS?
THE COIN TOSS DETERMINES WHETHER WE'RE TEAM A OR TEAM B...
BASICALLY, IT DETERMINES THE ORDER OF FENCING.
DANTE...
IS THAT FENCER...
...SHORTER THAN ME?!
HEADS!

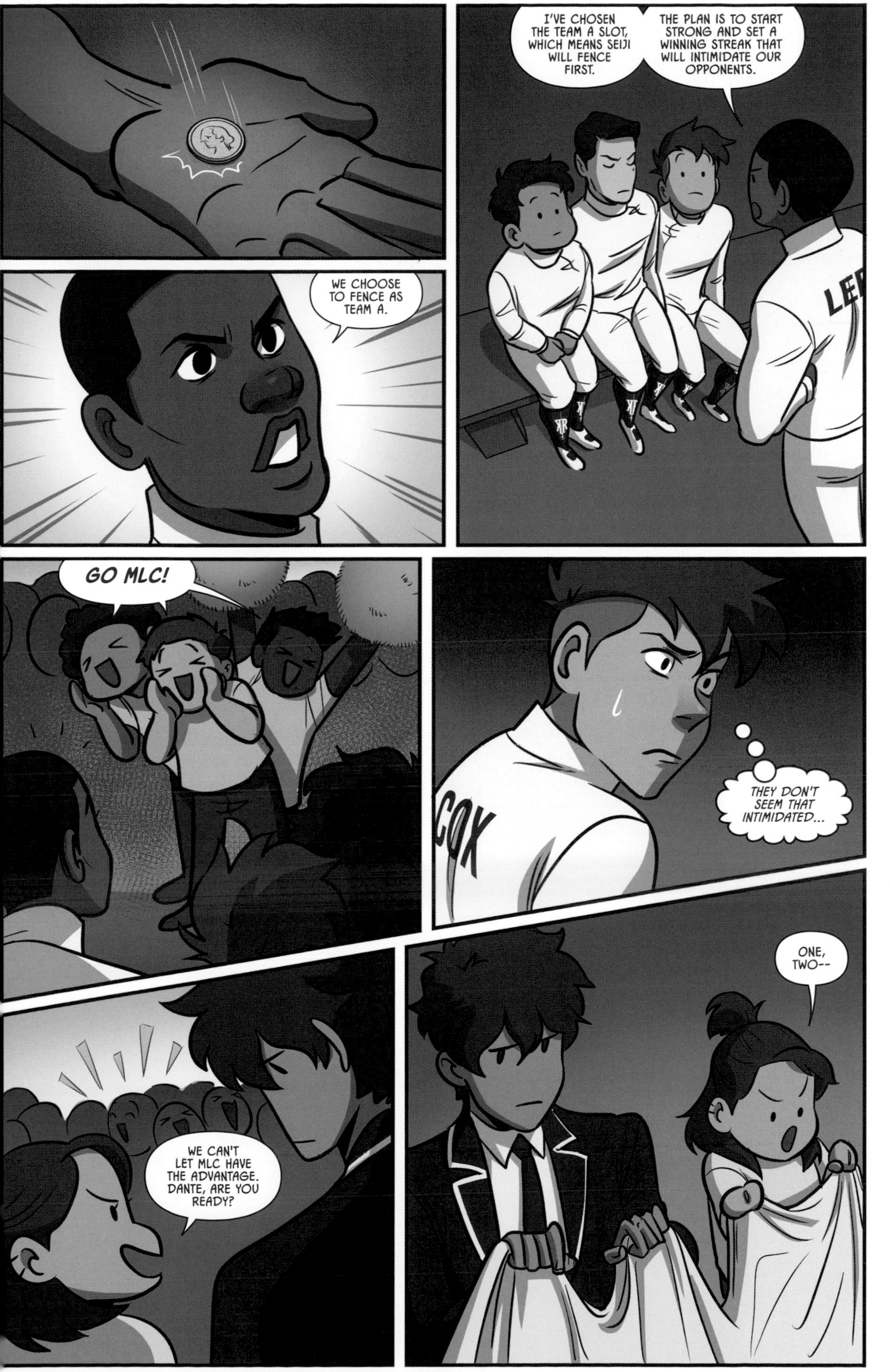
I'VE CHOSEN THE TEAM A SLOT, WHICH MEANS SEIJI WILL FENCE FIRST.
THE PLAN IS TO START STRONG AND SET A WINNING STREAK THAT WILL INTIMIDATE OUR OPPONENTS.
WE CHOOSE TO FENCE AS TEAM A.
LEE
GO MLC!
COX
THEY DON'T SEEM THAT INTIMIDATED...
WE CAN'T LET MLC HAVE THE ADVANTAGE. DANTE, ARE YOU READY?
ONE, TWO--

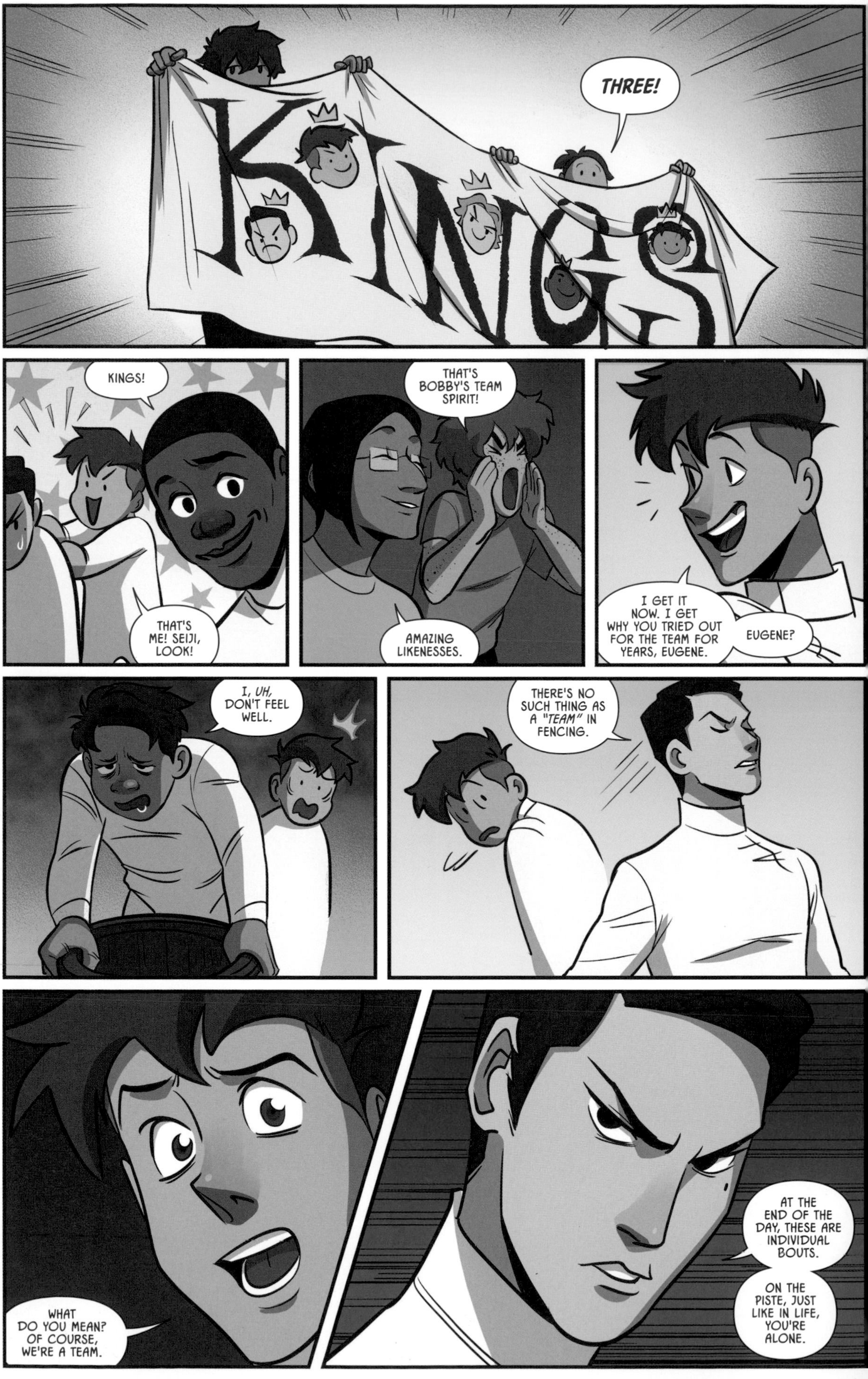
THREE!
KINGS!
THAT'S ME! SEIJI, LOOK!
THAT'S BOBBY'S TEAM SPIRIT!
AMAZING LIKENESSES.
I GET IT NOW. I GET WHY YOU TRIED OUT FOR THE TEAM FOR YEARS, EUGENE.
EUGENE?
I, *UH*, DON'T FEEL WELL.
THERE'S NO SUCH THING AS A *"TEAM"* IN FENCING.
WHAT DO YOU MEAN? OF COURSE, WE'RE A TEAM.
AT THE END OF THE DAY, THESE ARE INDIVIDUAL BOUTS.
ON THE PISTE, JUST LIKE IN LIFE, YOU'RE ALONE.

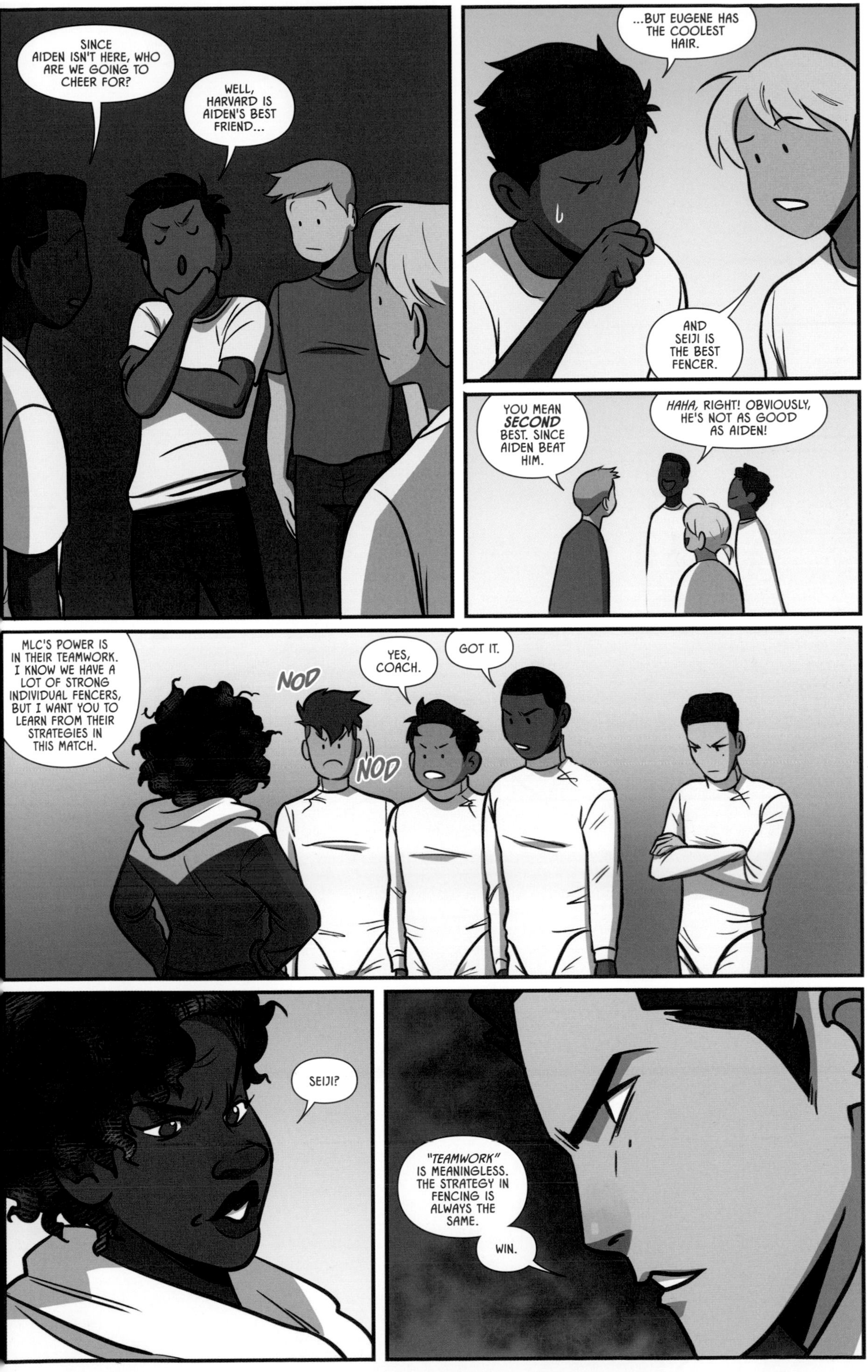
SINCE AIDEN ISN'T HERE, WHO ARE WE GOING TO CHEER FOR?
WELL, HARVARD IS AIDEN'S BEST FRIEND...
...BUT EUGENE HAS THE COOLEST HAIR.
AND SEIJI IS THE BEST FENCER.
YOU MEAN SECOND BEST. SINCE AIDEN BEAT HIM.
HAHA, RIGHT! OBVIOUSLY, HE'S NOT AS GOOD AS AIDEN!
MLC'S POWER IS IN THEIR TEAMWORK. I KNOW WE HAVE A LOT OF STRONG INDIVIDUAL FENCERS, BUT I WANT YOU TO LEARN FROM THEIR STRATEGIES IN THIS MATCH.
NOD
YES, COACH.
GOT IT.
NOD
SEIJI?
"TEAMWORK" IS MEANINGLESS. THE STRATEGY IN FENCING IS ALWAYS THE SAME.
WIN.

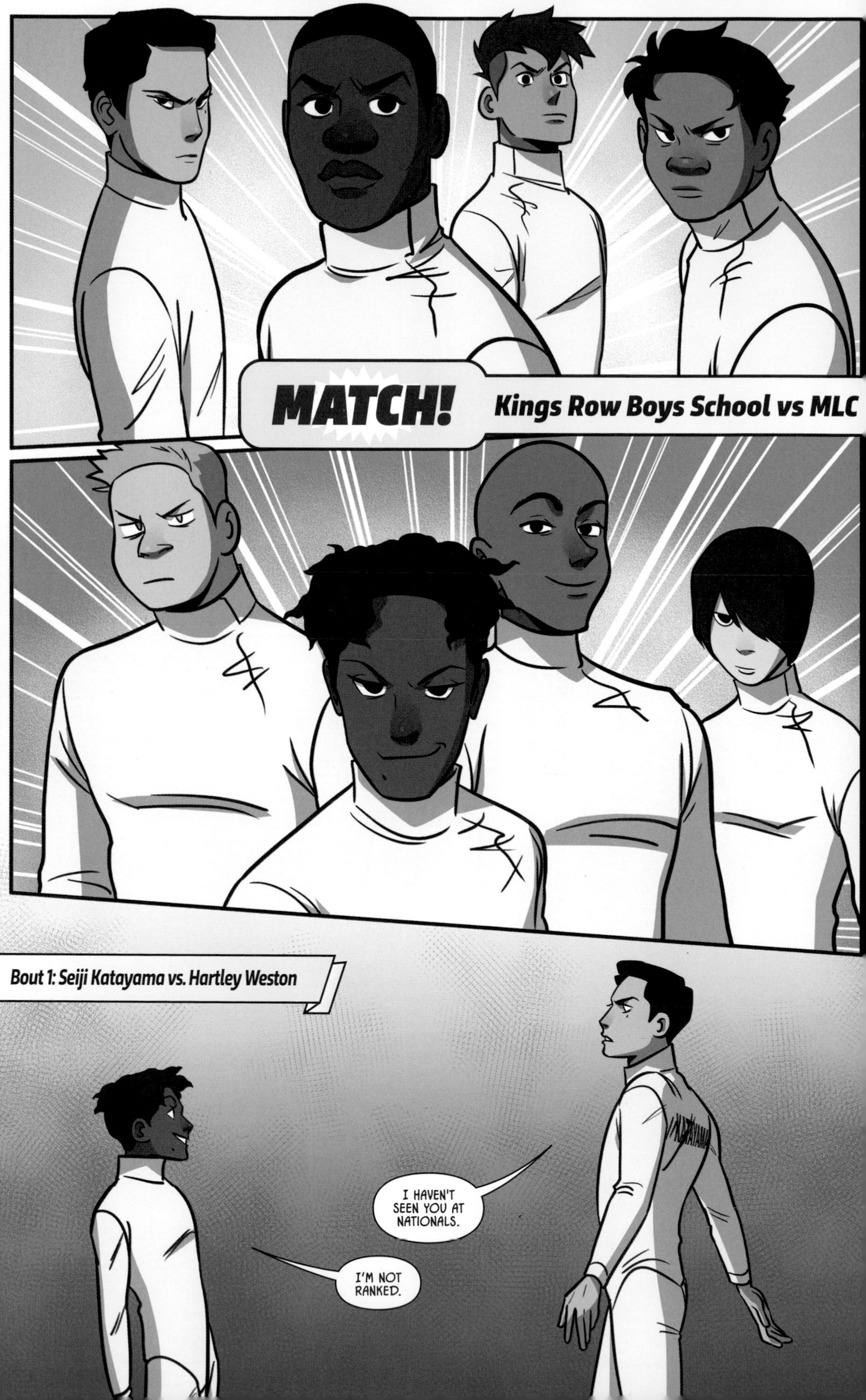
MATCH!
Kings Row Boys School vs MLC
Bout 1: Seiji Katayama vs. Hartley Weston
I HAVEN'T SEEN YOU AT NATIONALS.
I'M NOT RANKED.

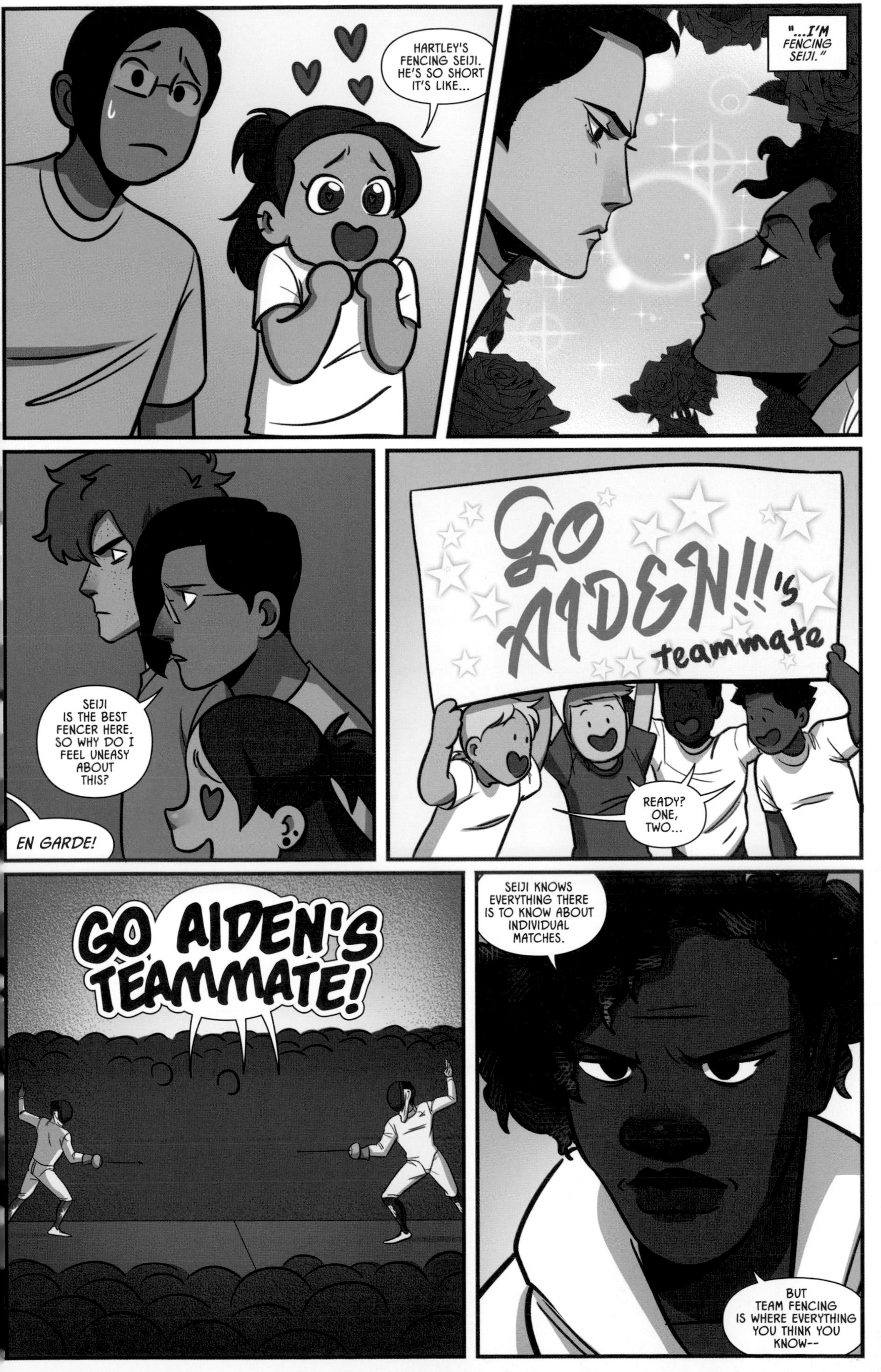
HARTLEY'S FENCING SEIJI. HE'S SO SHORT IT'S LIKE...
"...I'M FENCING SEIJI."
SEIJI IS THE BEST FENCER HERE. SO WHY DO I FEEL UNEASY ABOUT THIS?
EN GARDE!
GO AIDEN!!'s teammate
READY? ONE, TWO...
GO AIDEN'S TEAMMATE!
SEIJI KNOWS EVERYTHING THERE IS TO KNOW ABOUT INDIVIDUAL MATCHES.
BUT TEAM FENCING IS WHERE EVERYTHING YOU THINK YOU KNOW--

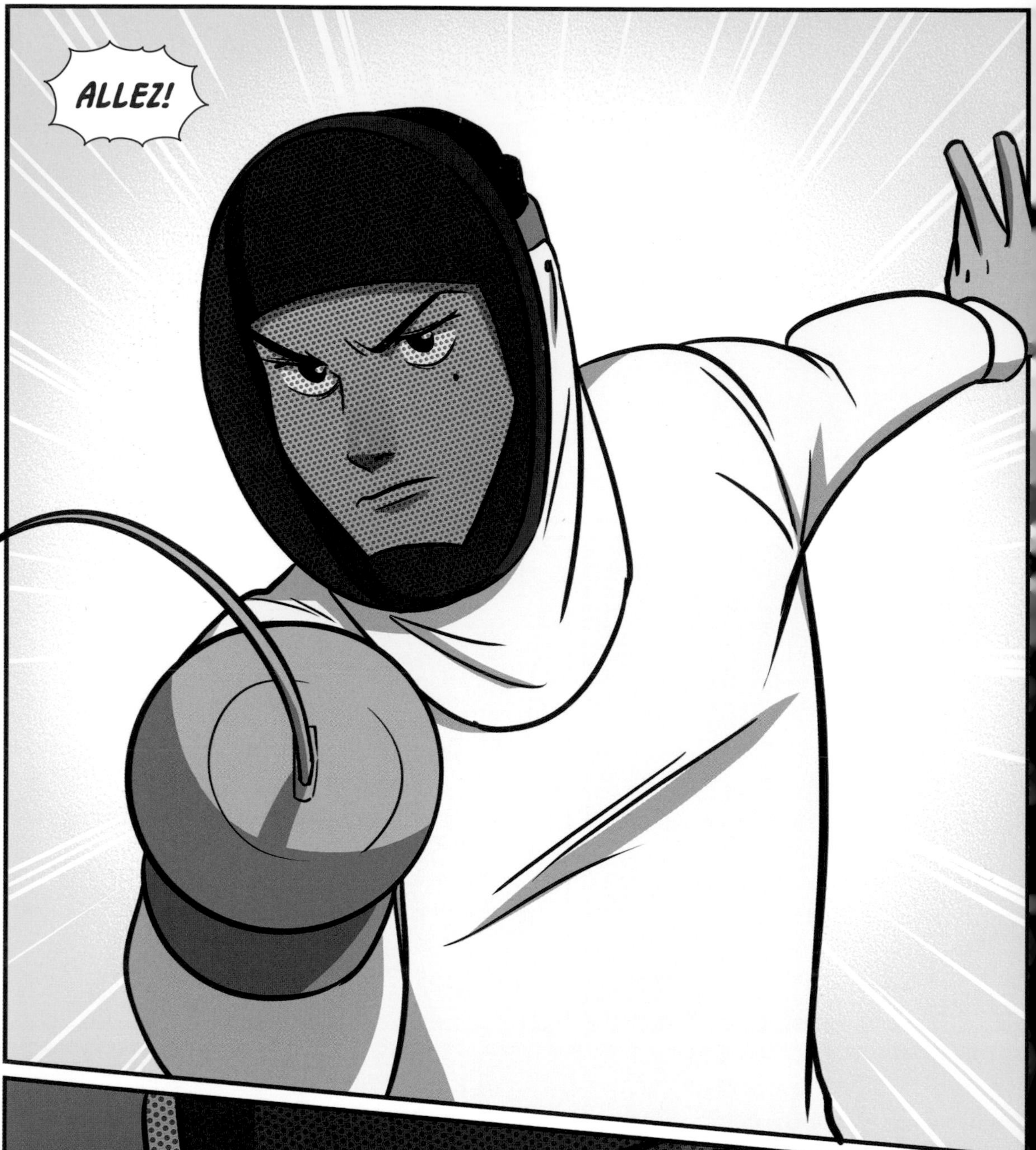
ALLEZ!

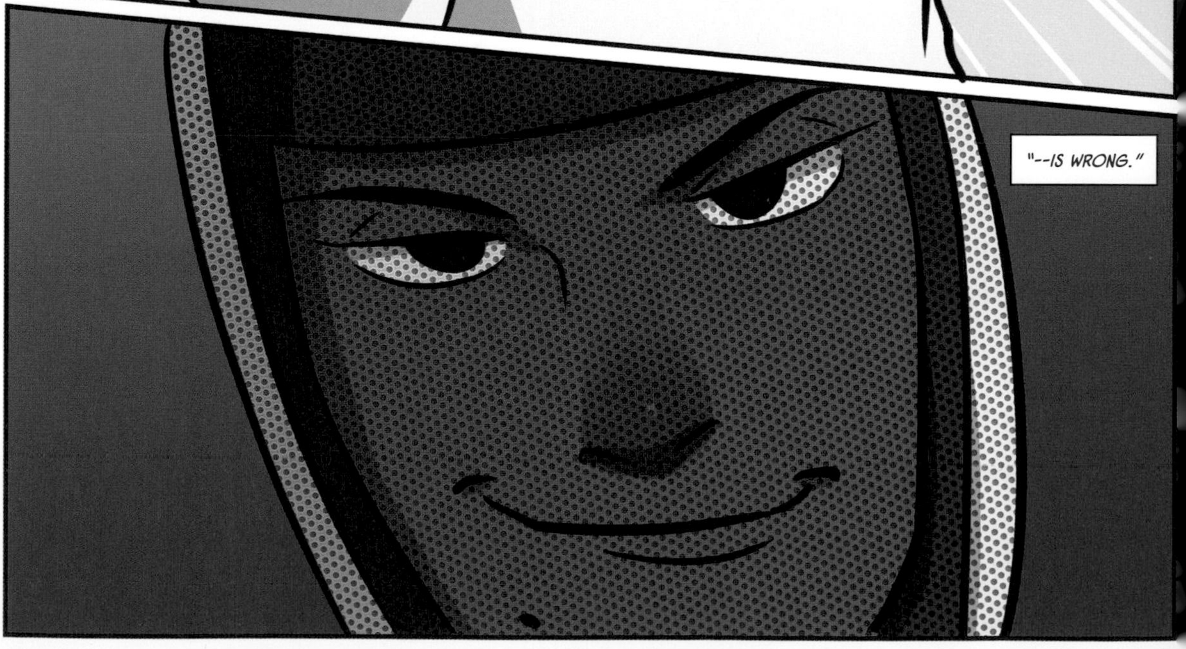
"--IS WRONG."

CHAPTER
FIFTEEN

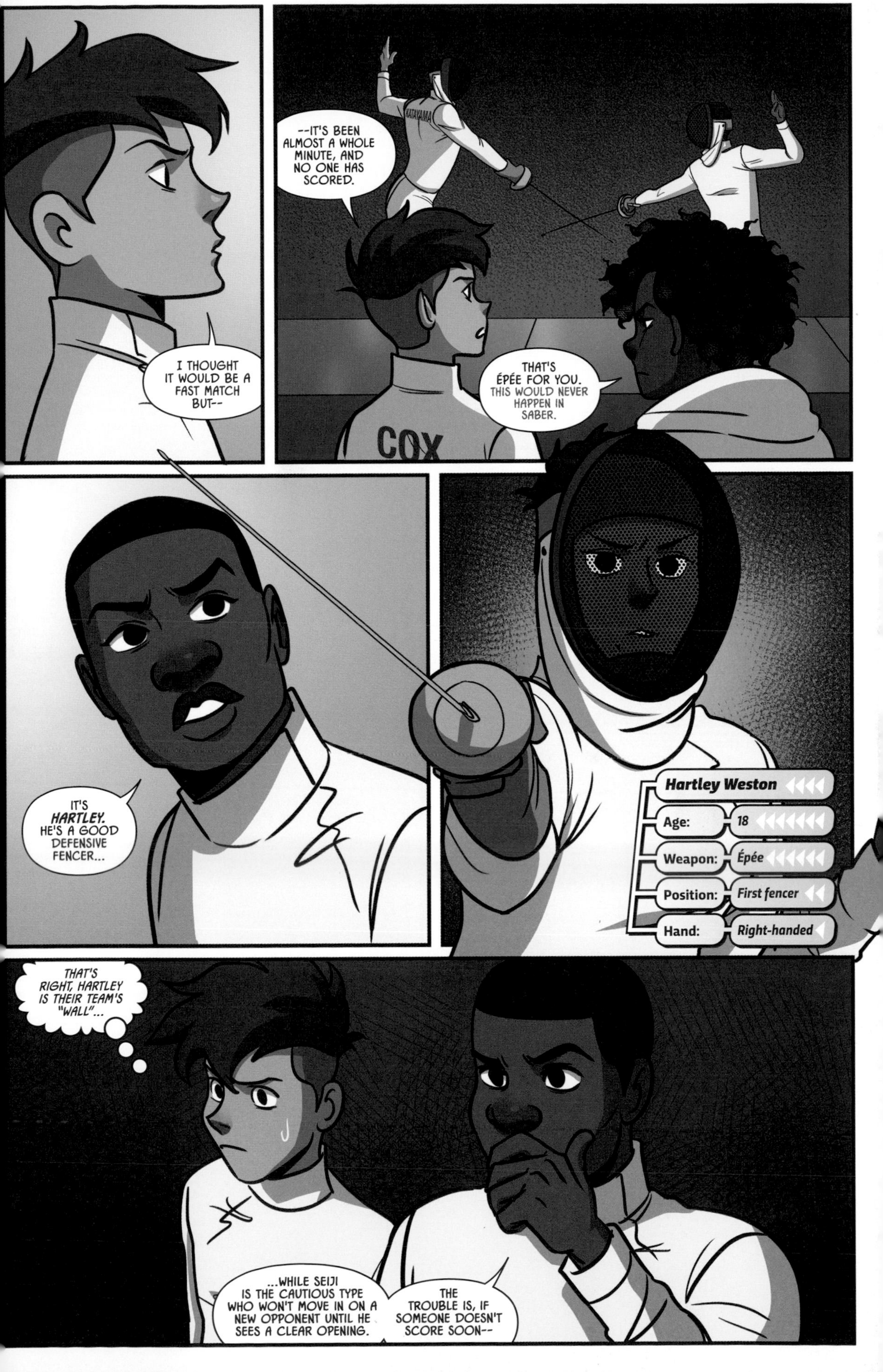
I THOUGHT IT WOULD BE A FAST MATCH BUT--
--IT'S BEEN ALMOST A WHOLE MINUTE, AND NO ONE HAS SCORED.
KATAYAMA
THAT'S ÉPÉE FOR YOU. THIS WOULD NEVER HAPPEN IN SABER.
COX
IT'S *HARTLEY.* HE'S A GOOD DEFENSIVE FENCER...
Hartley Weston
Age: 18
Weapon: Épée
Position: First fencer
Hand: Right-handed
THAT'S RIGHT, HARTLEY IS THEIR TEAM'S "WALL"...
...WHILE SEIJI IS THE CAUTIOUS TYPE WHO WON'T MOVE IN ON A NEW OPPONENT UNTIL HE SEES A CLEAR OPENING.
THE TROUBLE IS, IF SOMEONE DOESN'T SCORE SOON--

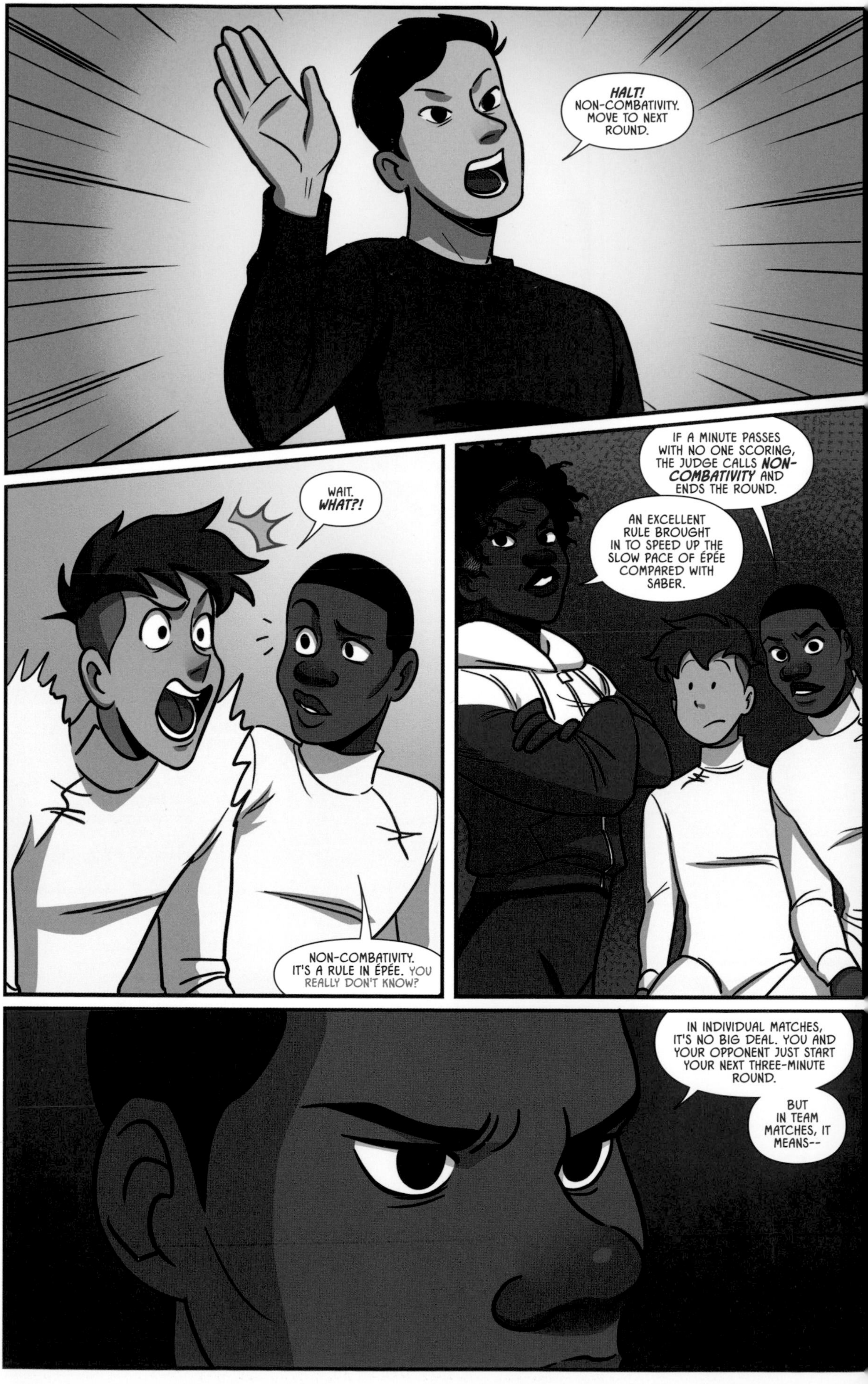
HALT! NON-COMBATIVITY. MOVE TO NEXT ROUND.
WAIT. WHAT?!
NON-COMBATIVITY. IT'S A RULE IN ÉPÉE. YOU REALLY DON'T KNOW?
IF A MINUTE PASSES WITH NO ONE SCORING, THE JUDGE CALLS NON-COMBATIVITY AND ENDS THE ROUND.
AN EXCELLENT RULE BROUGHT IN TO SPEED UP THE SLOW PACE OF ÉPÉE COMPARED WITH SABER.
IN INDIVIDUAL MATCHES, IT'S NO BIG DEAL. YOU AND YOUR OPPONENT JUST START YOUR NEXT THREE-MINUTE ROUND.
BUT IN TEAM MATCHES, IT MEANS--

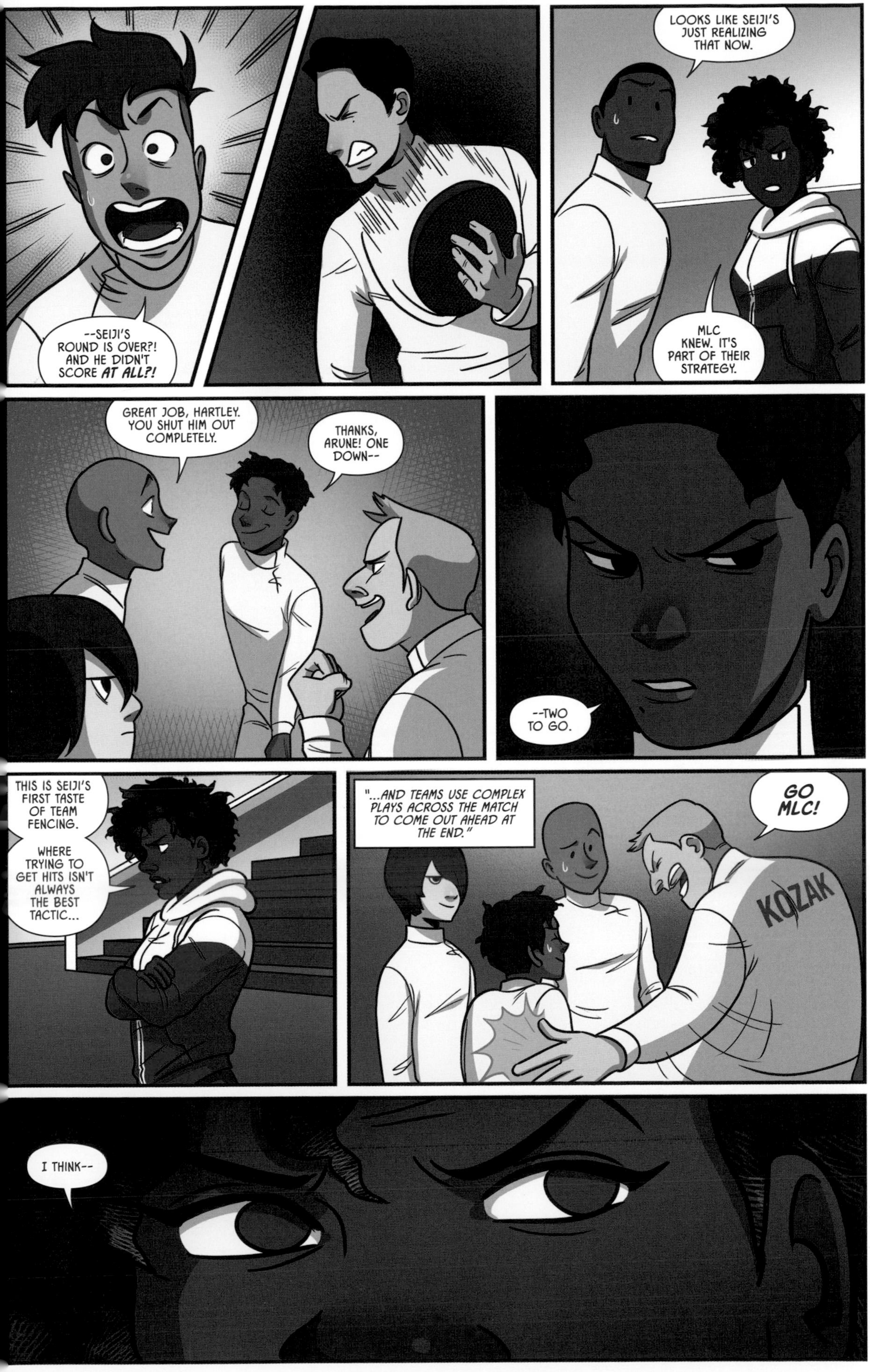
--SEIJI'S ROUND IS OVER?! AND HE DIDN'T SCORE *AT ALL?!*
LOOKS LIKE SEIJI'S JUST REALIZING THAT NOW.
MLC KNEW. IT'S PART OF THEIR STRATEGY.
GREAT JOB, HARTLEY. YOU SHUT HIM OUT COMPLETELY.
THANKS, ARUNE! ONE DOWN--
--TWO TO GO.
THIS IS SEIJI'S FIRST TASTE OF TEAM FENCING.
WHERE TRYING TO GET HITS ISN'T ALWAYS THE BEST TACTIC...
"...AND TEAMS USE COMPLEX PLAYS ACROSS THE MATCH TO COME OUT AHEAD AT THE END."
GO MLC!
KOZAK
I THINK--

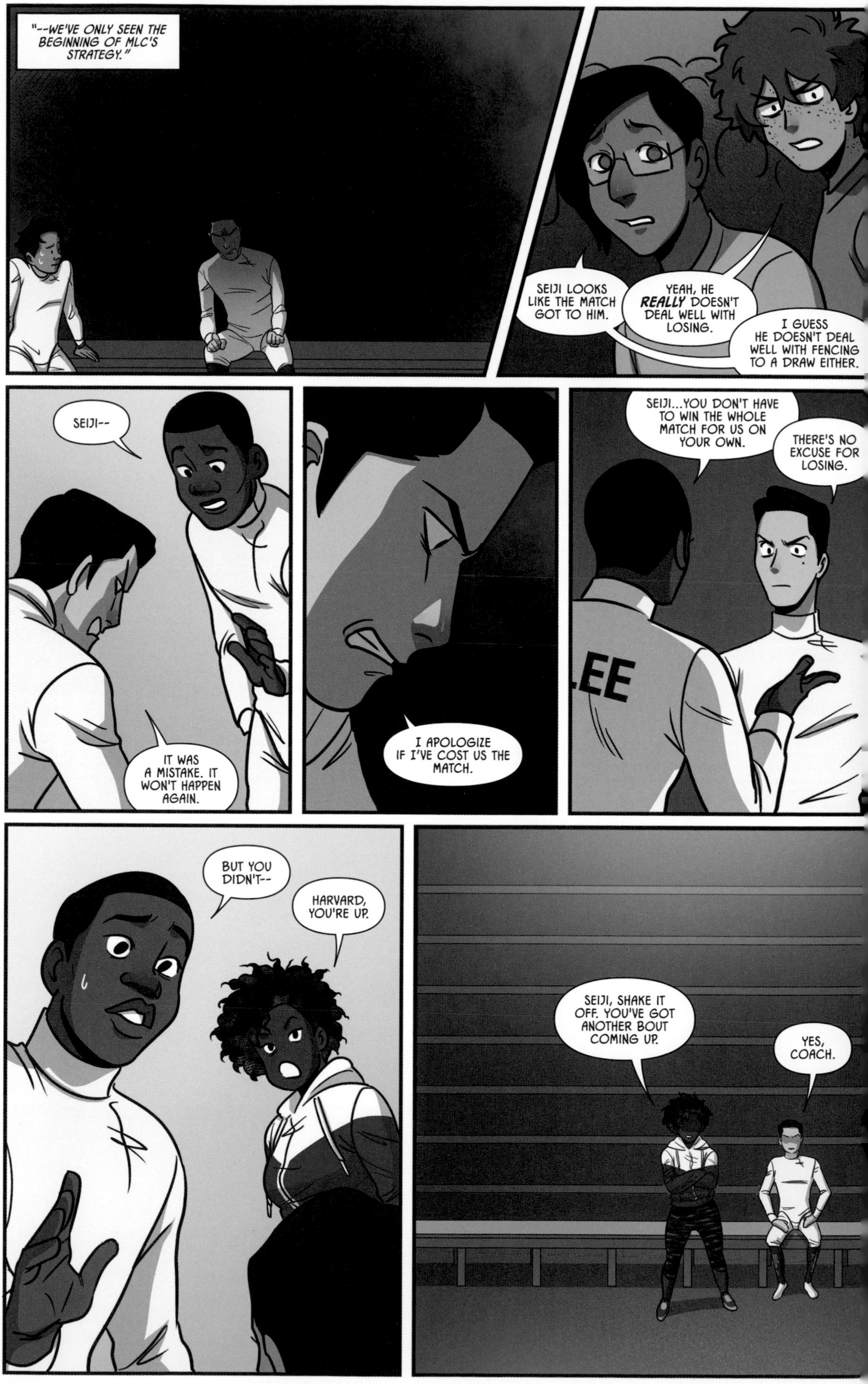
"--WE'VE ONLY SEEN THE BEGINNING OF MLC'S STRATEGY."
SEIJI LOOKS LIKE THE MATCH GOT TO HIM.
YEAH, HE *REALLY* DOESN'T DEAL WELL WITH LOSING.
I GUESS HE DOESN'T DEAL WELL WITH FENCING TO A DRAW EITHER.
SEIJI--
IT WAS A MISTAKE. IT WON'T HAPPEN AGAIN.
I APOLOGIZE IF I'VE COST US THE MATCH.
SEIJI...YOU DON'T HAVE TO WIN THE WHOLE MATCH FOR US ON YOUR OWN.
LEE
THERE'S NO EXCUSE FOR LOSING.
BUT YOU DIDN'T--
HARVARD, YOU'RE UP.
SEIJI, SHAKE IT OFF. YOU'VE GOT ANOTHER BOUT COMING UP.
YES, COACH.

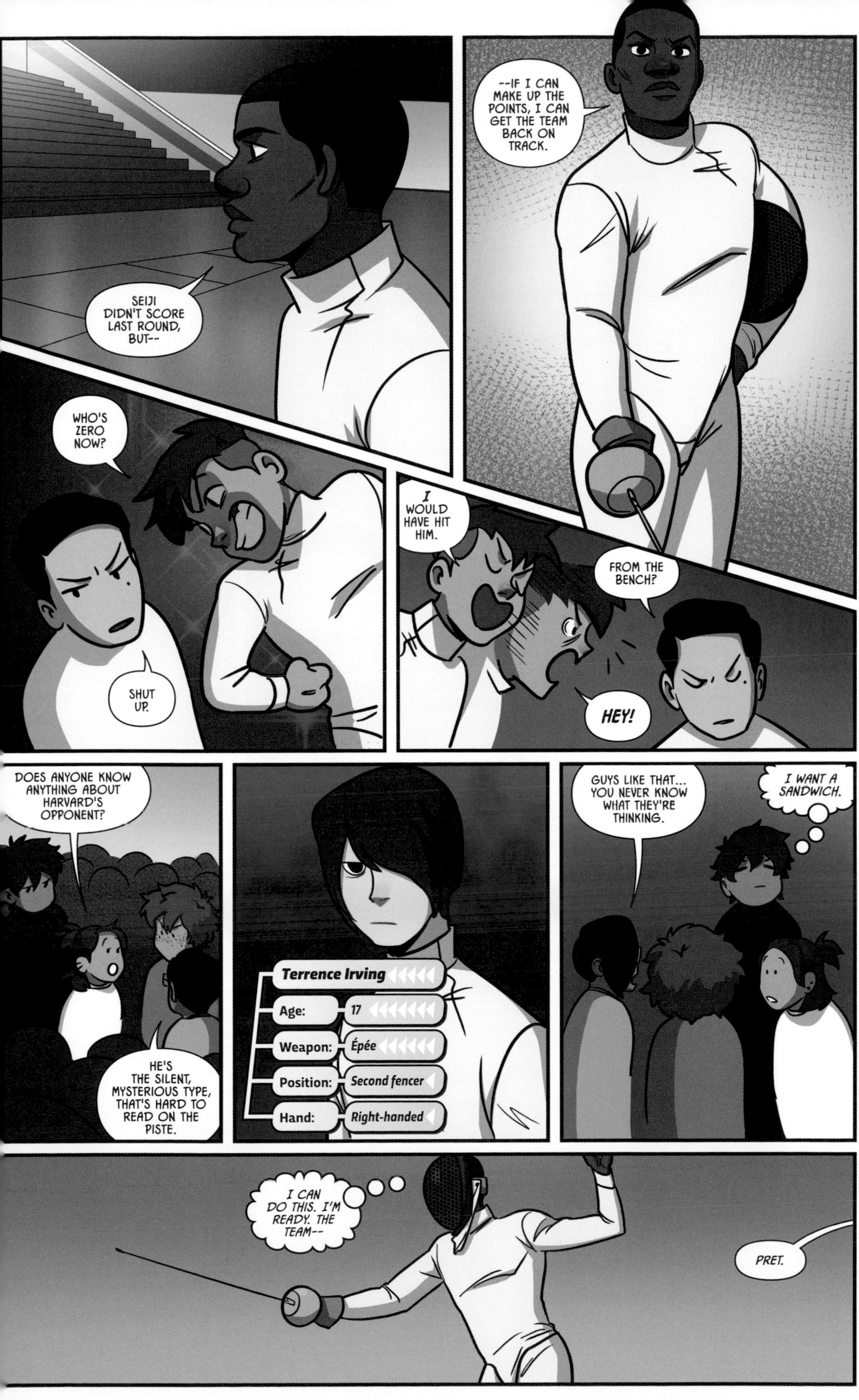
SEIJI DIDN'T SCORE LAST ROUND, BUT--
--IF I CAN MAKE UP THE POINTS, I CAN GET THE TEAM BACK ON TRACK.
WHO'S ZERO NOW?
SHUT UP.
I WOULD HAVE HIT HIM.
FROM THE BENCH?
HEY!
DOES ANYONE KNOW ANYTHING ABOUT HARVARD'S OPPONENT?
HE'S THE SILENT, MYSTERIOUS TYPE, THAT'S HARD TO READ ON THE PISTE.
Terrence Irving
Age: 17
Weapon: Épée
Position: Second fencer
Hand: Right-handed
GUYS LIKE THAT... YOU NEVER KNOW WHAT THEY'RE THINKING.
I WANT A SANDWICH.
I CAN DO THIS. I'M READY. THE TEAM--
PRET.

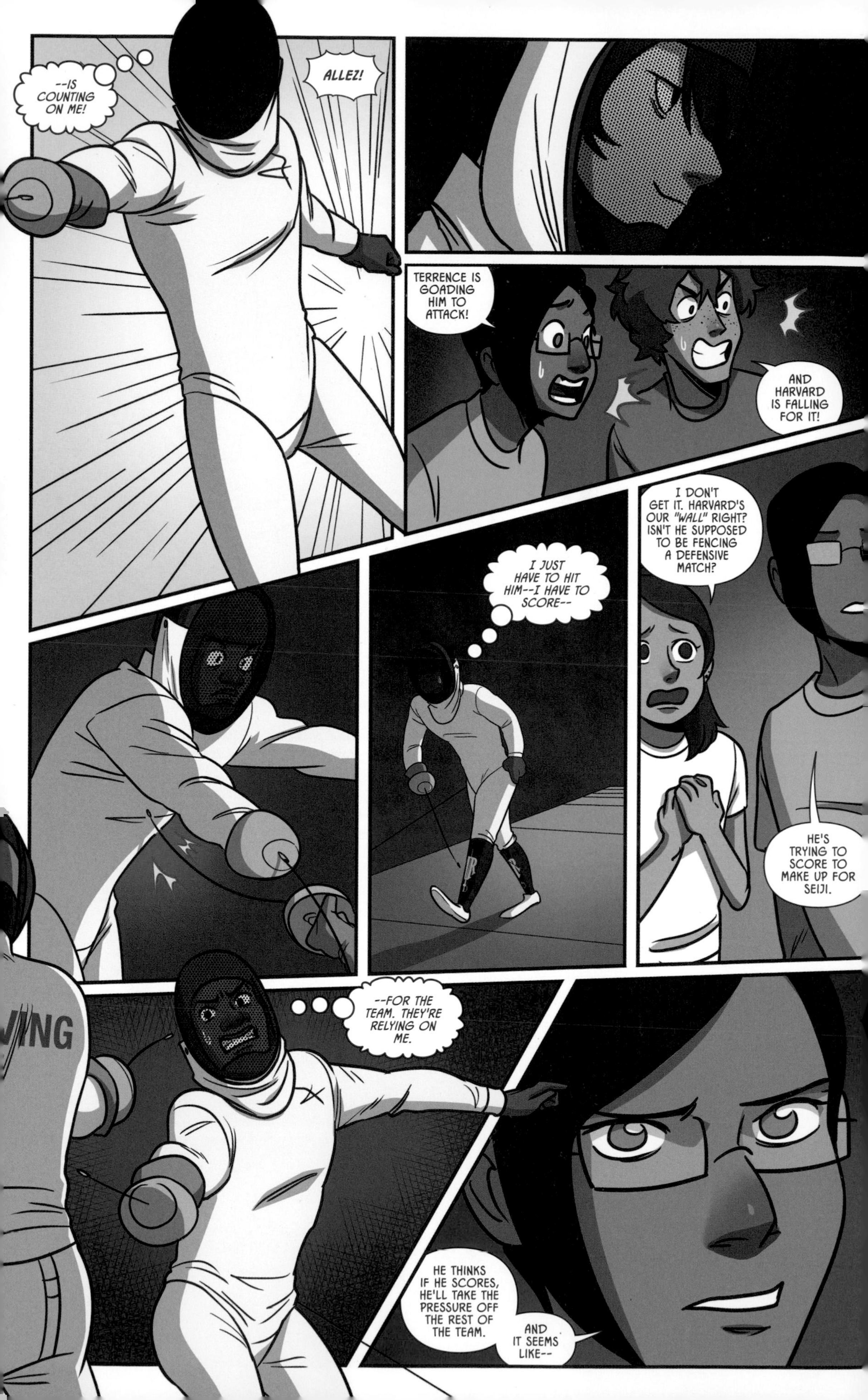
--IS COUNTING ON ME!
ALLEZ!
TERRENCE IS GOADING HIM TO ATTACK!
AND HARVARD IS FALLING FOR IT!
I JUST HAVE TO HIT HIM--I HAVE TO SCORE--
I DON'T GET IT. HARVARD'S OUR "WALL" RIGHT? ISN'T HE SUPPOSED TO BE FENCING A DEFENSIVE MATCH?
HE'S TRYING TO SCORE TO MAKE UP FOR SEIJI.
VING
--FOR THE TEAM. THEY'RE RELYING ON ME.
HE THINKS IF HE SCORES, HE'LL TAKE THE PRESSURE OFF THE REST OF THE TEAM.
AND IT SEEMS LIKE--

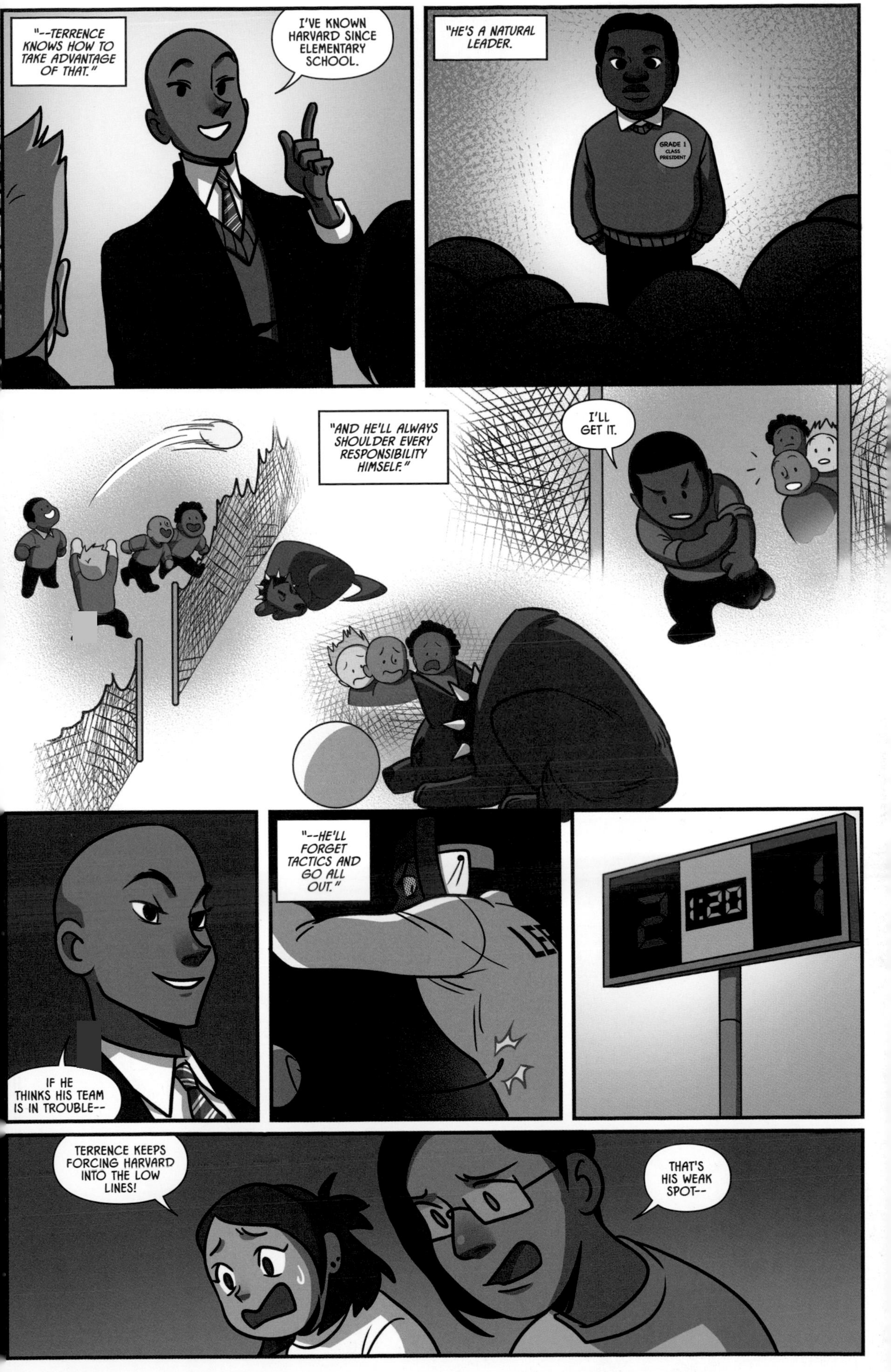
"--TERRENCE KNOWS HOW TO TAKE ADVANTAGE OF THAT."
I'VE KNOWN HARVARD SINCE ELEMENTARY SCHOOL.
"HE'S A NATURAL LEADER.
GRADE 1 CLASS PRESIDENT
"AND HE'LL ALWAYS SHOULDER EVERY RESPONSIBILITY HIMSELF."
I'LL GET IT.
IF HE THINKS HIS TEAM IS IN TROUBLE--
"--HE'LL FORGET TACTICS AND GO ALL OUT."
1:20
TERRENCE KEEPS FORCING HARVARD INTO THE LOW LINES!
THAT'S HIS WEAK SPOT--

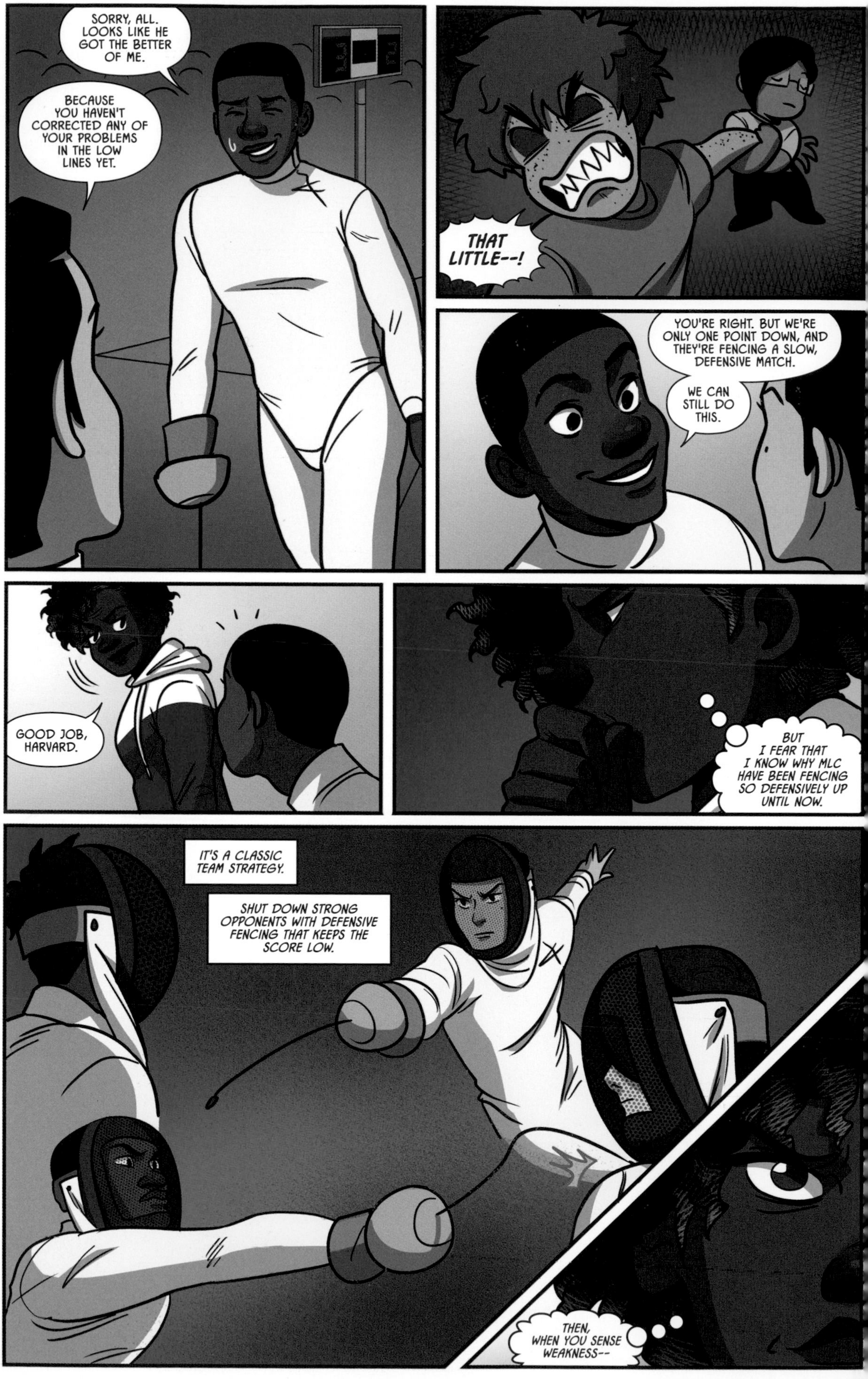
SORRY, ALL. LOOKS LIKE HE GOT THE BETTER OF ME.
BECAUSE YOU HAVEN'T CORRECTED ANY OF YOUR PROBLEMS IN THE LOW LINES YET.
THAT LITTLE--!
YOU'RE RIGHT. BUT WE'RE ONLY ONE POINT DOWN, AND THEY'RE FENCING A SLOW, DEFENSIVE MATCH.
WE CAN STILL DO THIS.
GOOD JOB, HARVARD.
BUT I FEAR THAT I KNOW WHY MLC HAVE BEEN FENCING SO DEFENSIVELY UP UNTIL NOW.
IT'S A CLASSIC TEAM STRATEGY.
SHUT DOWN STRONG OPPONENTS WITH DEFENSIVE FENCING THAT KEEPS THE SCORE LOW.
THEN, WHEN YOU SENSE WEAKNESS--

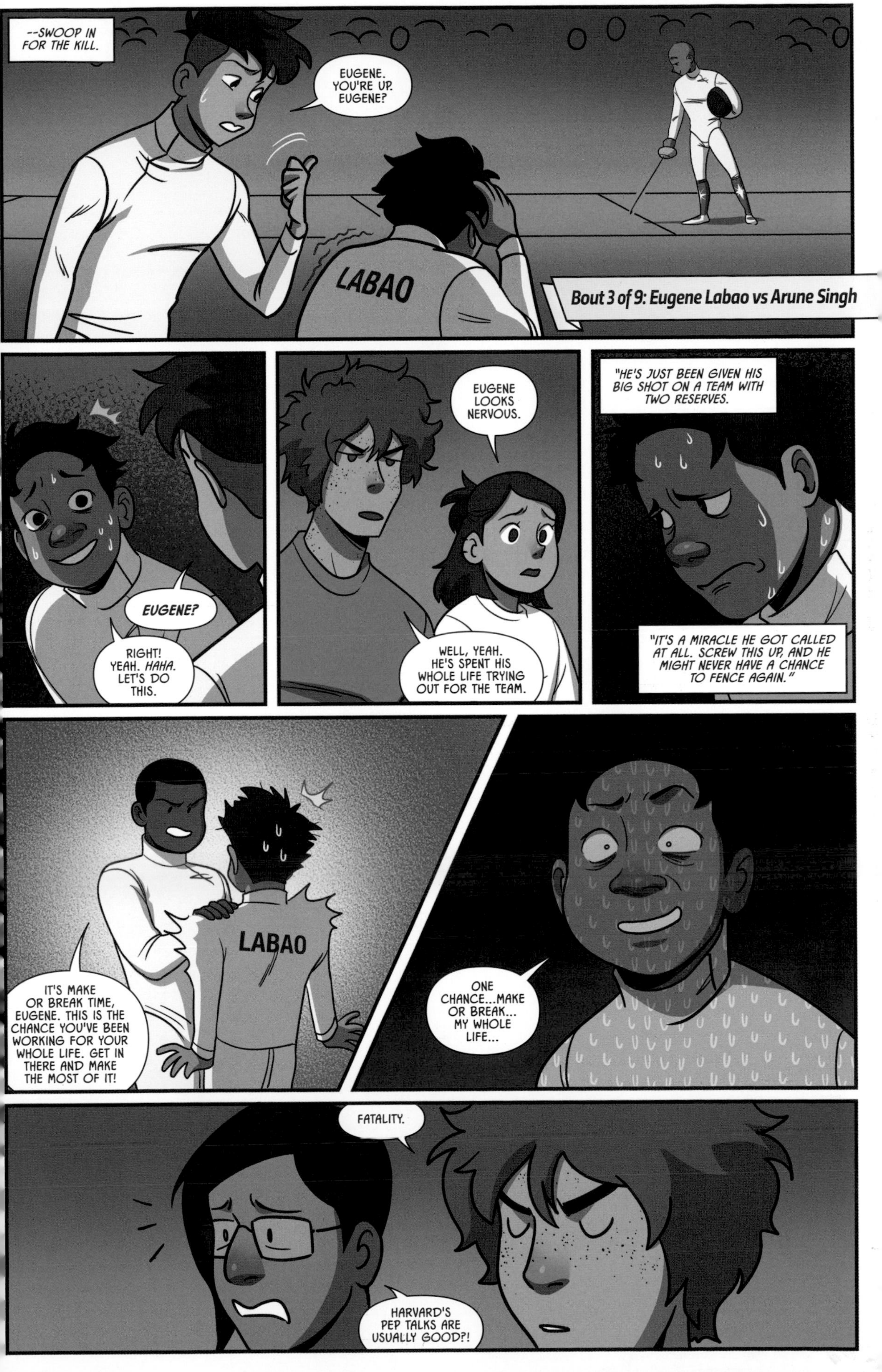
--SWOOP IN FOR THE KILL.
EUGENE. YOU'RE UP. EUGENE?
LABAO
Bout 3 of 9: Eugene Labao vs Arune Singh
EUGENE?
RIGHT! YEAH. HAHA. LET'S DO THIS.
EUGENE LOOKS NERVOUS.
WELL, YEAH. HE'S SPENT HIS WHOLE LIFE TRYING OUT FOR THE TEAM.
"HE'S JUST BEEN GIVEN HIS BIG SHOT ON A TEAM WITH TWO RESERVES.
"IT'S A MIRACLE HE GOT CALLED AT ALL. SCREW THIS UP, AND HE MIGHT NEVER HAVE A CHANCE TO FENCE AGAIN."
LABAO
IT'S MAKE OR BREAK TIME, EUGENE. THIS IS THE CHANCE YOU'VE BEEN WORKING FOR YOUR WHOLE LIFE. GET IN THERE AND MAKE THE MOST OF IT!
ONE CHANCE...MAKE OR BREAK... MY WHOLE LIFE...
FATALITY.
HARVARD'S PEP TALKS ARE USUALLY GOOD?!

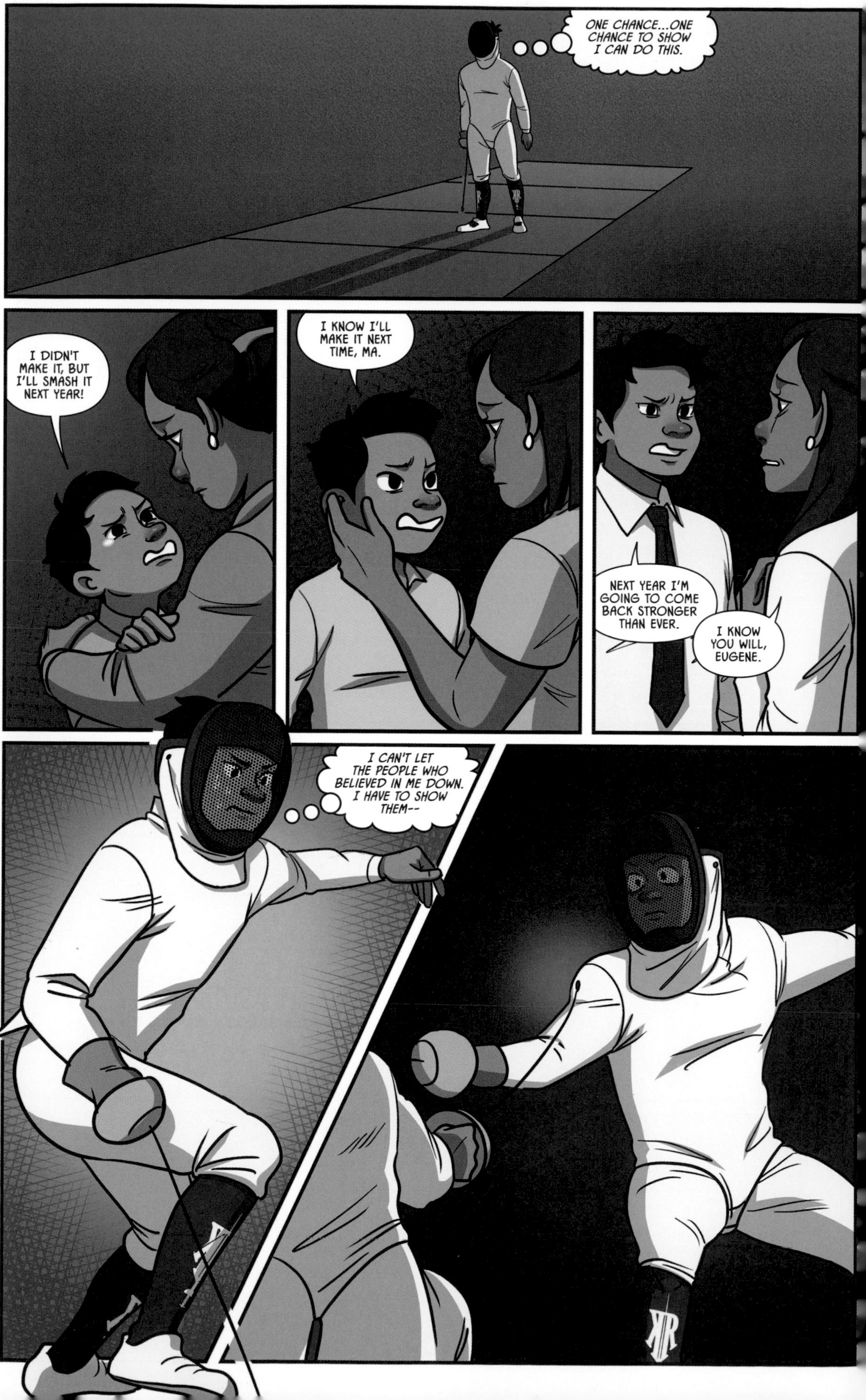
ONE CHANCE...ONE CHANCE TO SHOW I CAN DO THIS.
I DIDN'T MAKE IT, BUT I'LL SMASH IT NEXT YEAR!
I KNOW I'LL MAKE IT NEXT TIME, MA.
NEXT YEAR I'M GOING TO COME BACK STRONGER THAN EVER.
I KNOW YOU WILL, EUGENE.
I CAN'T LET THE PEOPLE WHO BELIEVED IN ME DOWN. I HAVE TO SHOW THEM--

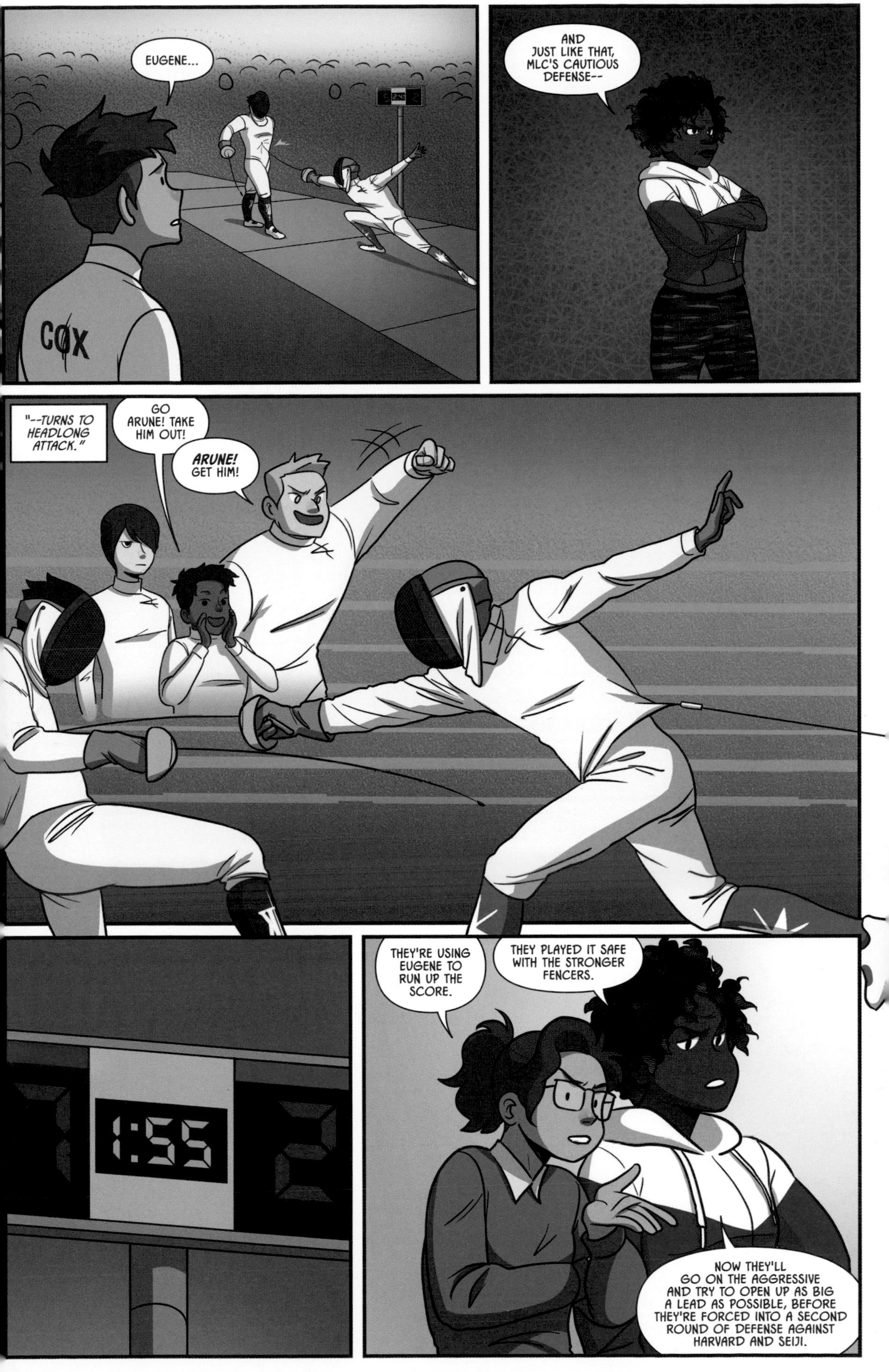
EUGENE...
AND JUST LIKE THAT, MLC'S CAUTIOUS DEFENSE--
"--TURNS TO HEADLONG ATTACK."
GO ARUNE! TAKE HIM OUT!
ARUNE! GET HIM!
1:55
THEY'RE USING EUGENE TO RUN UP THE SCORE.
THEY PLAYED IT SAFE WITH THE STRONGER FENCERS.
NOW THEY'LL GO ON THE AGGRESSIVE AND TRY TO OPEN UP AS BIG A LEAD AS POSSIBLE, BEFORE THEY'RE FORCED INTO A SECOND ROUND OF DEFENSE AGAINST HARVARD AND SEIJI.

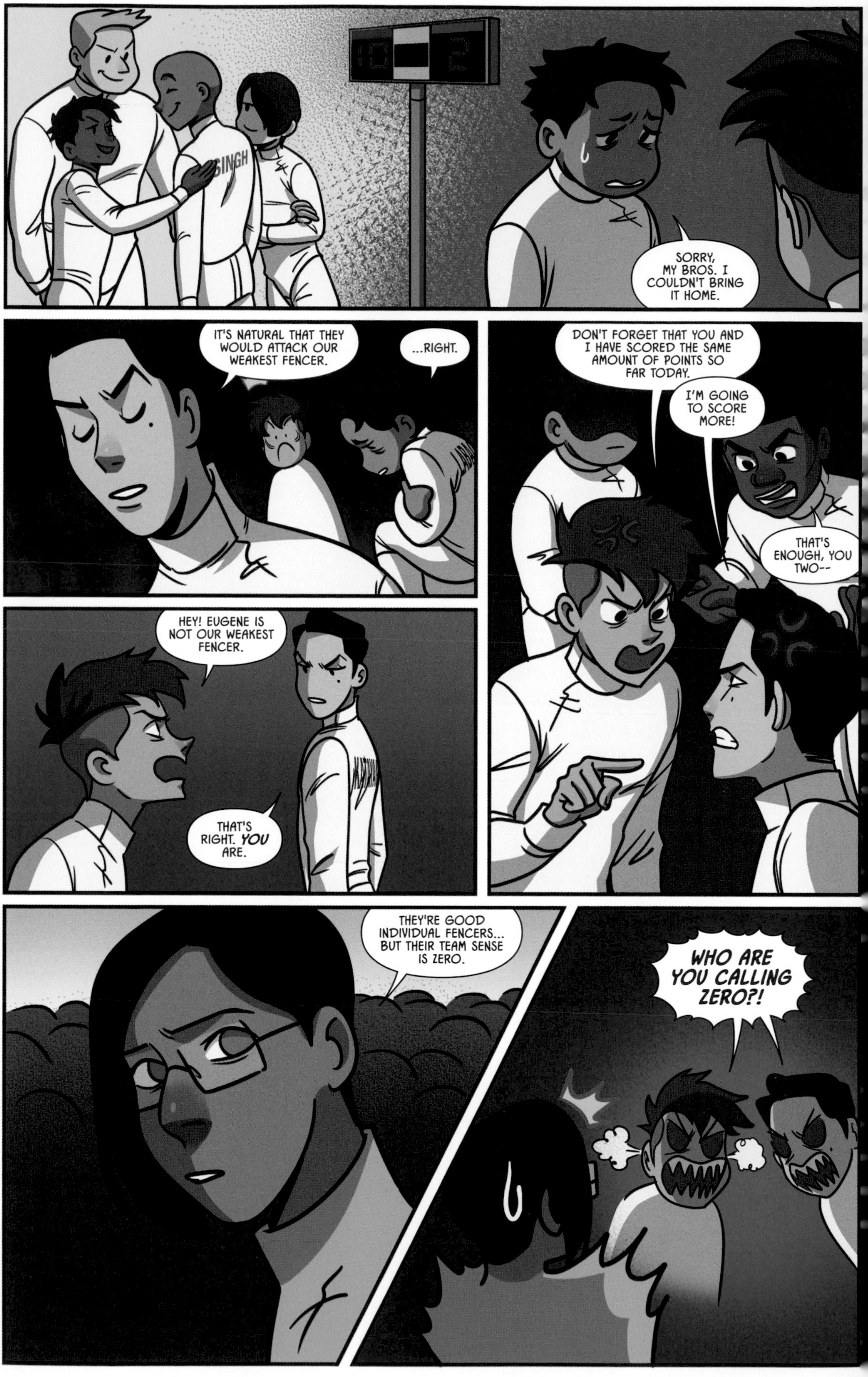
10 2
SINGH
SORRY, MY BROS. I COULDN'T BRING IT HOME.
IT'S NATURAL THAT THEY WOULD ATTACK OUR WEAKEST FENCER.
...RIGHT.
HEY! EUGENE IS NOT OUR WEAKEST FENCER.
THAT'S RIGHT. *YOU* ARE.
DON'T FORGET THAT YOU AND I HAVE SCORED THE SAME AMOUNT OF POINTS SO FAR TODAY.
I'M GOING TO SCORE MORE!
THAT'S ENOUGH, YOU TWO--
THEY'RE GOOD INDIVIDUAL FENCERS... BUT THEIR TEAM SENSE IS ZERO.
WHO ARE YOU CALLING ZERO?!

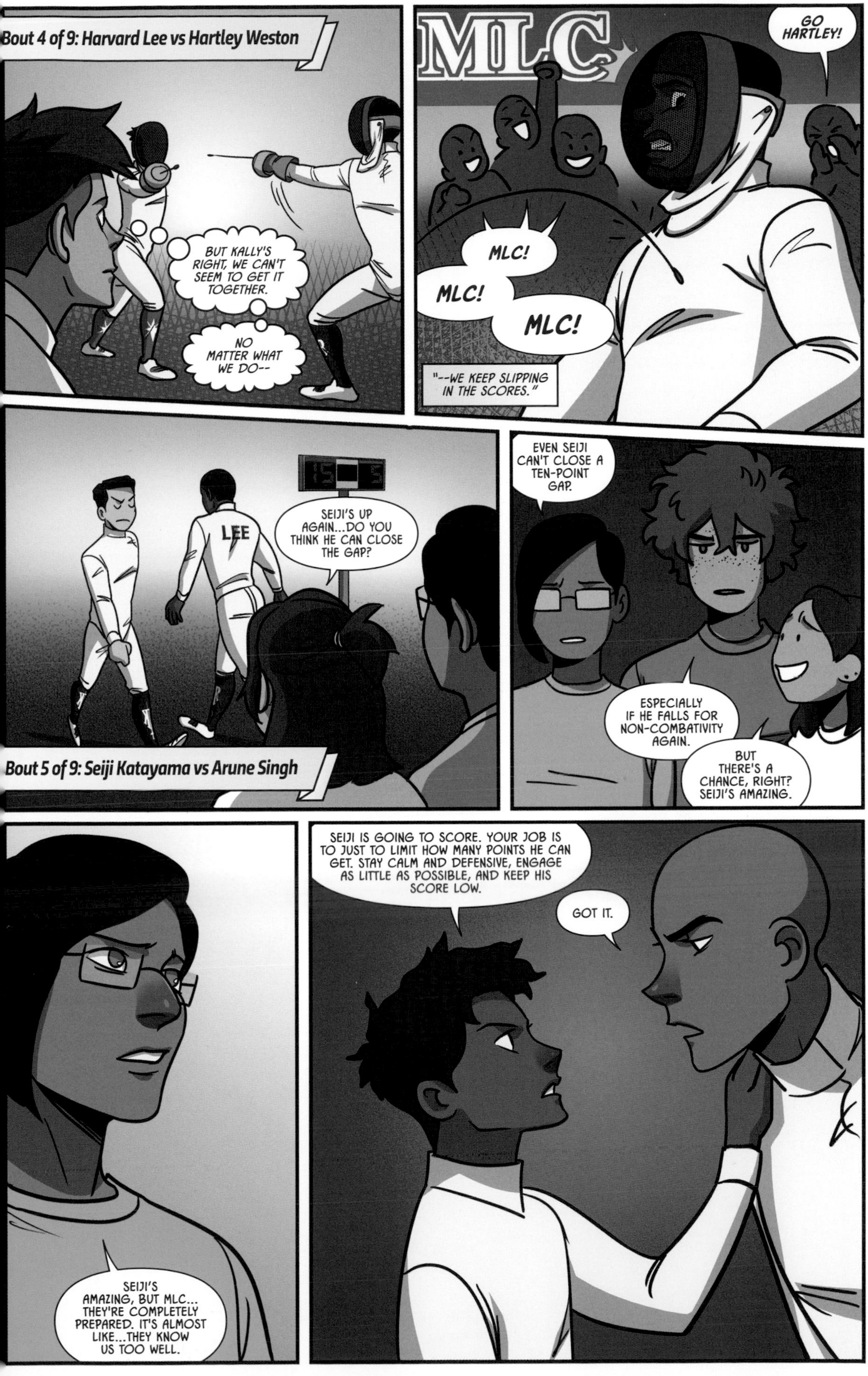
Bout 4 of 9: Harvard Lee vs Hartley Weston
BUT KALLY'S RIGHT, WE CAN'T SEEM TO GET IT TOGETHER.
NO MATTER WHAT WE DO--
MLC
GO HARTLEY!
MLC!
MLC!
MLC!
"--WE KEEP SLIPPING IN THE SCORES."
LEE
SEIJI'S UP AGAIN...DO YOU THINK HE CAN CLOSE THE GAP?
Bout 5 of 9: Seiji Katayama vs Arune Singh
EVEN SEIJI CAN'T CLOSE A TEN-POINT GAP.
ESPECIALLY IF HE FALLS FOR NON-COMBATIVITY AGAIN.
BUT THERE'S A CHANCE, RIGHT? SEIJI'S AMAZING.
SEIJI'S AMAZING, BUT MLC... THEY'RE COMPLETELY PREPARED. IT'S ALMOST LIKE...THEY KNOW US TOO WELL.
SEIJI IS GOING TO SCORE. YOUR JOB IS TO JUST TO LIMIT HOW MANY POINTS HE CAN GET. STAY CALM AND DEFENSIVE, ENGAGE AS LITTLE AS POSSIBLE, AND KEEP HIS SCORE LOW.
GOT IT.

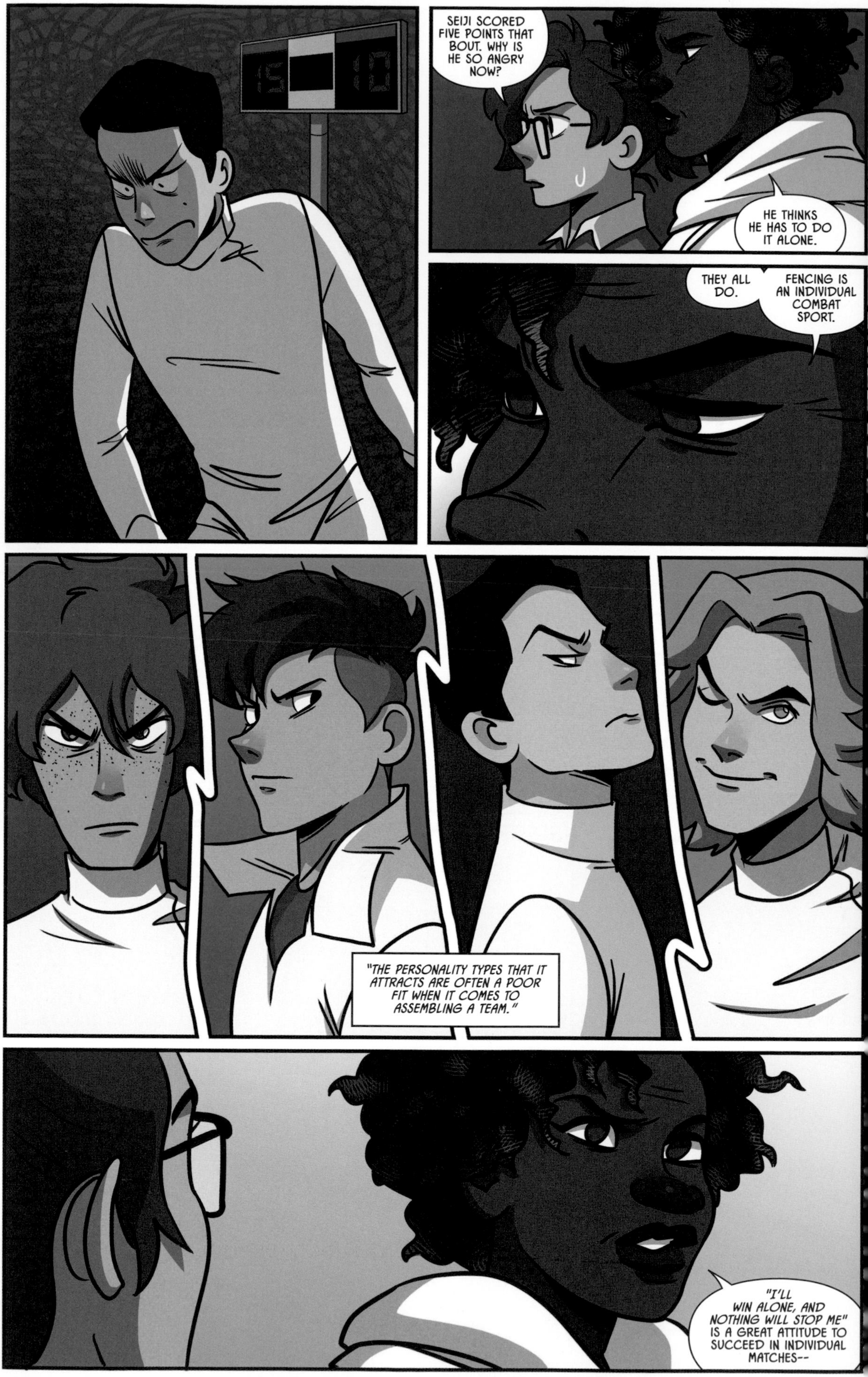
SEIJI SCORED FIVE POINTS THAT BOUT. WHY IS HE SO ANGRY NOW?
HE THINKS HE HAS TO DO IT ALONE.
THEY ALL DO.
FENCING IS AN INDIVIDUAL COMBAT SPORT.
"THE PERSONALITY TYPES THAT IT ATTRACTS ARE OFTEN A POOR FIT WHEN IT COMES TO ASSEMBLING A TEAM."
"I'LL WIN ALONE, AND NOTHING WILL STOP ME" IS A GREAT ATTITUDE TO SUCCEED IN INDIVIDUAL MATCHES--

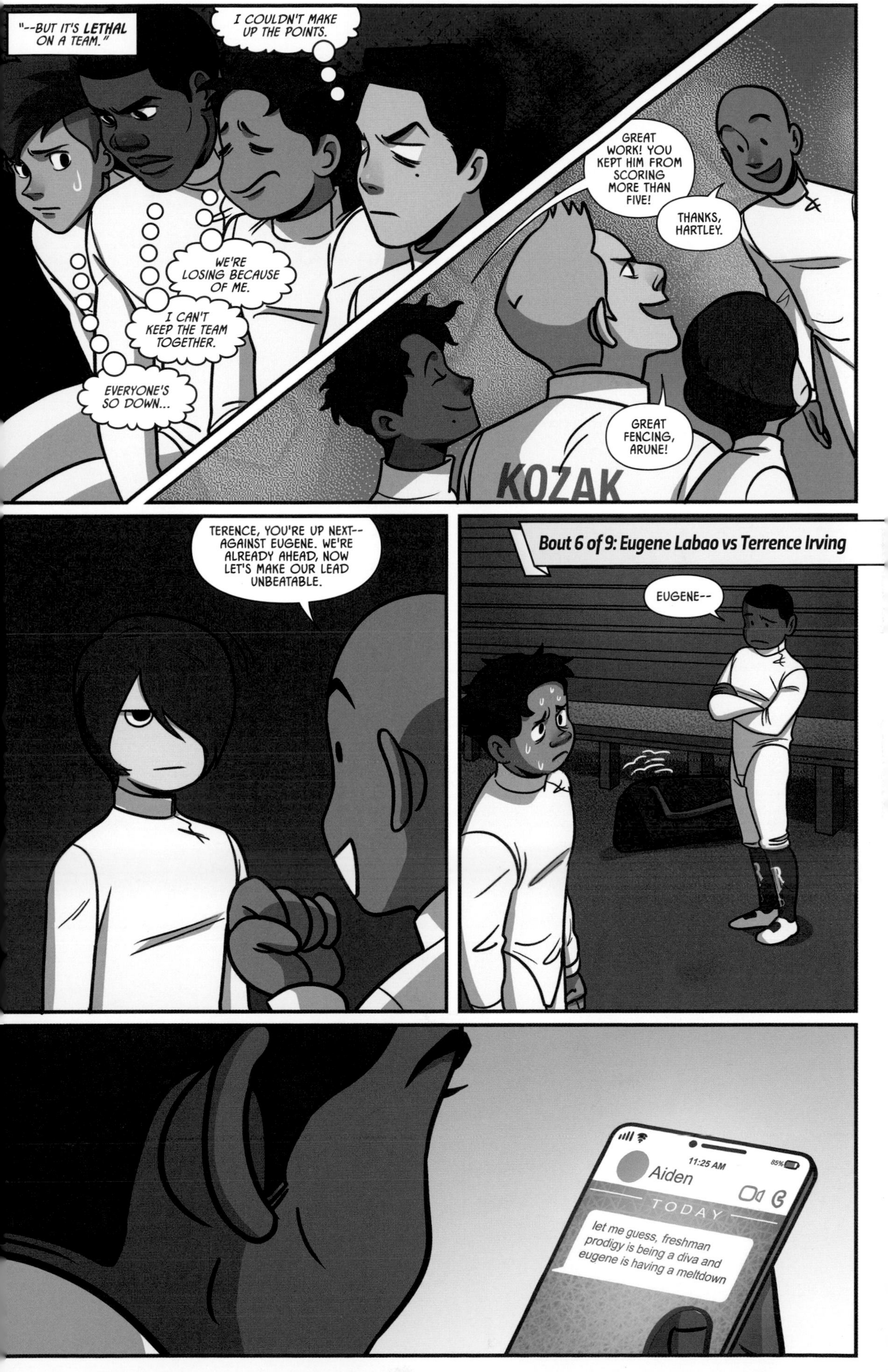
"--BUT IT'S **LETHAL** ON A TEAM."
I COULDN'T MAKE UP THE POINTS.
WE'RE LOSING BECAUSE OF ME.
I CAN'T KEEP THE TEAM TOGETHER.
EVERYONE'S SO DOWN...
GREAT WORK! YOU KEPT HIM FROM SCORING MORE THAN FIVE!
THANKS, HARTLEY.
GREAT FENCING, ARUNE!
KOZAK
TERENCE, YOU'RE UP NEXT--AGAINST EUGENE. WE'RE ALREADY AHEAD, NOW LET'S MAKE OUR LEAD UNBEATABLE.
Bout 6 of 9: Eugene Labao vs Terrence Irving
EUGENE--
11:25 AM
85%
Aiden
TODAY
let me guess, freshman prodigy is being a diva and eugene is having a meltdown

TODAY

let me guess, freshman prodigy is being a diva and eugene is having a meltdown

Let me guess, you're at Rosie's Cafe eating strawberry cupcakes.

...

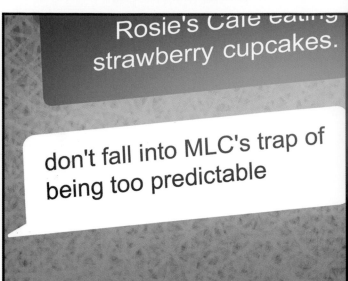

Rosie's Cafe eating strawberry cupcakes.

don't fall into MLC's trap of being too predictable

PREDICTABLE...

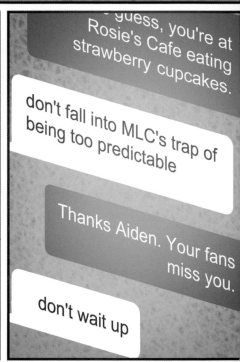

...guess, you're at Rosie's Cafe eating strawberry cupcakes.

don't fall into MLC's trap of being too predictable

Thanks Aiden. Your fans miss you.

don't wait up

WHAT ARE YOU SMILING ABOUT?

NOTHING.

Harvard

Save me a cupcake.

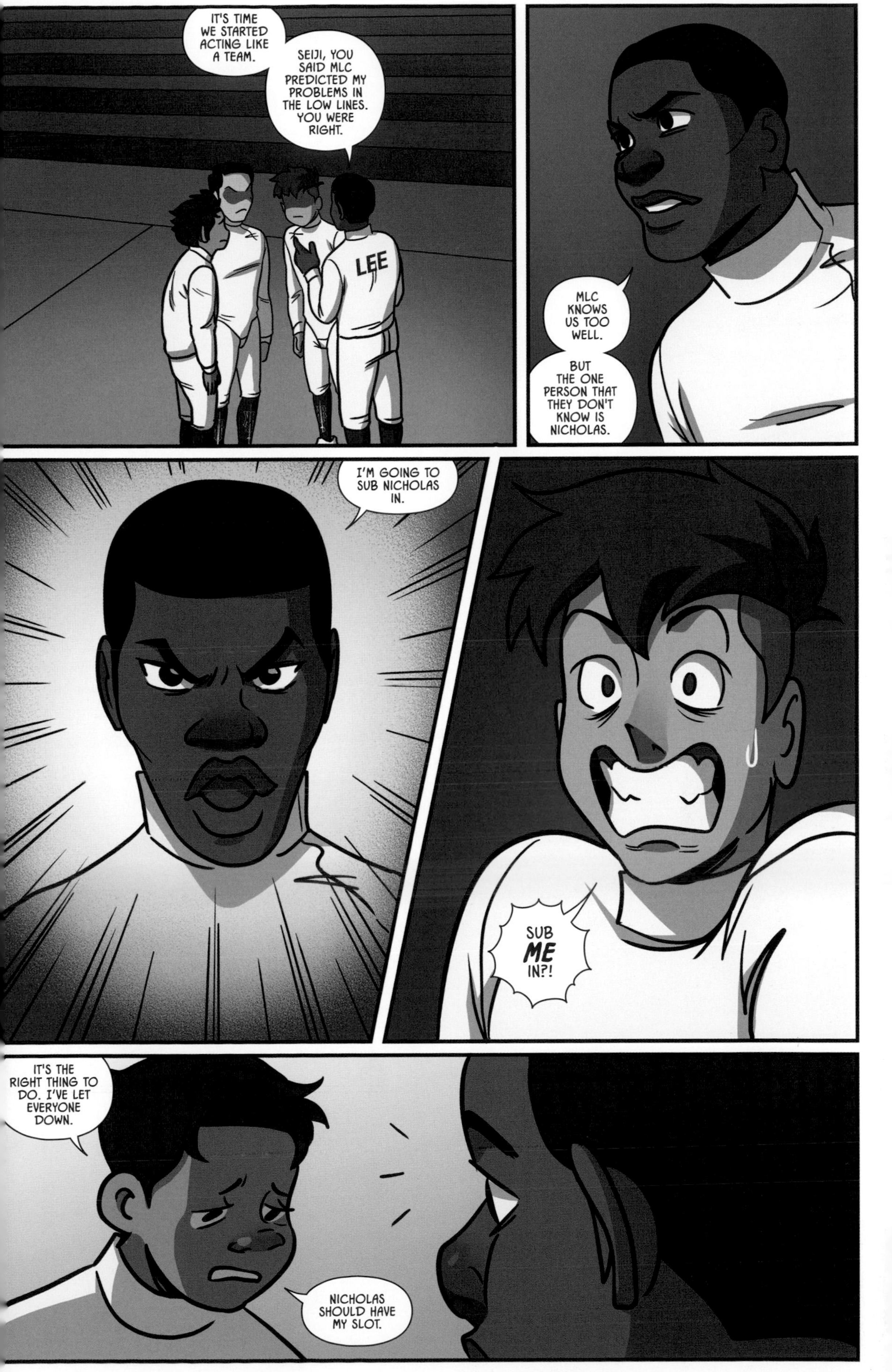
IT'S TIME WE STARTED ACTING LIKE A TEAM.
SEIJI, YOU SAID MLC PREDICTED MY PROBLEMS IN THE LOW LINES. YOU WERE RIGHT.
LEE
MLC KNOWS US TOO WELL.
BUT THE ONE PERSON THAT THEY DON'T KNOW IS NICHOLAS.
I'M GOING TO SUB NICHOLAS IN.
SUB ***ME*** IN?!
IT'S THE RIGHT THING TO DO. I'VE LET EVERYONE DOWN.
NICHOLAS SHOULD HAVE MY SLOT.

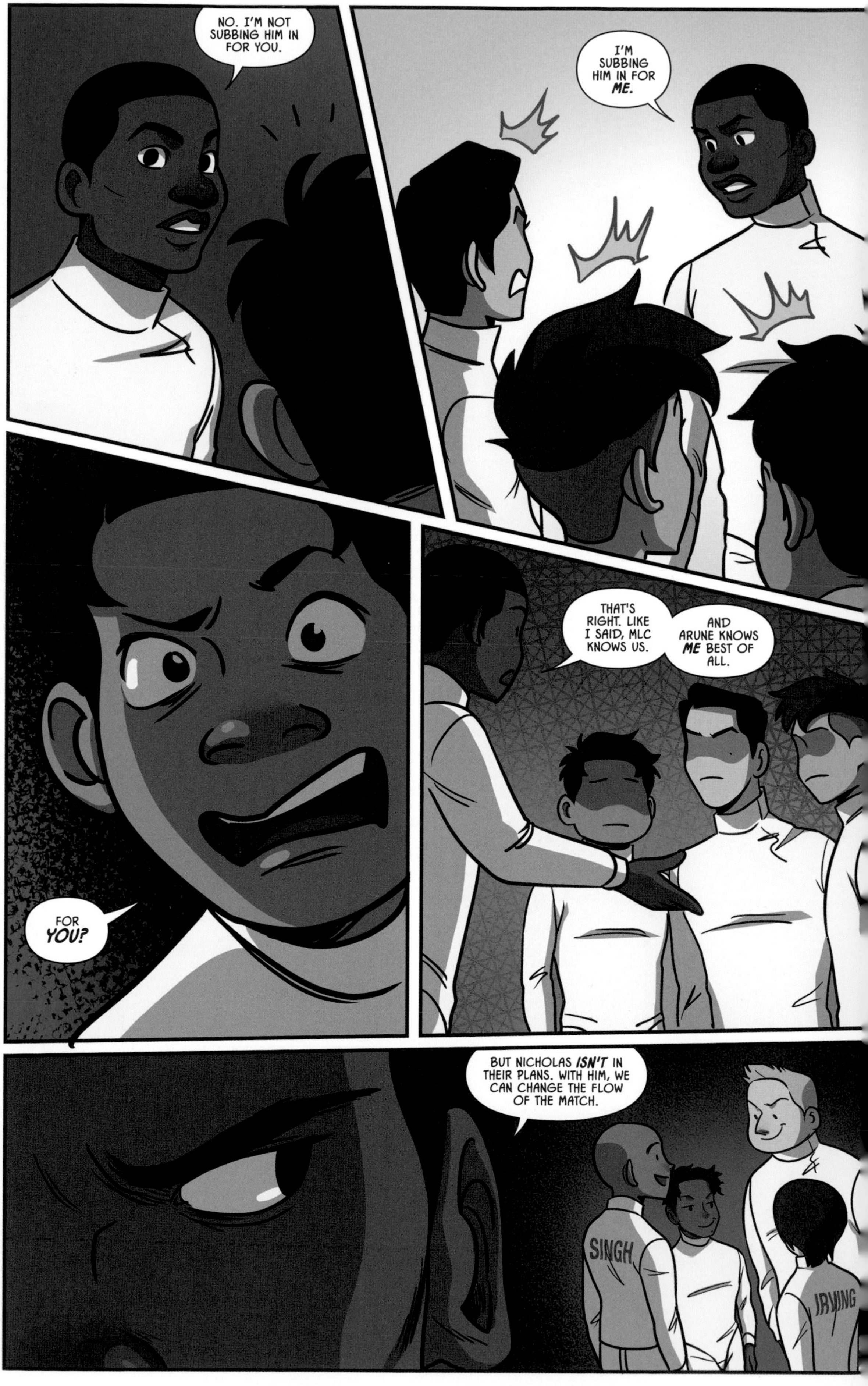
NO. I'M NOT SUBBING HIM IN FOR YOU.
I'M SUBBING HIM IN FOR ME.
FOR YOU?
THAT'S RIGHT. LIKE I SAID, MLC KNOWS US.
AND ARUNE KNOWS ME BEST OF ALL.
BUT NICHOLAS ISN'T IN THEIR PLANS. WITH HIM, WE CAN CHANGE THE FLOW OF THE MATCH.
SINGH
IRVING

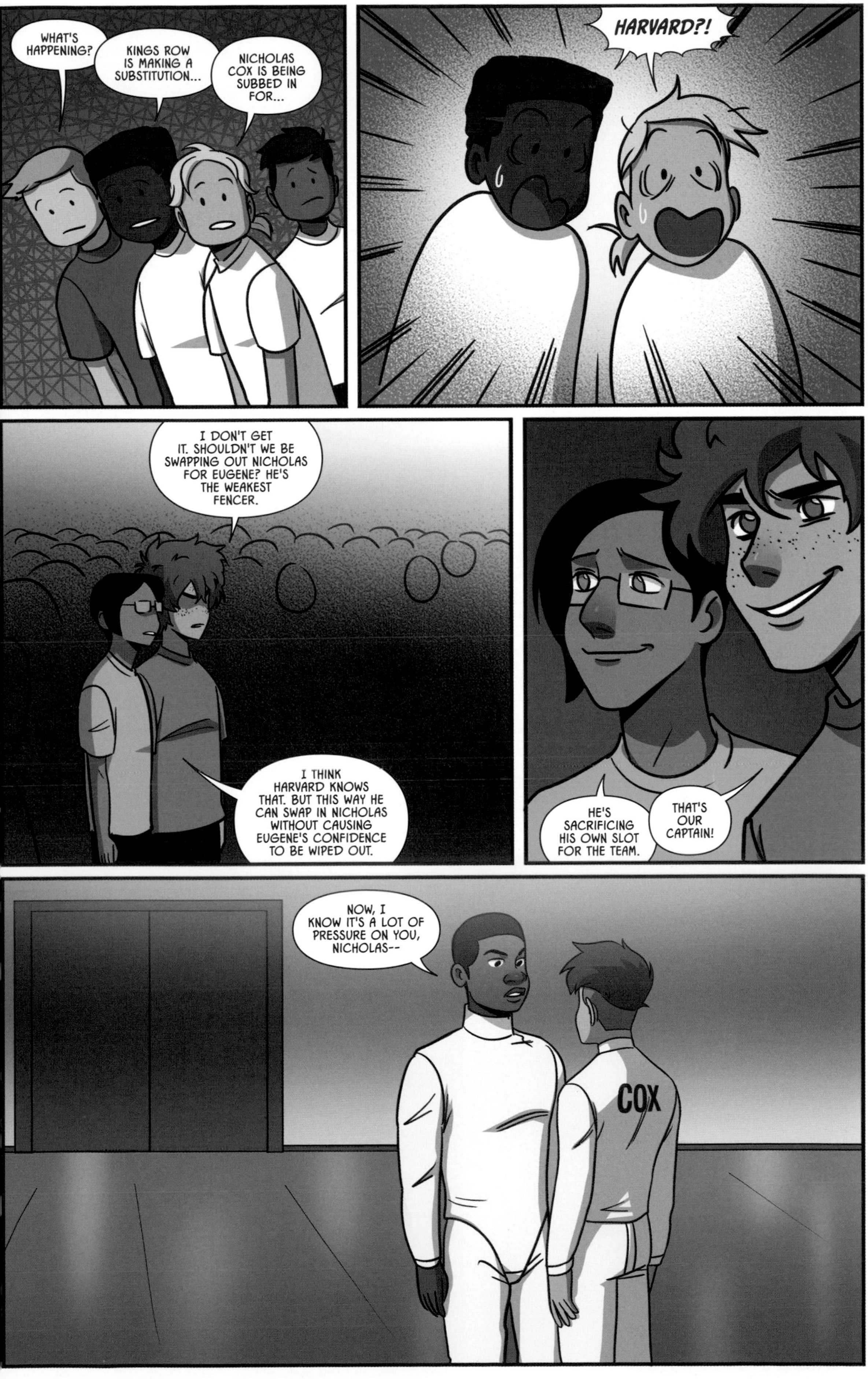
WHAT'S HAPPENING?
KINGS ROW IS MAKING A SUBSTITUTION...
NICHOLAS COX IS BEING SUBBED IN FOR...
HARVARD?!
I DON'T GET IT. SHOULDN'T WE BE SWAPPING OUT NICHOLAS FOR EUGENE? HE'S THE WEAKEST FENCER.
I THINK HARVARD KNOWS THAT. BUT THIS WAY HE CAN SWAP IN NICHOLAS WITHOUT CAUSING EUGENE'S CONFIDENCE TO BE WIPED OUT.
HE'S SACRIFICING HIS OWN SLOT FOR THE TEAM.
THAT'S OUR CAPTAIN!
NOW, I KNOW IT'S A LOT OF PRESSURE ON YOU, NICHOLAS--
COX

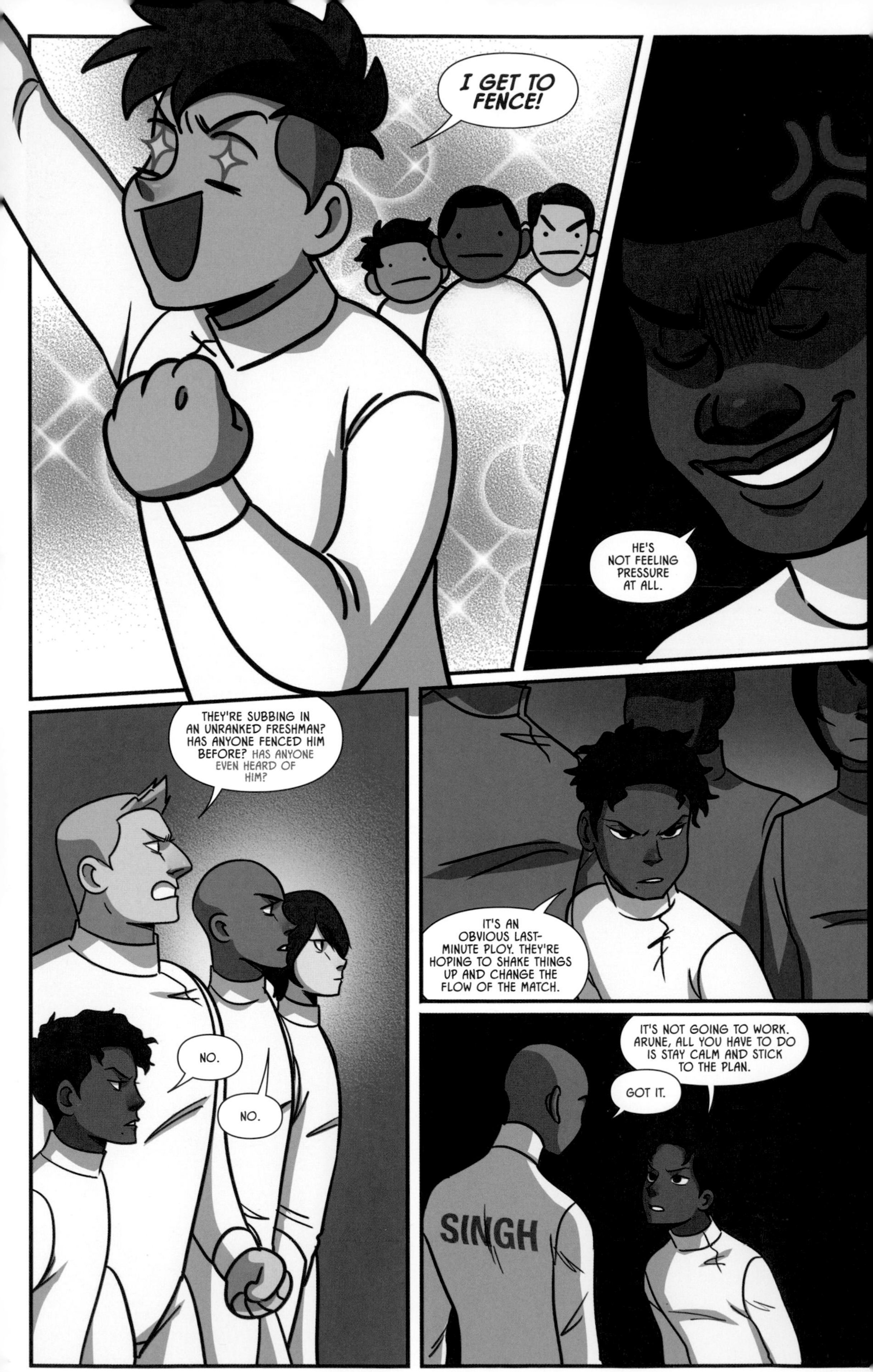
I GET TO FENCE!
HE'S NOT FEELING PRESSURE AT ALL.
THEY'RE SUBBING IN AN UNRANKED FRESHMAN? HAS ANYONE FENCED HIM BEFORE? HAS ANYONE EVEN HEARD OF HIM?
NO.
NO.
IT'S AN OBVIOUS LAST-MINUTE PLOY. THEY'RE HOPING TO SHAKE THINGS UP AND CHANGE THE FLOW OF THE MATCH.
IT'S NOT GOING TO WORK. ARUNE, ALL YOU HAVE TO DO IS STAY CALM AND STICK TO THE PLAN.
GOT IT.
SINGH

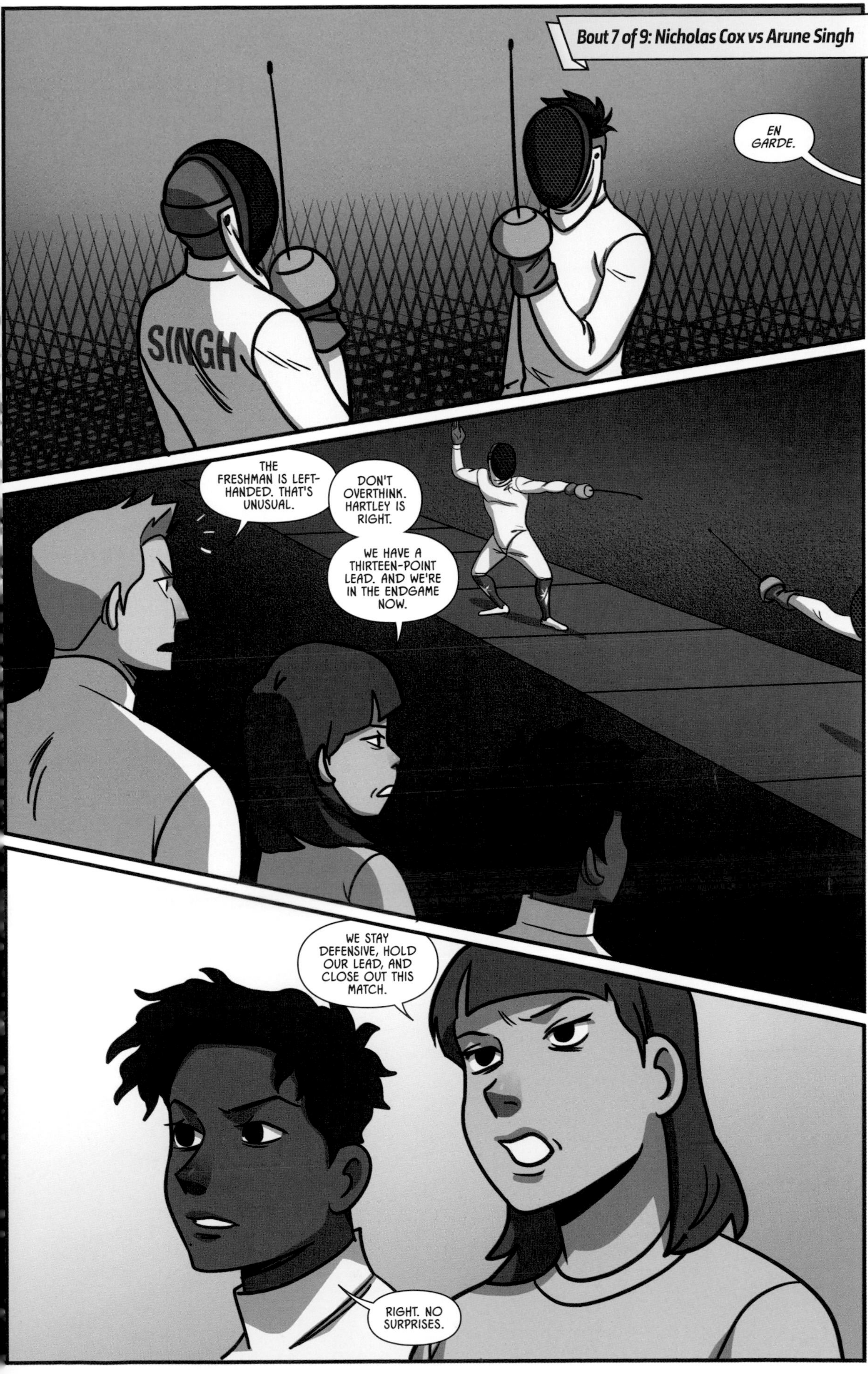
Bout 7 of 9: Nicholas Cox vs Arune Singh
EN GARDE.
SINGH
THE FRESHMAN IS LEFT-HANDED. THAT'S UNUSUAL.
DON'T OVERTHINK. HARTLEY IS RIGHT.
WE HAVE A THIRTEEN-POINT LEAD. AND WE'RE IN THE ENDGAME NOW.
WE STAY DEFENSIVE, HOLD OUR LEAD, AND CLOSE OUT THIS MATCH.
RIGHT. NO SURPRISES.

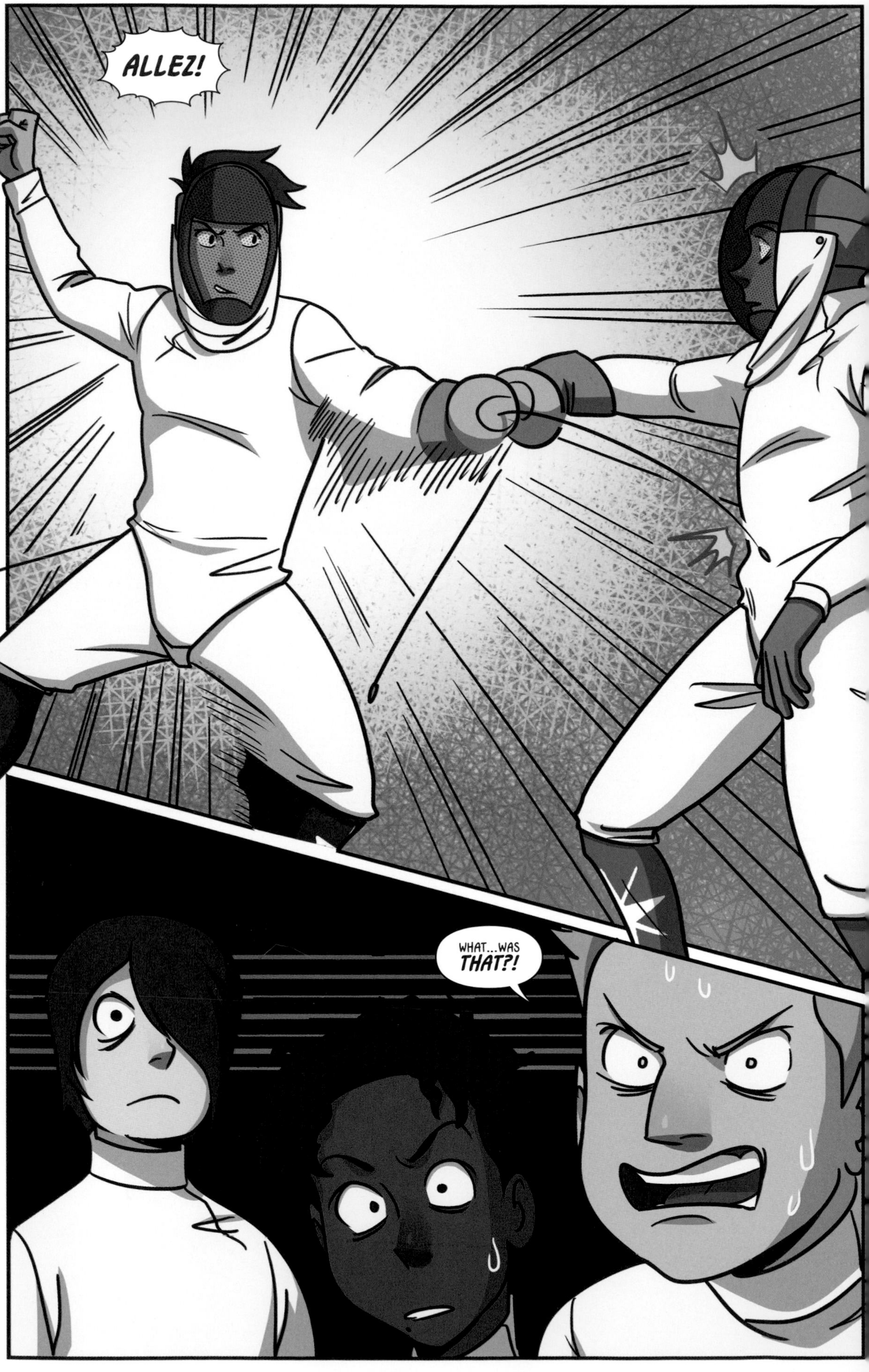
ALLEZ!
WHAT...WAS THAT?!

CHAPTER
SIXTEEN

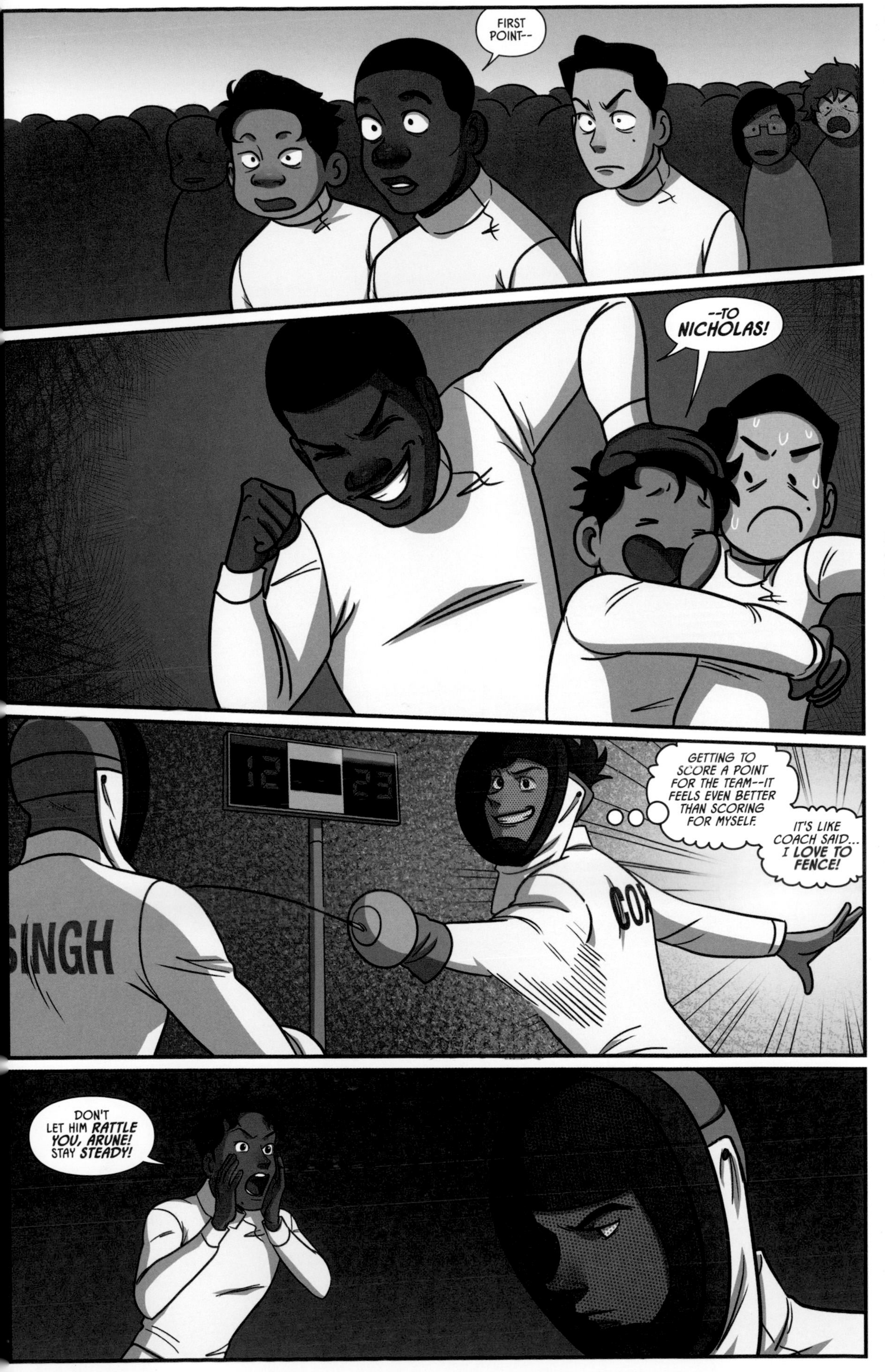
FIRST POINT--
--TO NICHOLAS!
GETTING TO SCORE A POINT FOR THE TEAM--IT FEELS EVEN BETTER THAN SCORING FOR MYSELF.
IT'S LIKE COACH SAID... I LOVE TO FENCE!
SINGH
DON'T LET HIM RATTLE YOU, ARUNE! STAY STEADY!

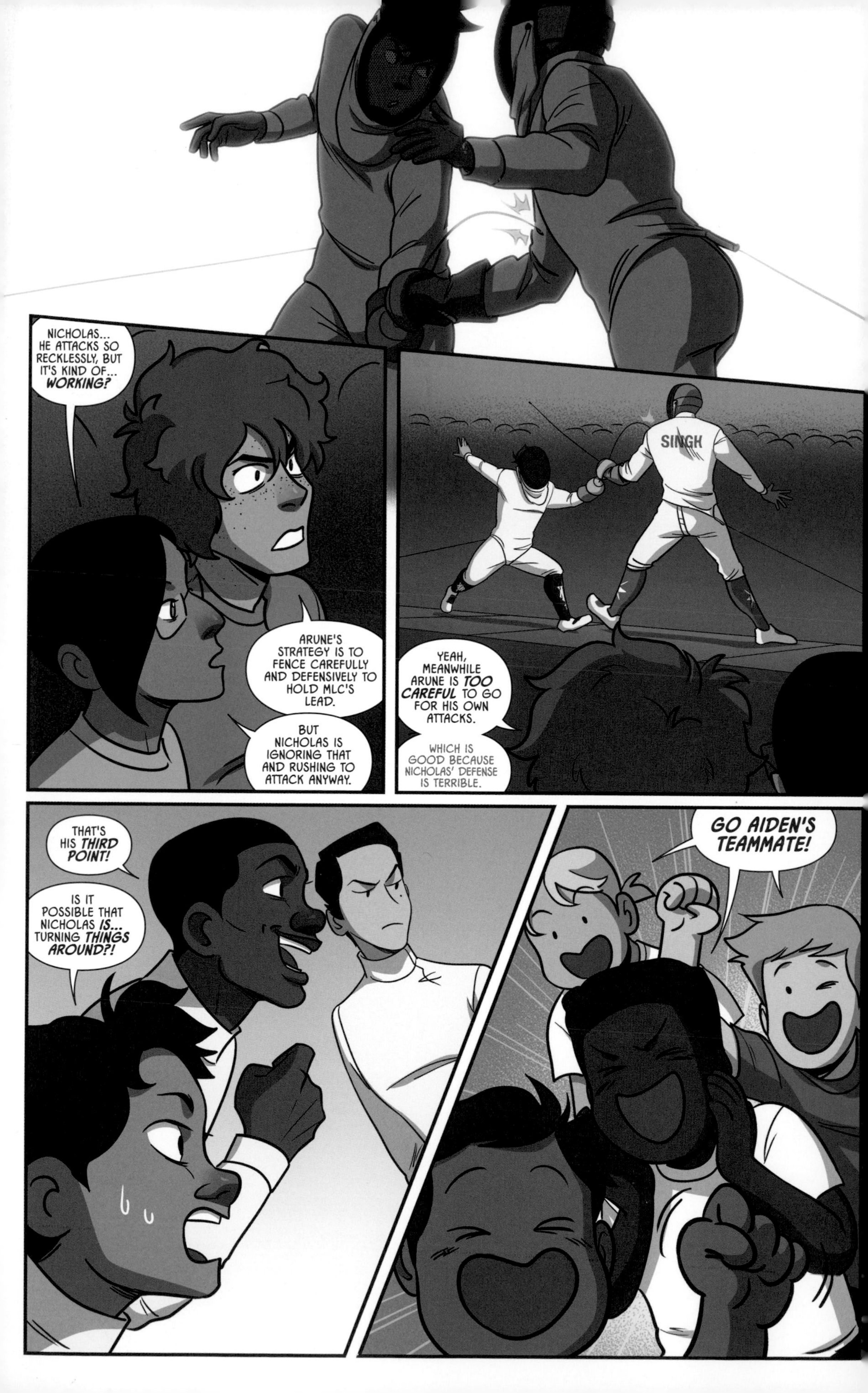
NICHOLAS... HE ATTACKS SO RECKLESSLY, BUT IT'S KIND OF... **WORKING?**
ARUNE'S STRATEGY IS TO FENCE CAREFULLY AND DEFENSIVELY TO HOLD MLC'S LEAD.
BUT NICHOLAS IS IGNORING THAT AND RUSHING TO ATTACK ANYWAY.
SINGH
YEAH, MEANWHILE ARUNE IS **TOO CAREFUL** TO GO FOR HIS OWN ATTACKS.
WHICH IS GOOD BECAUSE NICHOLAS' DEFENSE IS TERRIBLE.
THAT'S HIS **THIRD POINT!**
IS IT POSSIBLE THAT NICHOLAS **IS...** TURNING **THINGS AROUND?!**
GO AIDEN'S TEAMMATE!

A BENT WRIST! I USED TO MAKE THAT MISTAKE!
IT'S A TINY OPENING NO LARGER THAN--
--A TENNIS BALL!
DID NICHOLAS JUST GET A HIT TO THE WRIST?!
I HAD NO IDEA HIS ACCURACY HAD IMPROVED THAT MUCH!
HAHA, I STILL MISS THE TENNIS BALL ALMOST HALF THE TIME, SO THAT WAS LUCKY.
complete fluke
23
17
HALT! TIME!

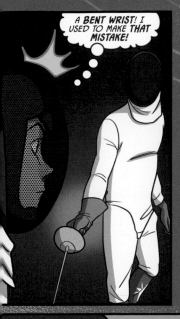

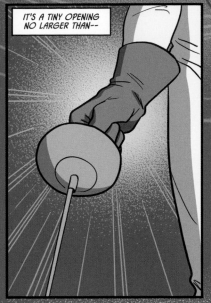

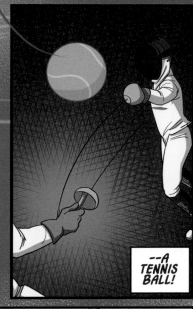

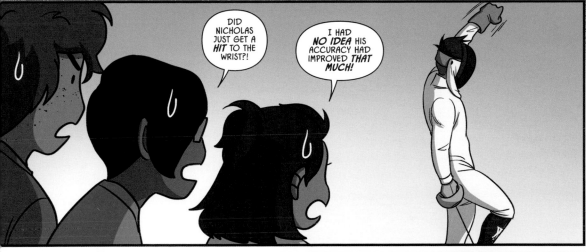

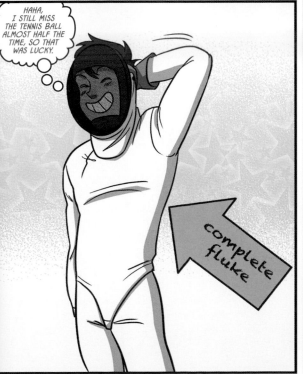

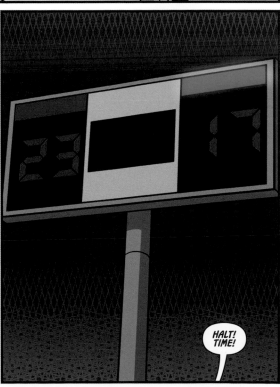

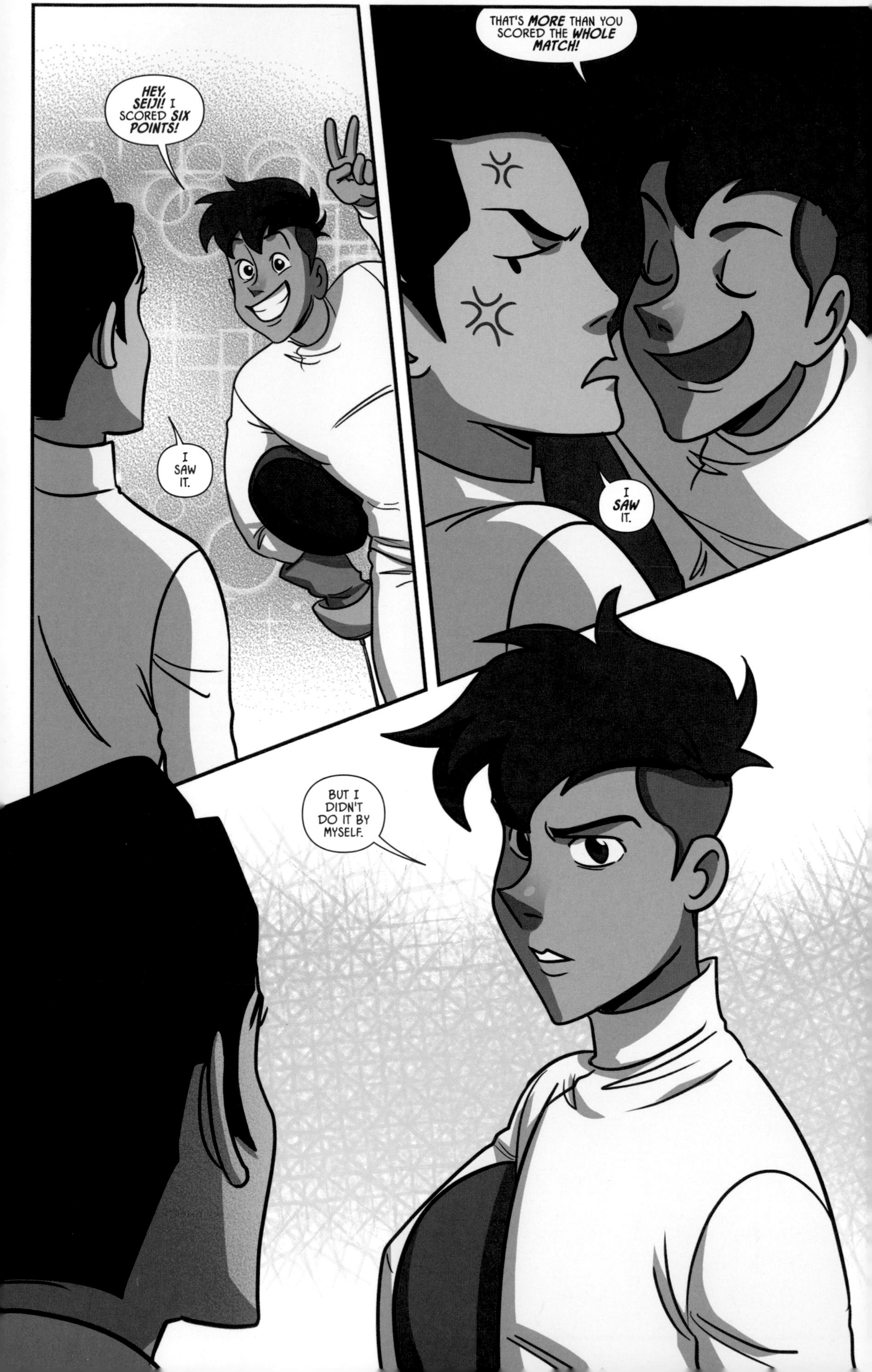
HEY, SEIJI! I SCORED SIX POINTS!
I SAW IT.
THAT'S MORE THAN YOU SCORED THE WHOLE MATCH!
I SAW IT.
BUT I DIDN'T DO IT BY MYSELF.

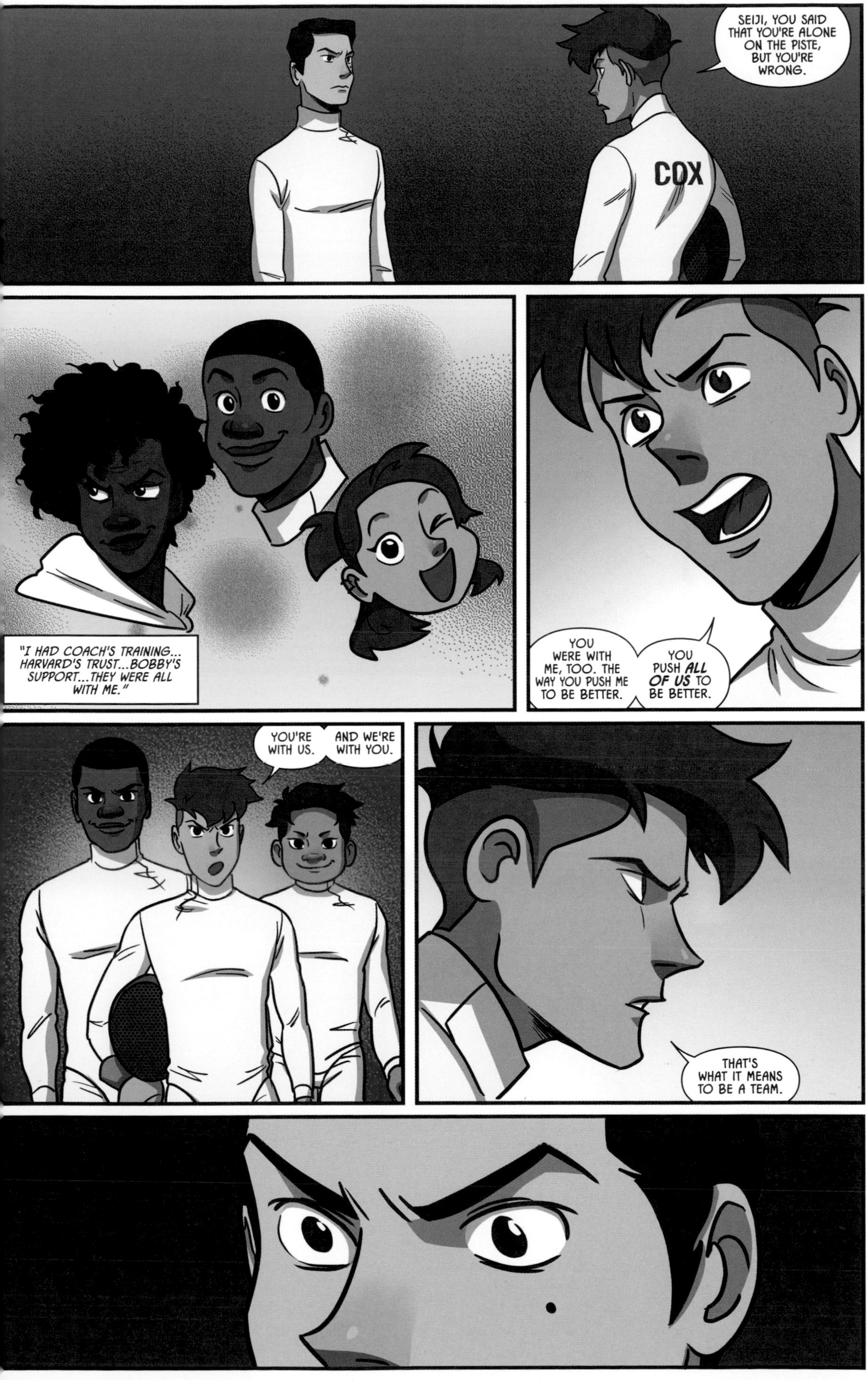
COX
SEIJI, YOU SAID THAT YOU'RE ALONE ON THE PISTE, BUT YOU'RE WRONG.
"I HAD COACH'S TRAINING... HARVARD'S TRUST...BOBBY'S SUPPORT...THEY WERE ALL WITH ME."
YOU WERE WITH ME, TOO. THE WAY YOU PUSH ME TO BE BETTER.
YOU PUSH ALL OF US TO BE BETTER.
YOU'RE WITH US.
AND WE'RE WITH YOU.
THAT'S WHAT IT MEANS TO BE A TEAM.

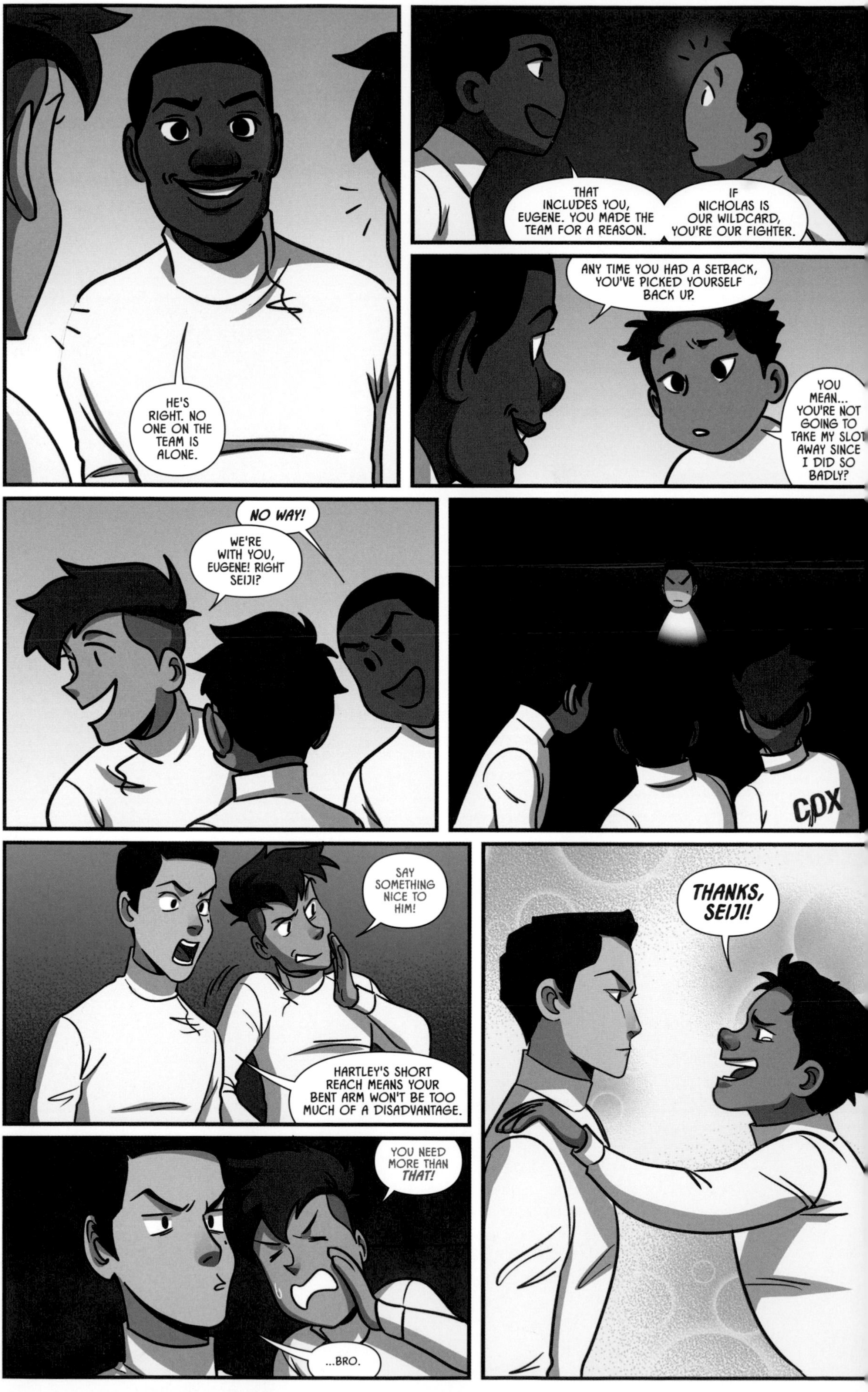
HE'S RIGHT. NO ONE ON THE TEAM IS ALONE.
THAT INCLUDES YOU, EUGENE. YOU MADE THE TEAM FOR A REASON.
IF NICHOLAS IS OUR WILDCARD, YOU'RE OUR FIGHTER.
ANY TIME YOU HAD A SETBACK, YOU'VE PICKED YOURSELF BACK UP.
YOU MEAN... YOU'RE NOT GOING TO TAKE MY SLOT AWAY SINCE I DID SO BADLY?
NO WAY!
WE'RE WITH YOU, EUGENE! RIGHT SEIJI?
CDX
SAY SOMETHING NICE TO HIM!
HARTLEY'S SHORT REACH MEANS YOUR BENT ARM WON'T BE TOO MUCH OF A DISADVANTAGE.
YOU NEED MORE THAN THAT!
...BRO.
THANKS, SEIJI!

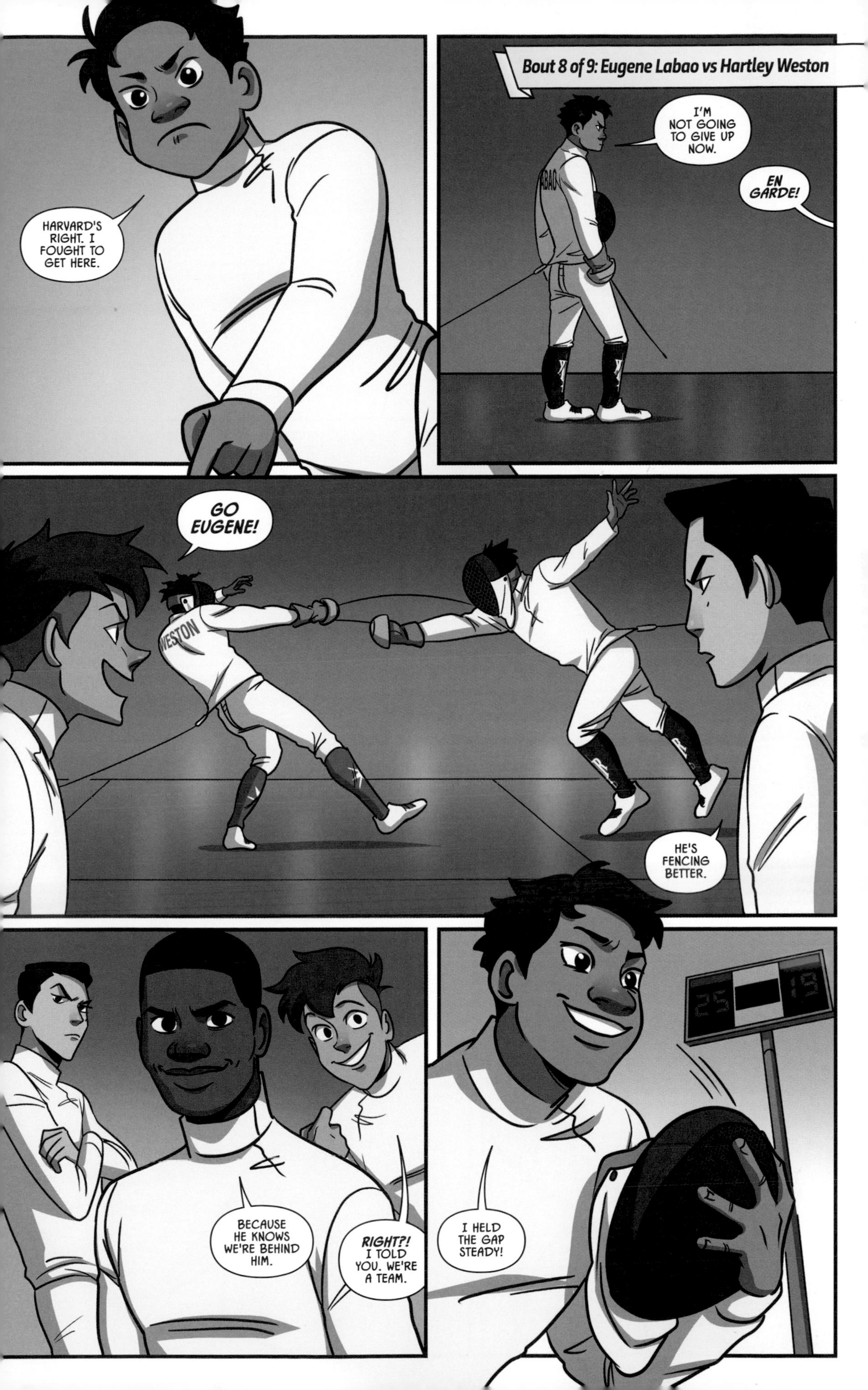
HARVARD'S RIGHT. I FOUGHT TO GET HERE.
Bout 8 of 9: Eugene Labao vs Hartley Weston
I'M NOT GOING TO GIVE UP NOW.
EN GARDE!
GO EUGENE!
WESTON
HE'S FENCING BETTER.
BECAUSE HE KNOWS WE'RE BEHIND HIM.
RIGHT?! I TOLD YOU. WE'RE A TEAM.
I HELD THE GAP STEADY!
25
19

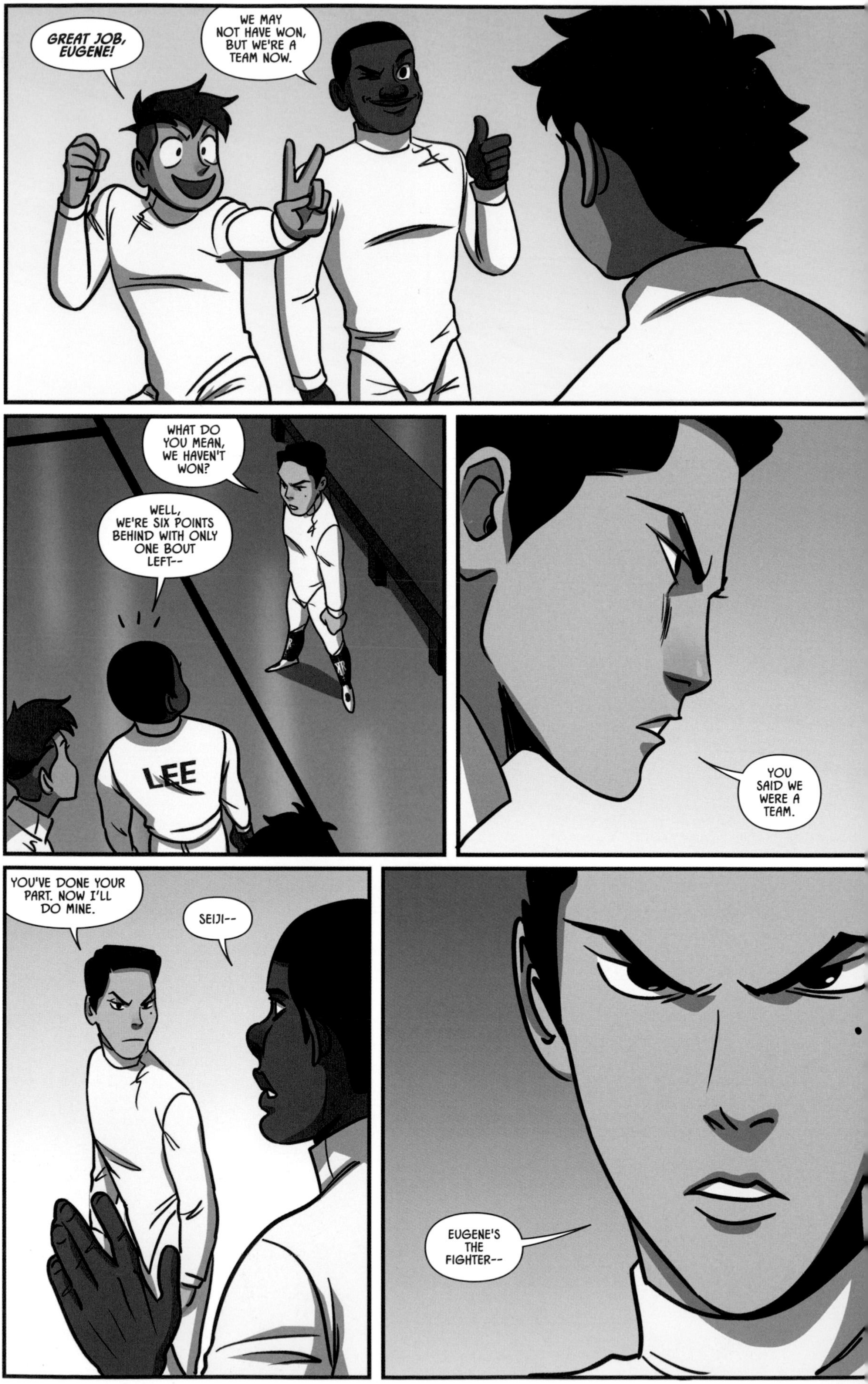
GREAT JOB, EUGENE!
WE MAY NOT HAVE WON, BUT WE'RE A TEAM NOW.
WHAT DO YOU MEAN, WE HAVEN'T WON?
WELL, WE'RE SIX POINTS BEHIND WITH ONLY ONE BOUT LEFT--
LEE
YOU SAID WE WERE A TEAM.
YOU'VE DONE YOUR PART. NOW I'LL DO MINE.
SEIJI--
EUGENE'S THE FIGHTER--

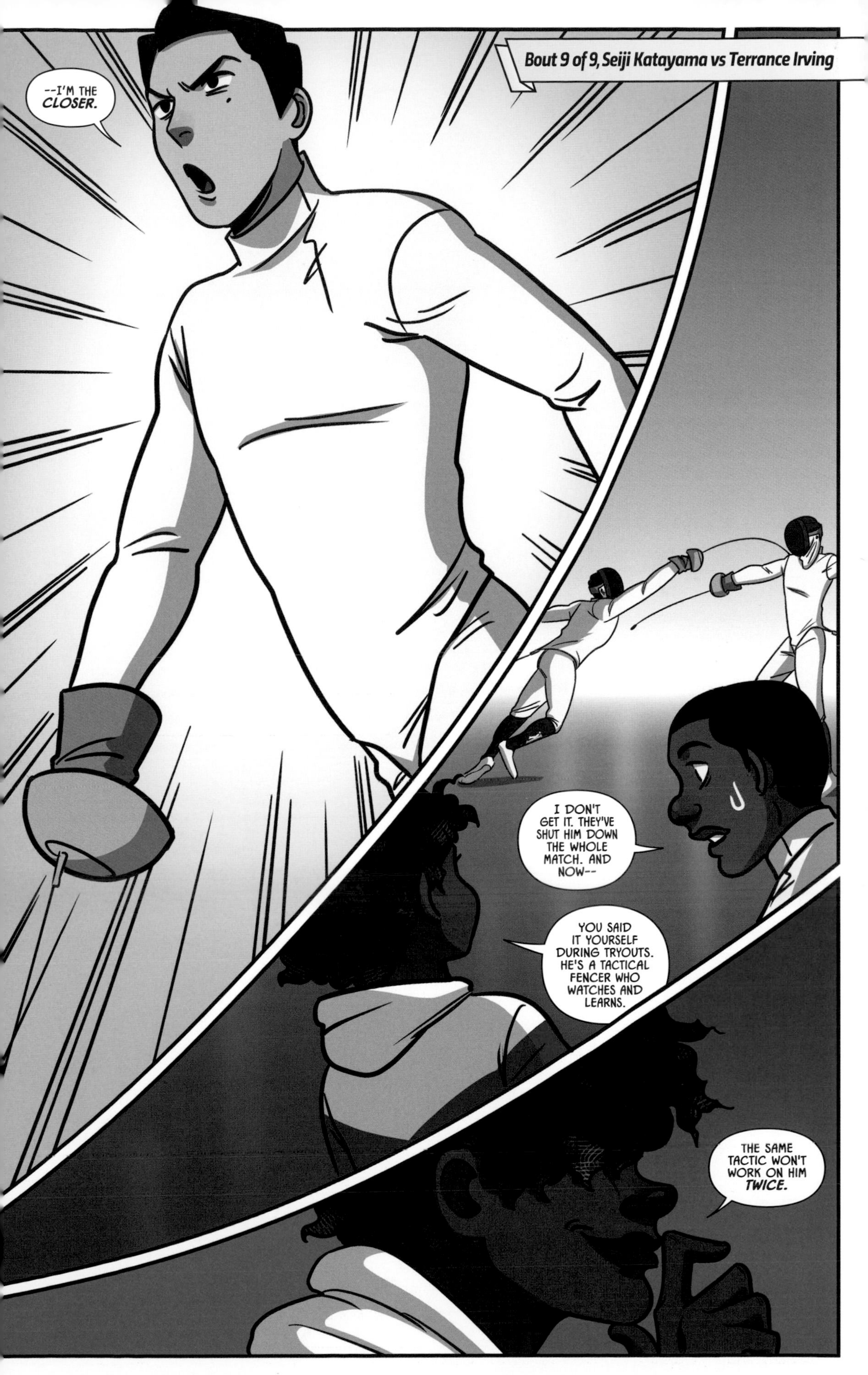
Bout 9 of 9, Seiji Katayama vs Terrance Irving
--I'M THE *CLOSER.*
I DON'T GET IT. THEY'VE SHUT HIM DOWN THE WHOLE MATCH. AND NOW--
YOU SAID IT YOURSELF DURING TRYOUTS. HE'S A TACTICAL FENCER WHO WATCHES AND LEARNS.
THE SAME TACTIC WON'T WORK ON HIM *TWICE.*

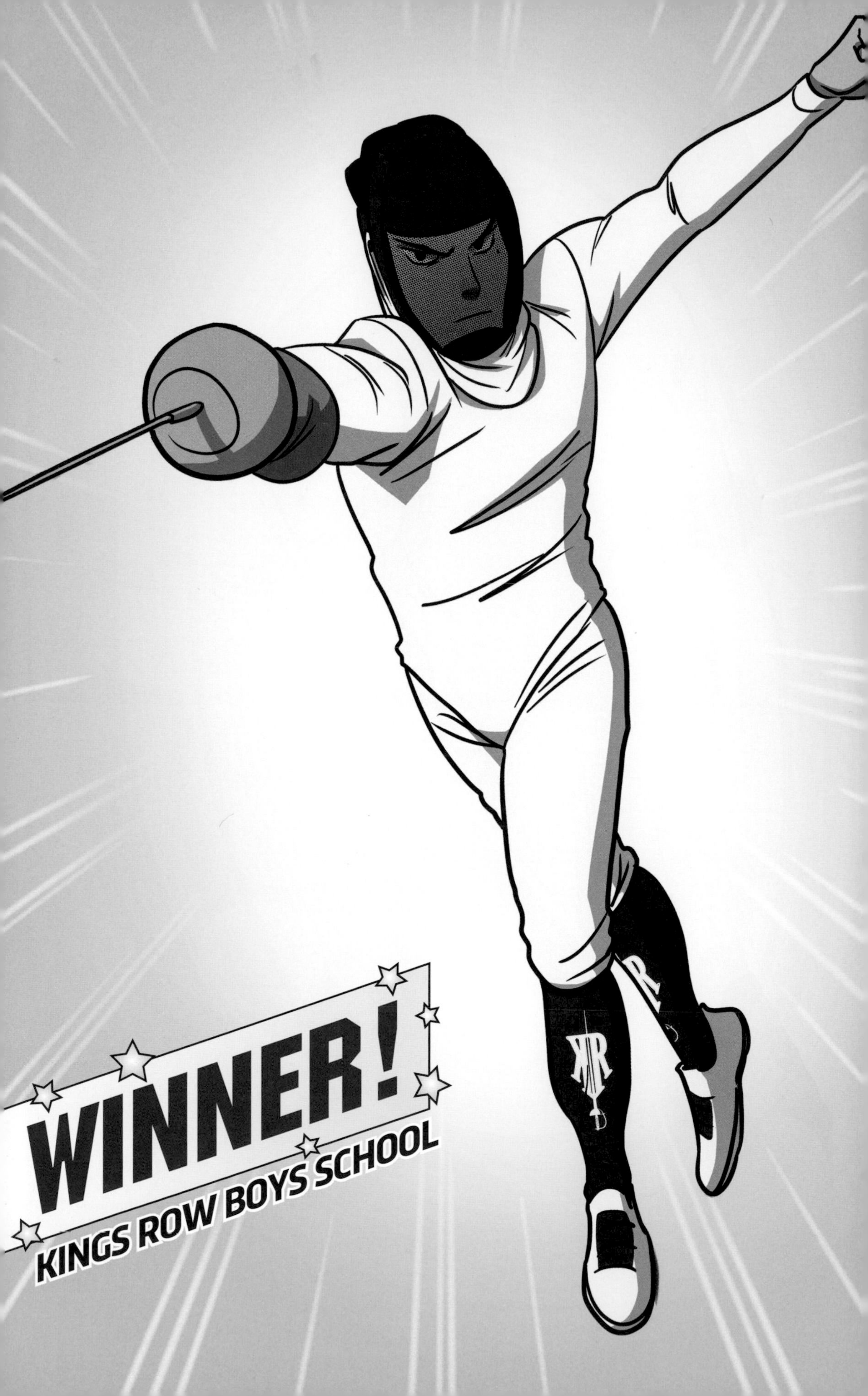
WINNER!
KINGS ROW BOYS SCHOOL

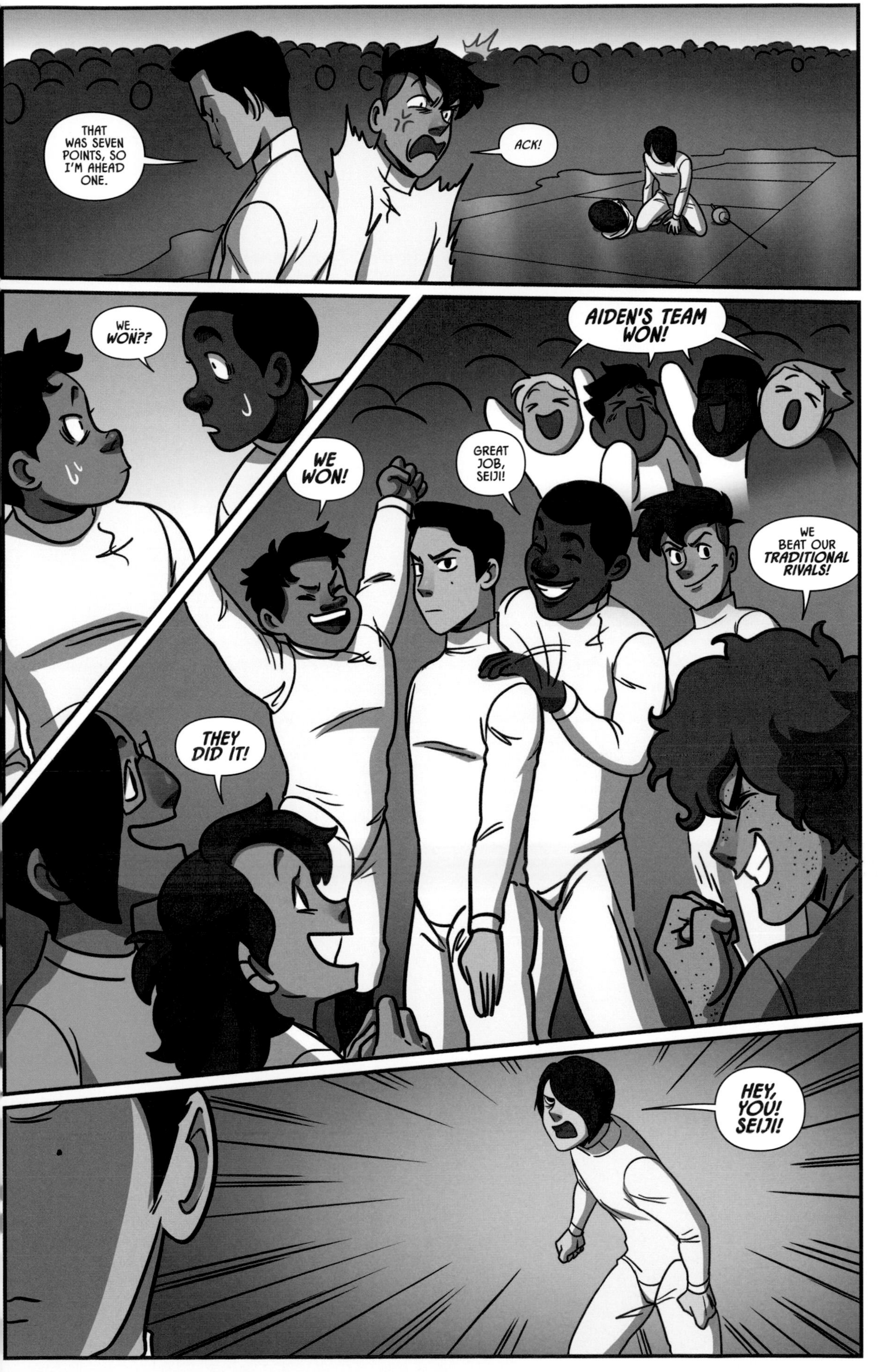
THAT WAS SEVEN POINTS, SO I'M AHEAD ONE.
ACK!
WE... WON??
AIDEN'S TEAM WON!
WE WON!
GREAT JOB, SEIJI!
WE BEAT OUR TRADITIONAL RIVALS!
THEY DID IT!
HEY, YOU! SEIJI!

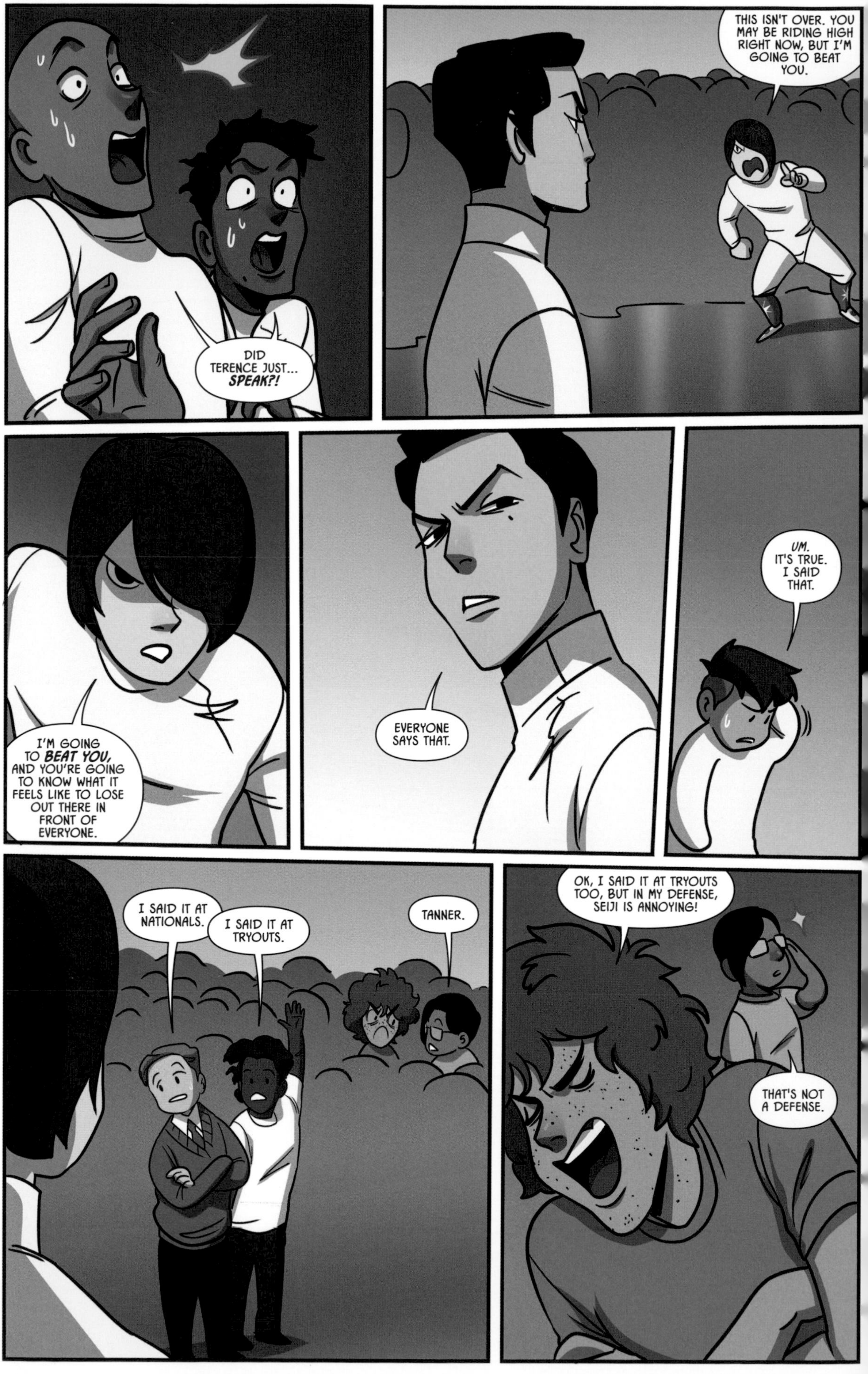
DID TERENCE JUST... ***SPEAK?!***
THIS ISN'T OVER. YOU MAY BE RIDING HIGH RIGHT NOW, BUT I'M GOING TO BEAT YOU.
I'M GOING TO ***BEAT YOU***, AND YOU'RE GOING TO KNOW WHAT IT FEELS LIKE TO LOSE OUT THERE IN FRONT OF EVERYONE.
EVERYONE SAYS THAT.
UM. IT'S TRUE. I SAID THAT.
I SAID IT AT NATIONALS.
I SAID IT AT TRYOUTS.
TANNER.
OK, I SAID IT AT TRYOUTS TOO, BUT IN MY DEFENSE, SEIJI IS ANNOYING!
THAT'S NOT A DEFENSE.

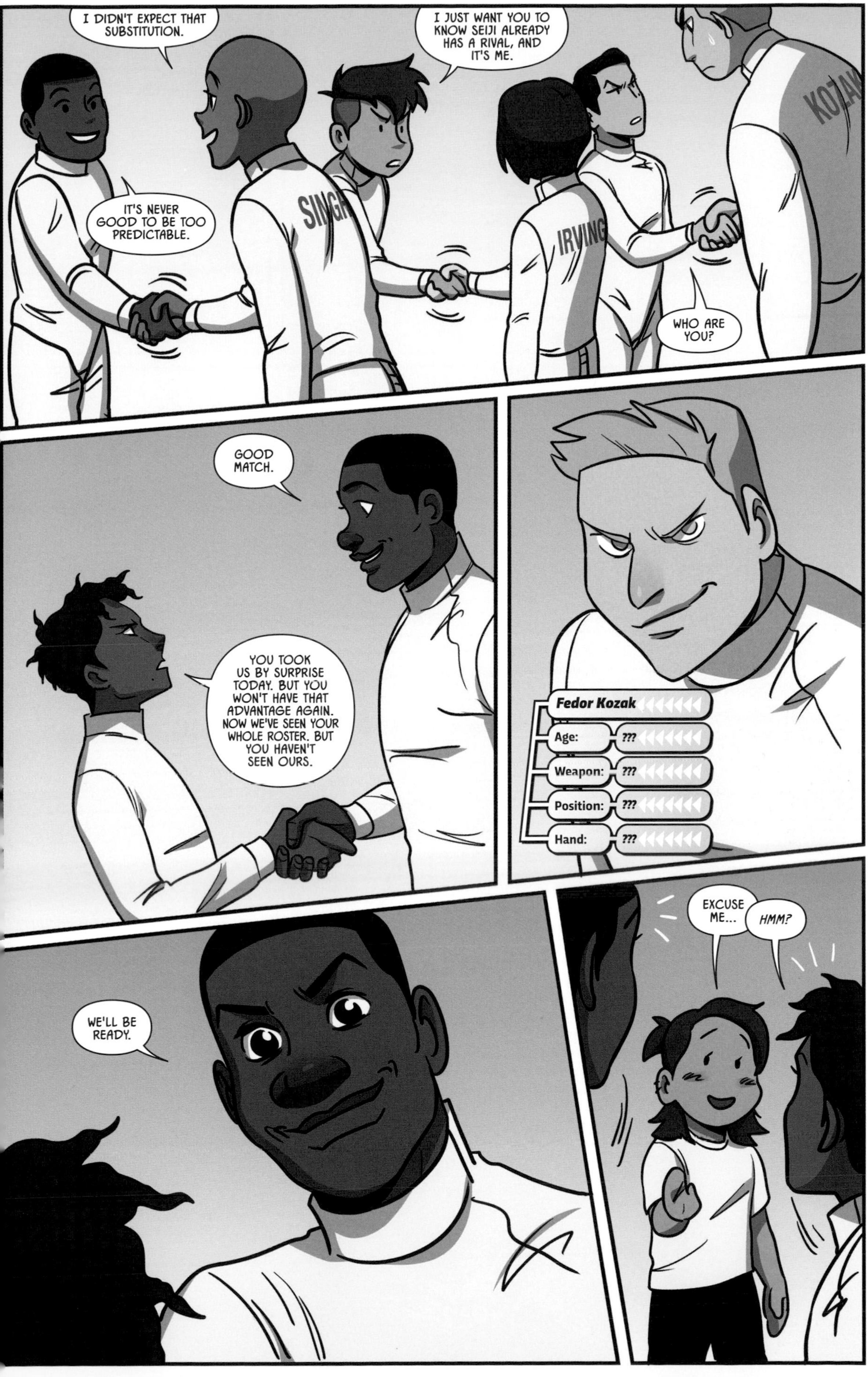
I DIDN'T EXPECT THAT SUBSTITUTION.
IT'S NEVER GOOD TO BE TOO PREDICTABLE.
SINGH
I JUST WANT YOU TO KNOW SEIJI ALREADY HAS A RIVAL, AND IT'S ME.
IRVING
KOZAK
WHO ARE YOU?
GOOD MATCH.
YOU TOOK US BY SURPRISE TODAY. BUT YOU WON'T HAVE THAT ADVANTAGE AGAIN. NOW WE'VE SEEN YOUR WHOLE ROSTER. BUT YOU HAVEN'T SEEN OURS.
Fedor Kozak
Age: ???
Weapon: ???
Position: ???
Hand: ???
WE'LL BE READY.
EXCUSE ME...
HMM?

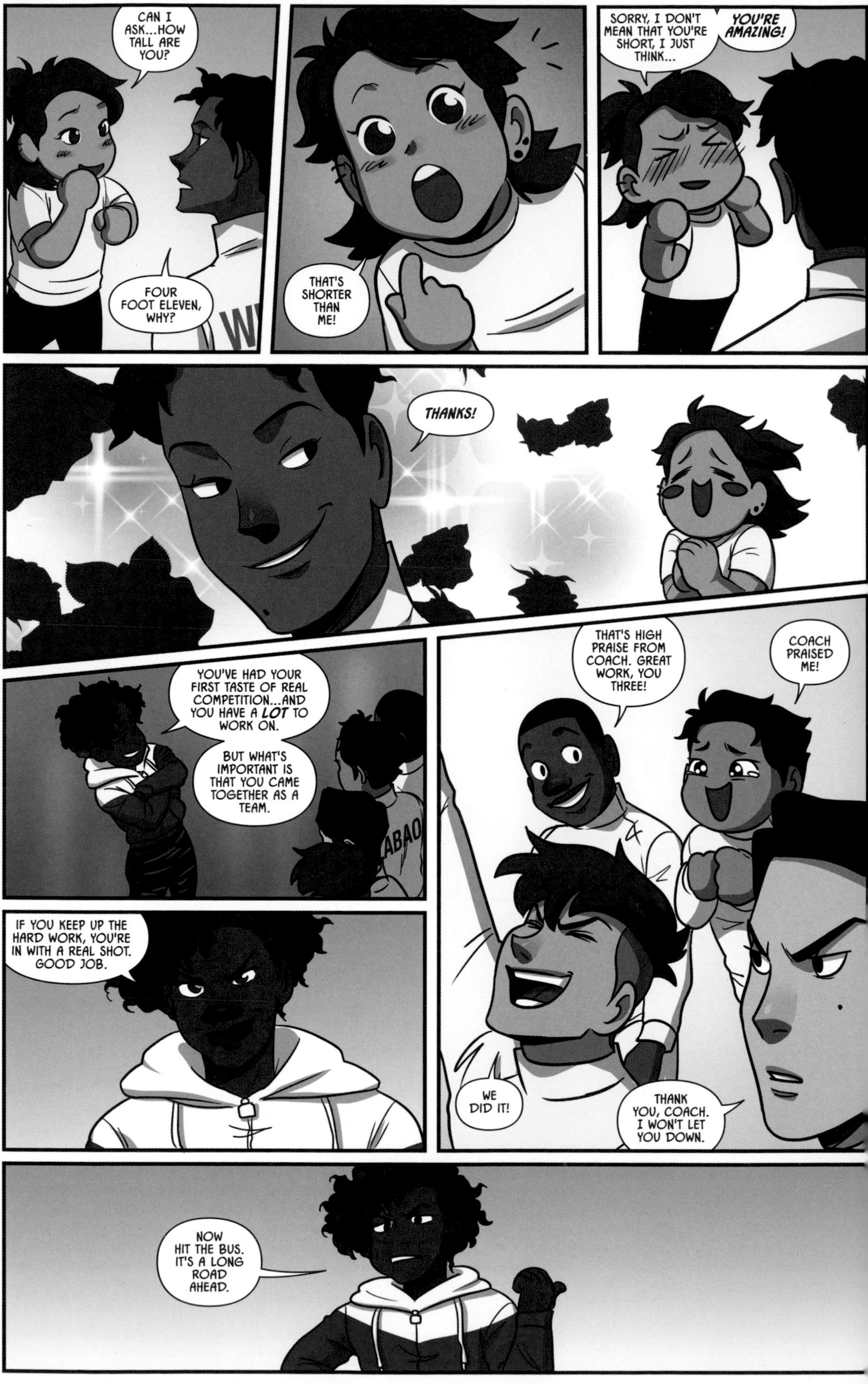
CAN I ASK...HOW TALL ARE YOU?
FOUR FOOT ELEVEN, WHY?
THAT'S SHORTER THAN ME!
SORRY, I DON'T MEAN THAT YOU'RE SHORT, I JUST THINK...
YOU'RE AMAZING!
THANKS!
YOU'VE HAD YOUR FIRST TASTE OF REAL COMPETITION...AND YOU HAVE A LOT TO WORK ON.
BUT WHAT'S IMPORTANT IS THAT YOU CAME TOGETHER AS A TEAM.
IF YOU KEEP UP THE HARD WORK, YOU'RE IN WITH A REAL SHOT. GOOD JOB.
THAT'S HIGH PRAISE FROM COACH. GREAT WORK, YOU THREE!
COACH PRAISED ME!
WE DID IT!
THANK YOU, COACH. I WON'T LET YOU DOWN.
NOW HIT THE BUS. IT'S A LONG ROAD AHEAD.

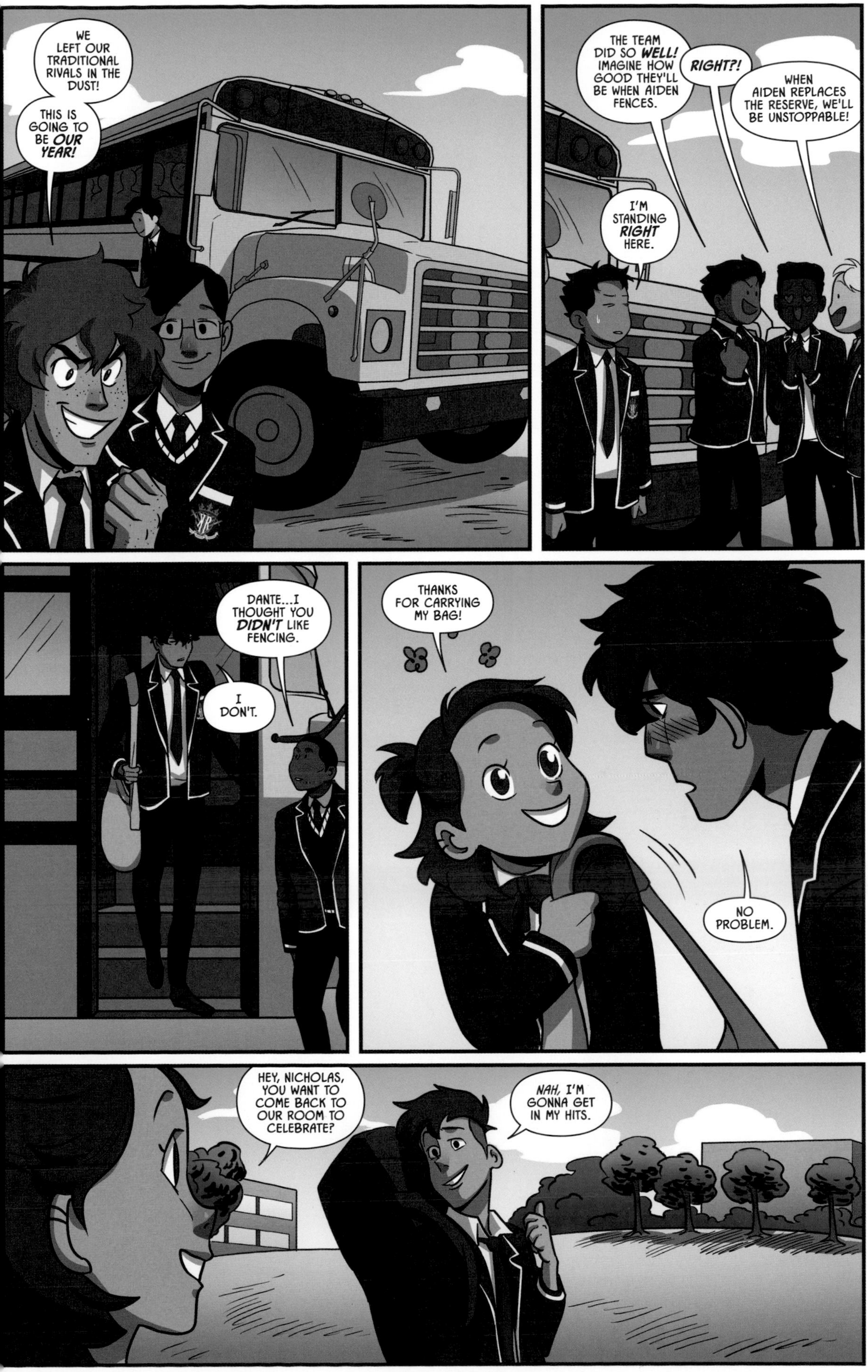
WE LEFT OUR TRADITIONAL RIVALS IN THE DUST!
THIS IS GOING TO BE *OUR YEAR!*
THE TEAM DID SO **WELL!** IMAGINE HOW GOOD THEY'LL BE WHEN AIDEN FENCES.
RIGHT?!
WHEN AIDEN REPLACES THE RESERVE, WE'LL BE UNSTOPPABLE!
I'M STANDING ***RIGHT*** HERE.
DANTE...I THOUGHT YOU ***DIDN'T*** LIKE FENCING.
I DON'T.
THANKS FOR CARRYING MY BAG!
NO PROBLEM.
HEY, NICHOLAS, YOU WANT TO COME BACK TO OUR ROOM TO CELEBRATE?
NAH, I'M GONNA GET IN MY HITS.

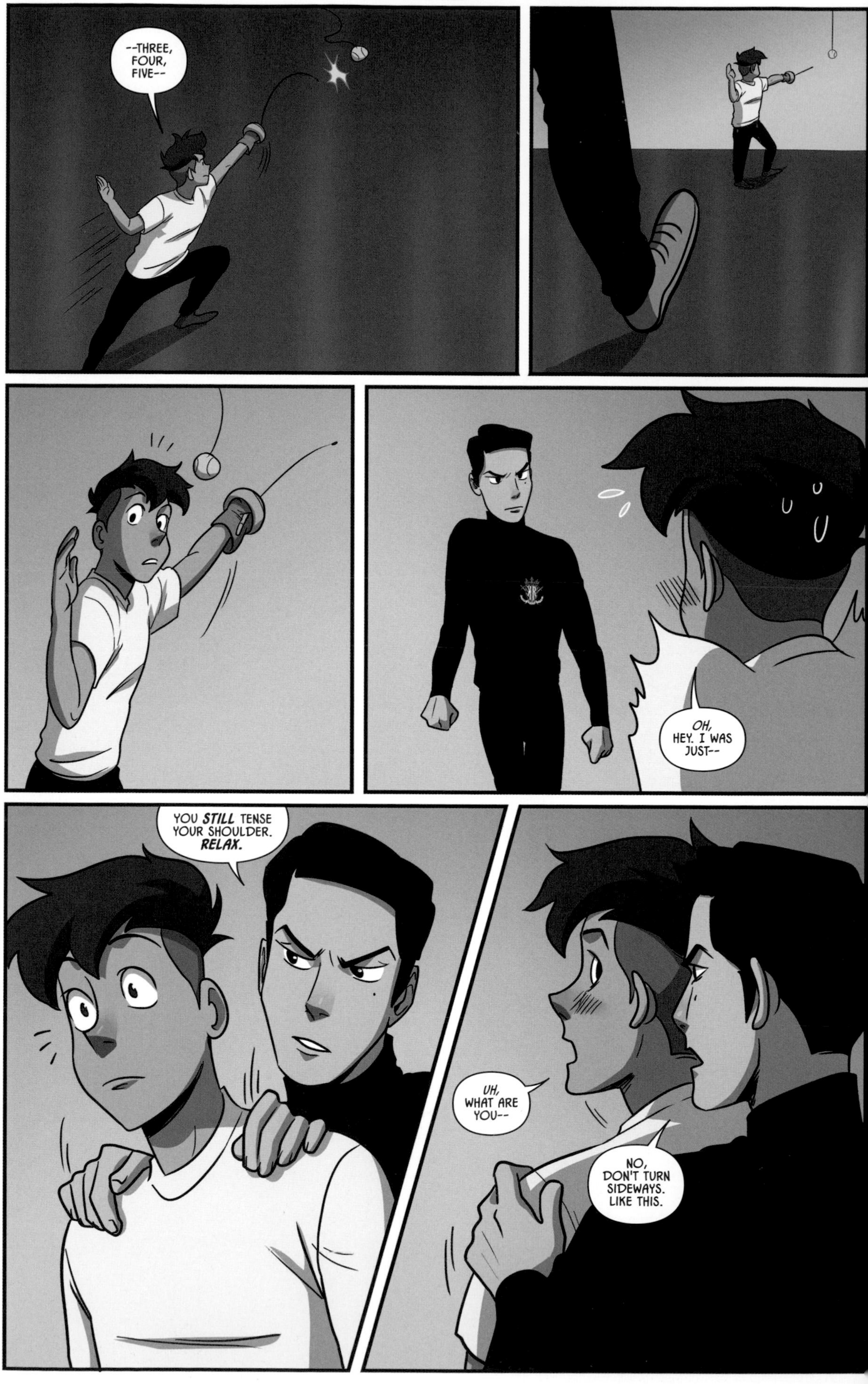
--THREE, FOUR, FIVE--
OH, HEY. I WAS JUST--
YOU **STILL** TENSE YOUR SHOULDER. ***RELAX.***
UH, WHAT ARE YOU--
NO, DON'T TURN SIDEWAYS. LIKE THIS.

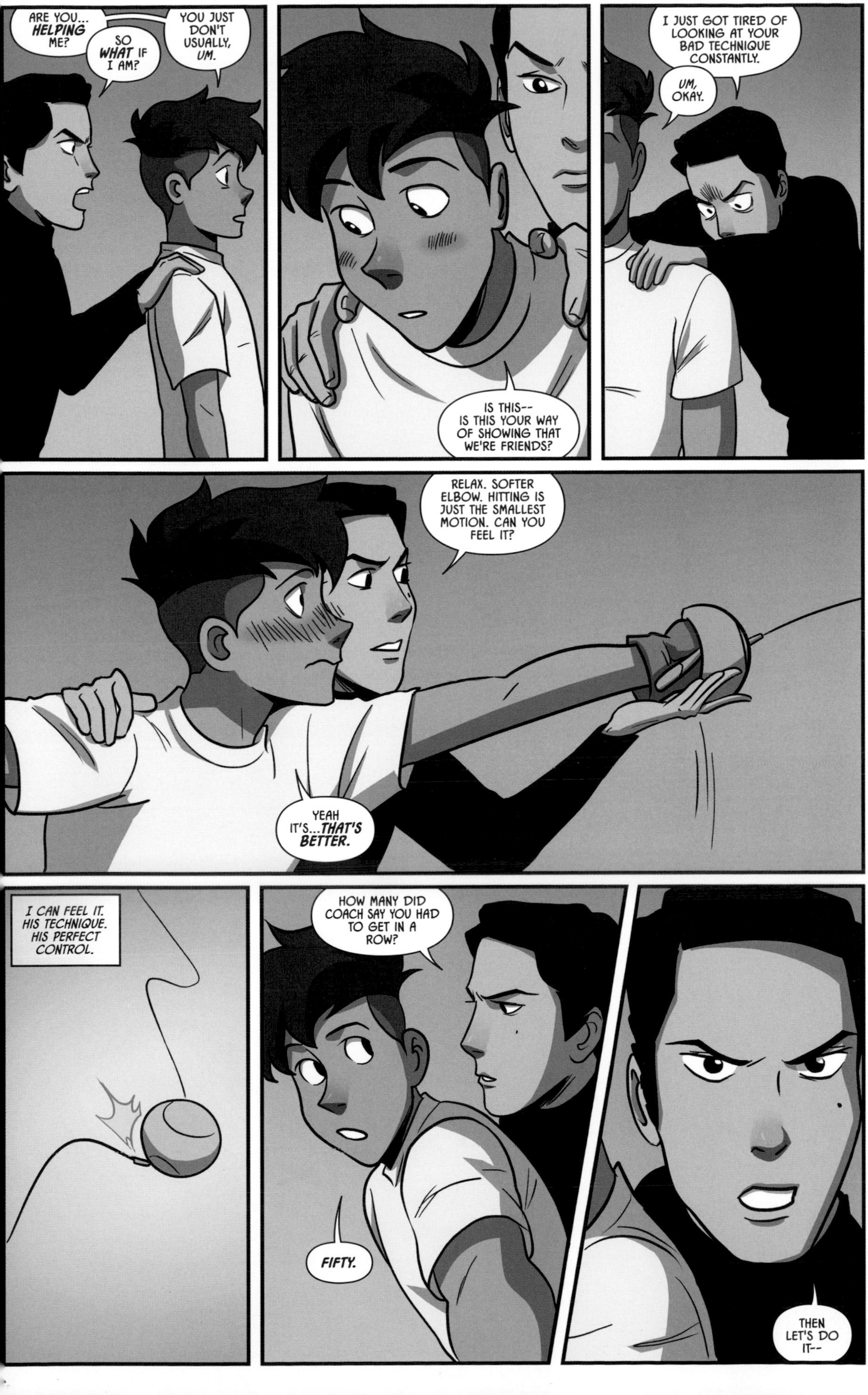
ARE YOU... **HELPING** ME?
SO **WHAT** IF I AM?
YOU JUST DON'T USUALLY, UM.
IS THIS-- IS THIS YOUR WAY OF SHOWING THAT WE'RE FRIENDS?
I JUST GOT TIRED OF LOOKING AT YOUR BAD TECHNIQUE CONSTANTLY.
UM, OKAY.
RELAX. SOFTER ELBOW. HITTING IS JUST THE SMALLEST MOTION. CAN YOU FEEL IT?
YEAH IT'S...**THAT'S BETTER.**
I CAN FEEL IT. HIS TECHNIQUE. HIS PERFECT CONTROL.
HOW MANY DID COACH SAY YOU HAD TO GET IN A ROW?
FIFTY.
THEN LET'S DO IT--

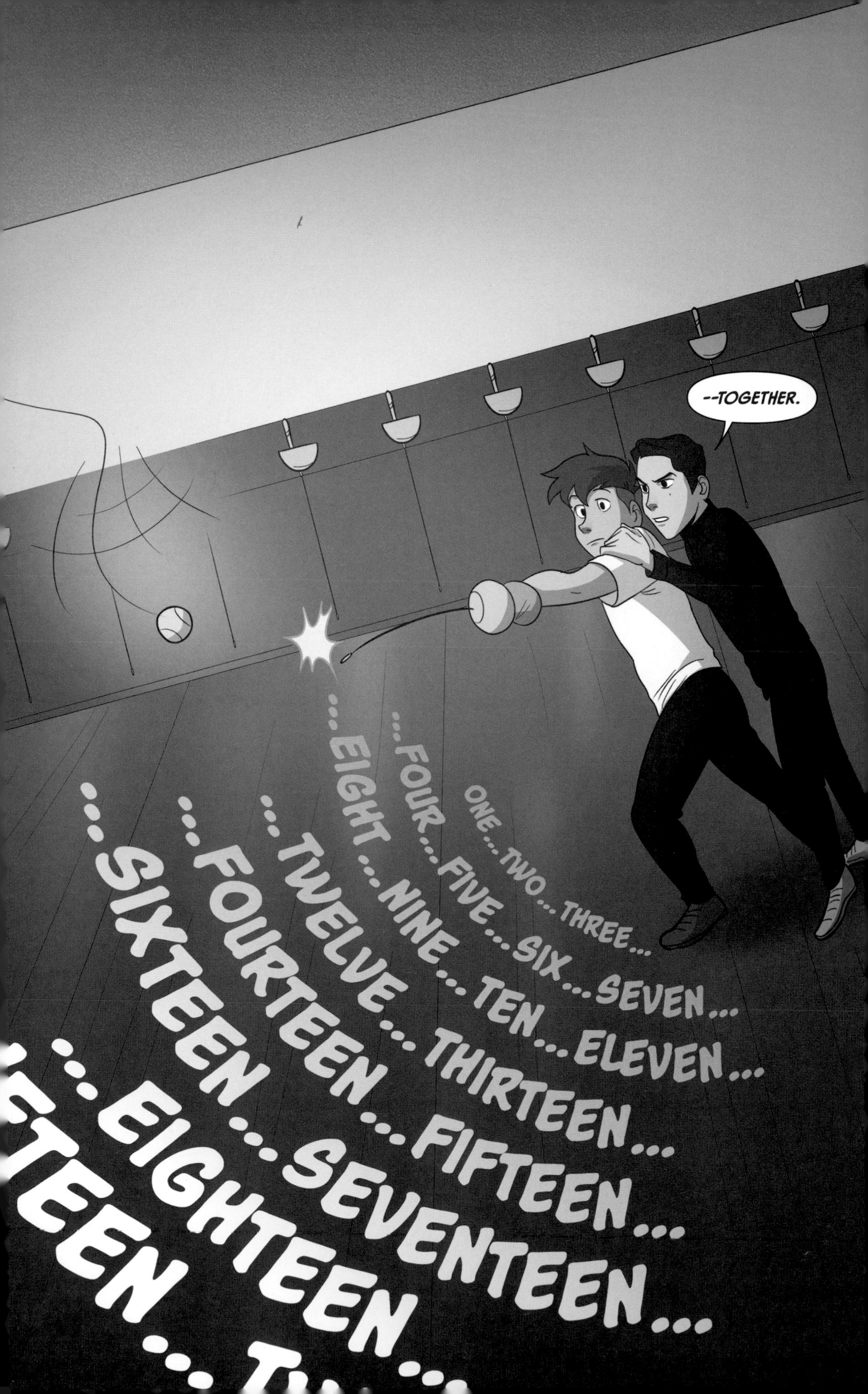
--TOGETHER.
ONE...TWO...THREE...
...FOUR...FIVE...SIX...SEVEN...
...EIGHT...NINE...TEN...ELEVEN...
...TWELVE...THIRTEEN...
...FOURTEEN...FIFTEEN...
...SIXTEEN...SEVENTEEN...
...EIGHTEEN...
TEEN...

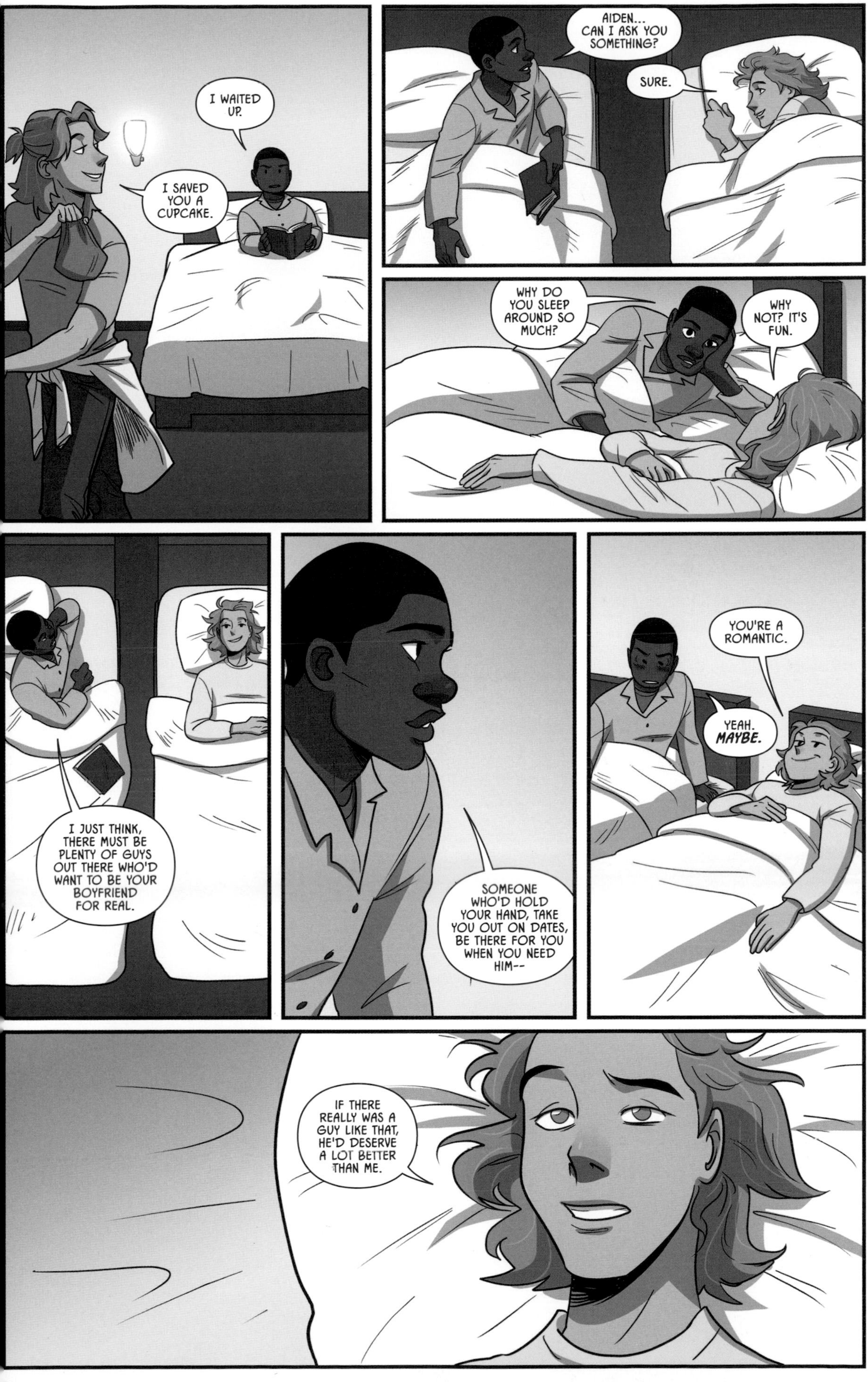
I WAITED UP.
I SAVED YOU A CUPCAKE.
AIDEN... CAN I ASK YOU SOMETHING?
SURE.
WHY DO YOU SLEEP AROUND SO MUCH?
WHY NOT? IT'S FUN.
I JUST THINK, THERE MUST BE PLENTY OF GUYS OUT THERE WHO'D WANT TO BE YOUR BOYFRIEND FOR REAL.
SOMEONE WHO'D HOLD YOUR HAND, TAKE YOU OUT ON DATES, BE THERE FOR YOU WHEN YOU NEED HIM--
YOU'RE A ROMANTIC.
YEAH. ***MAYBE.***
IF THERE REALLY WAS A GUY LIKE THAT, HE'D DESERVE A LOT BETTER THAN ME.

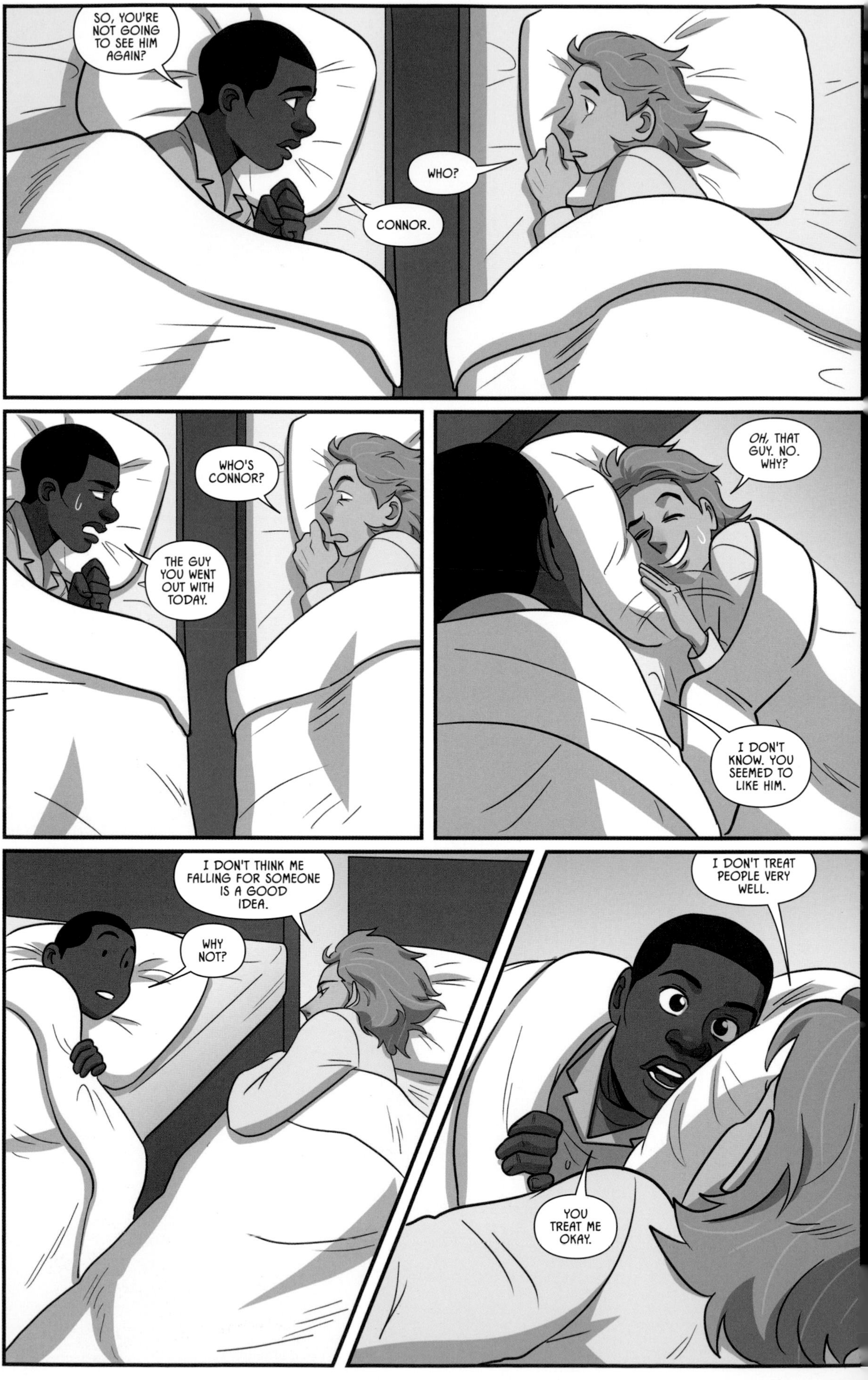
SO, YOU'RE NOT GOING TO SEE HIM AGAIN?
WHO?
CONNOR.
WHO'S CONNOR?
THE GUY YOU WENT OUT WITH TODAY.
OH, THAT GUY. NO. WHY?
I DON'T KNOW. YOU SEEMED TO LIKE HIM.
I DON'T THINK ME FALLING FOR SOMEONE IS A GOOD IDEA.
WHY NOT?
I DON'T TREAT PEOPLE VERY WELL.
YOU TREAT ME OKAY.

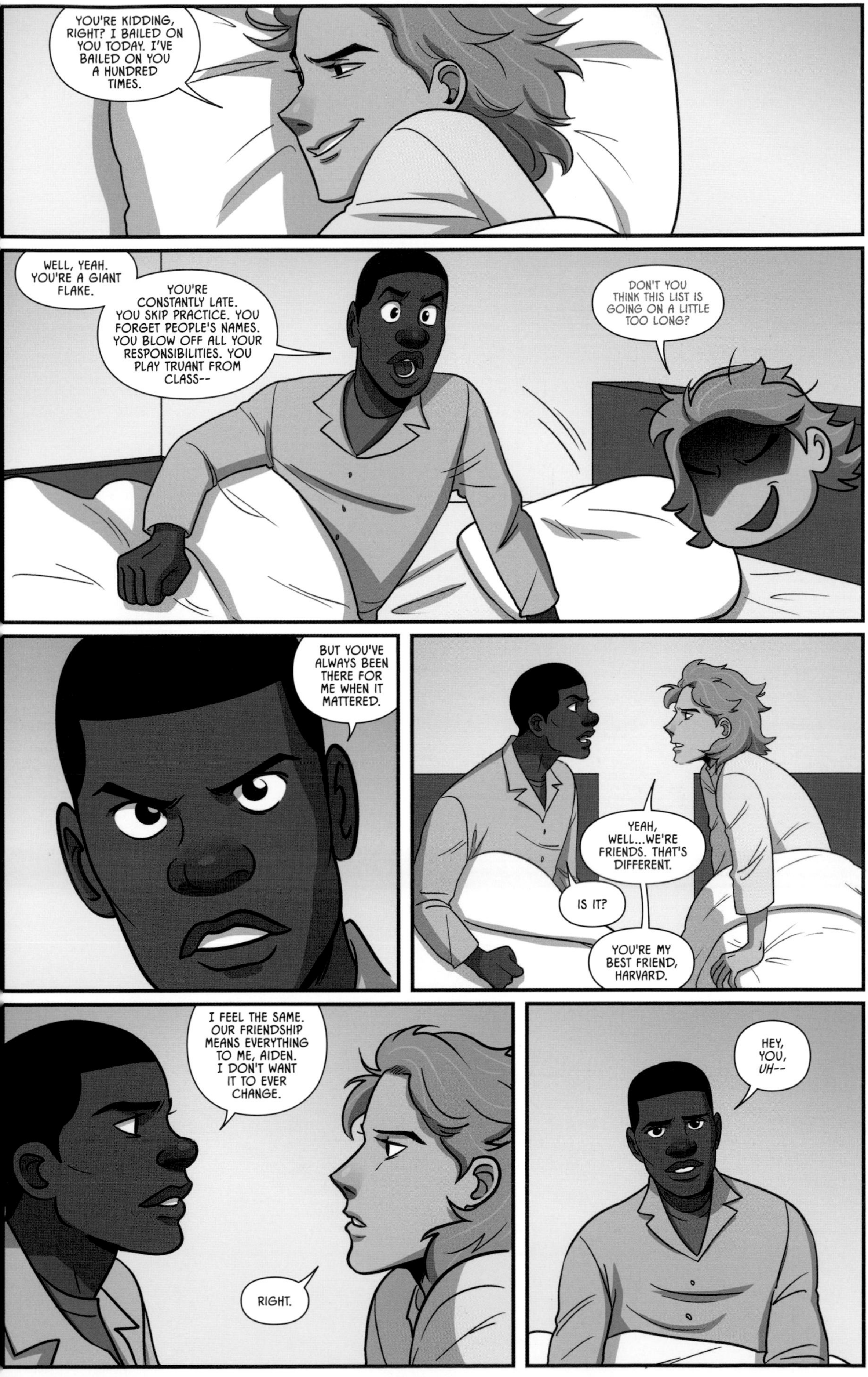
YOU'RE KIDDING, RIGHT? I BAILED ON YOU TODAY. I'VE BAILED ON YOU A HUNDRED TIMES.
WELL, YEAH. YOU'RE A GIANT FLAKE.
YOU'RE CONSTANTLY LATE. YOU SKIP PRACTICE. YOU FORGET PEOPLE'S NAMES. YOU BLOW OFF ALL YOUR RESPONSIBILITIES. YOU PLAY TRUANT FROM CLASS--
DON'T YOU THINK THIS LIST IS GOING ON A LITTLE TOO LONG?
BUT YOU'VE ALWAYS BEEN THERE FOR ME WHEN IT MATTERED.
YEAH, WELL...WE'RE FRIENDS. THAT'S DIFFERENT.
IS IT?
YOU'RE MY BEST FRIEND, HARVARD.
I FEEL THE SAME. OUR FRIENDSHIP MEANS EVERYTHING TO ME, AIDEN. I DON'T WANT IT TO EVER CHANGE.
RIGHT.
HEY, YOU, *UH--*

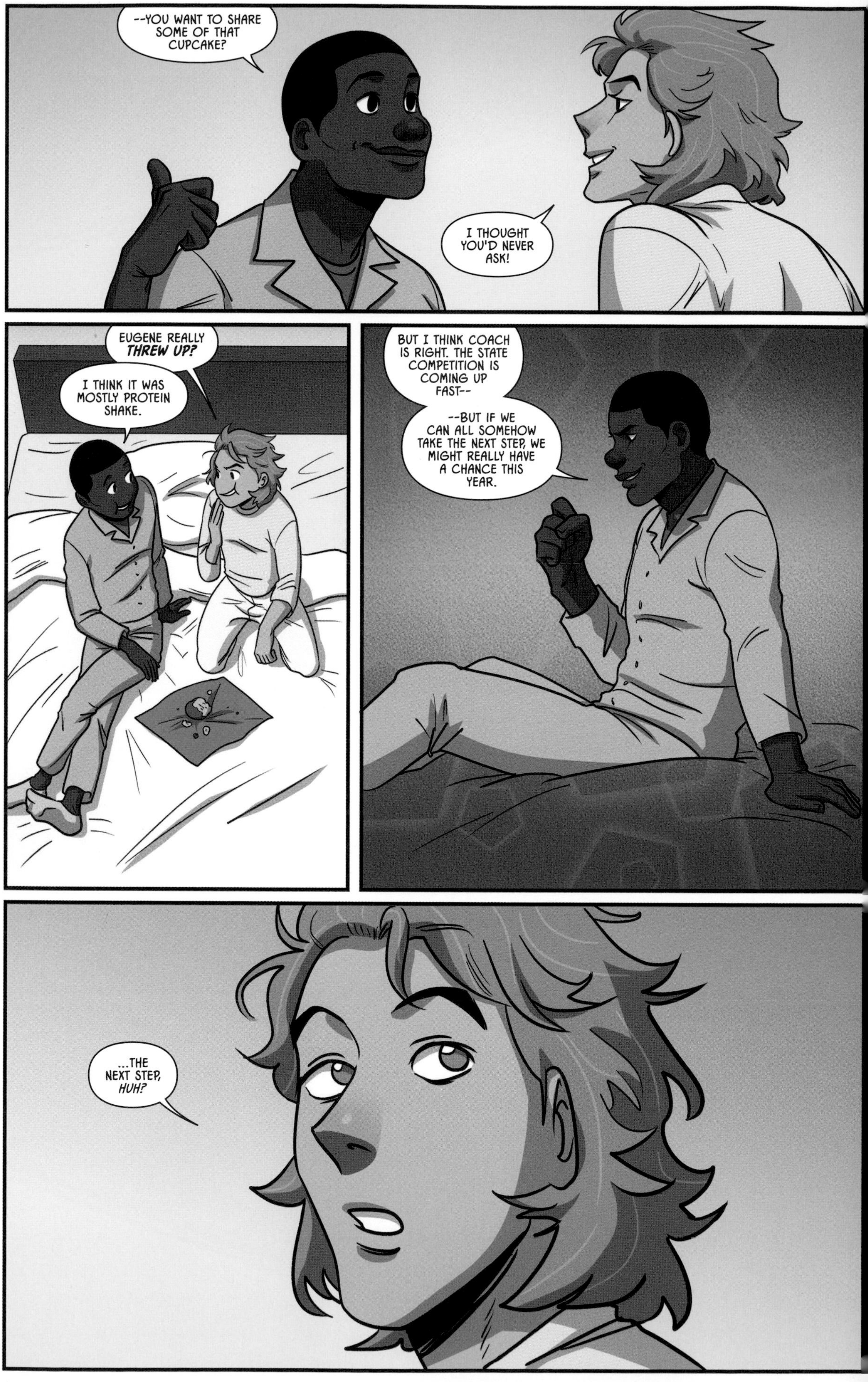
--YOU WANT TO SHARE SOME OF THAT CUPCAKE?
I THOUGHT YOU'D NEVER ASK!
EUGENE REALLY *THREW UP?*
I THINK IT WAS MOSTLY PROTEIN SHAKE.
BUT I THINK COACH IS RIGHT. THE STATE COMPETITION IS COMING UP FAST--
--BUT IF WE CAN ALL SOMEHOW TAKE THE NEXT STEP, WE MIGHT REALLY HAVE A CHANCE THIS YEAR.
...THE NEXT STEP, *HUH?*

BEHIND THE
SCENES

SEIJI

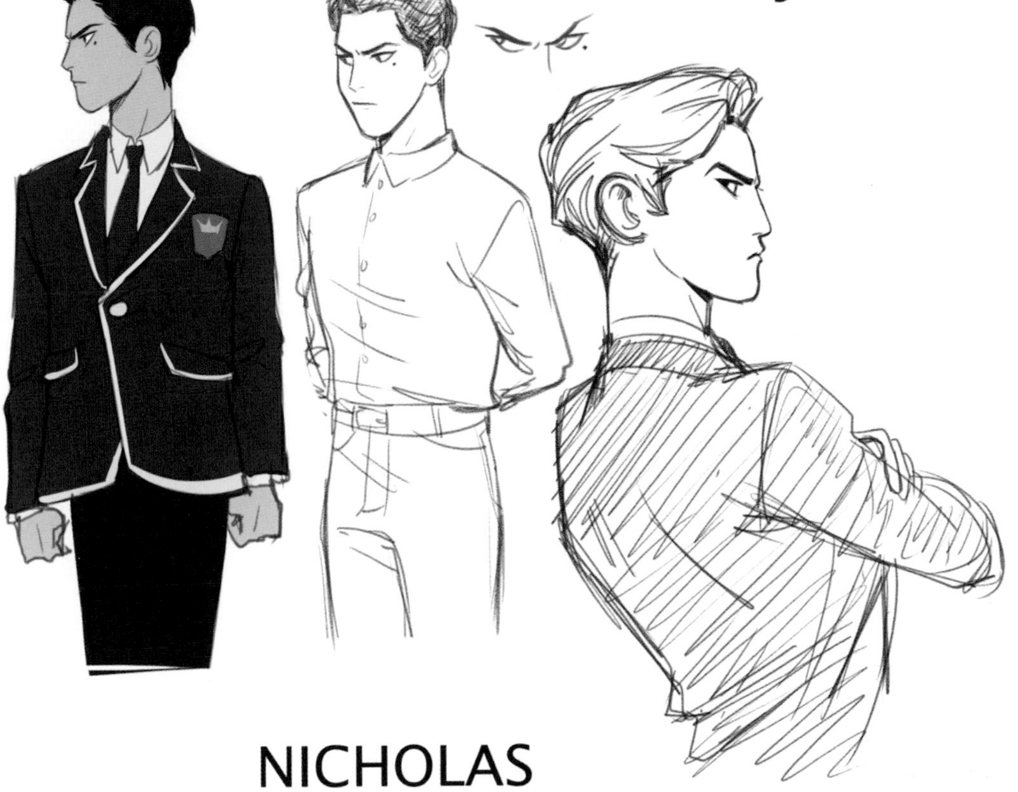

NICHOLAS

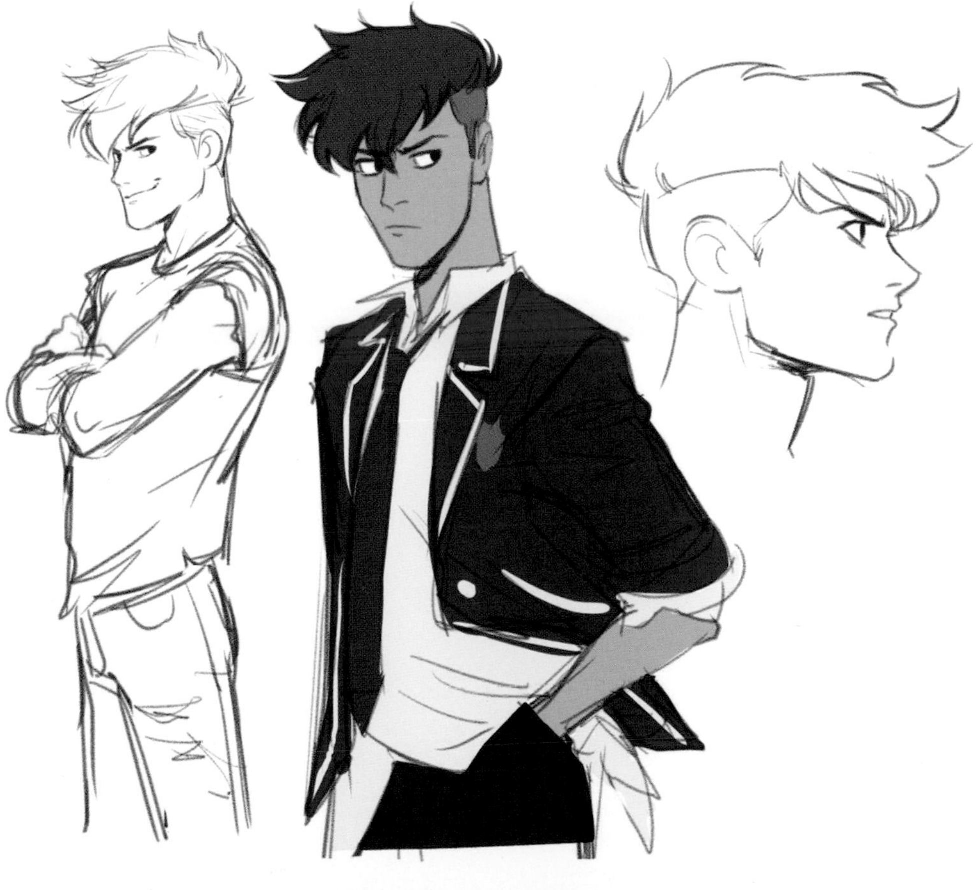

CHARACTER DESIGNS BY **JOHANNA THE MAD**

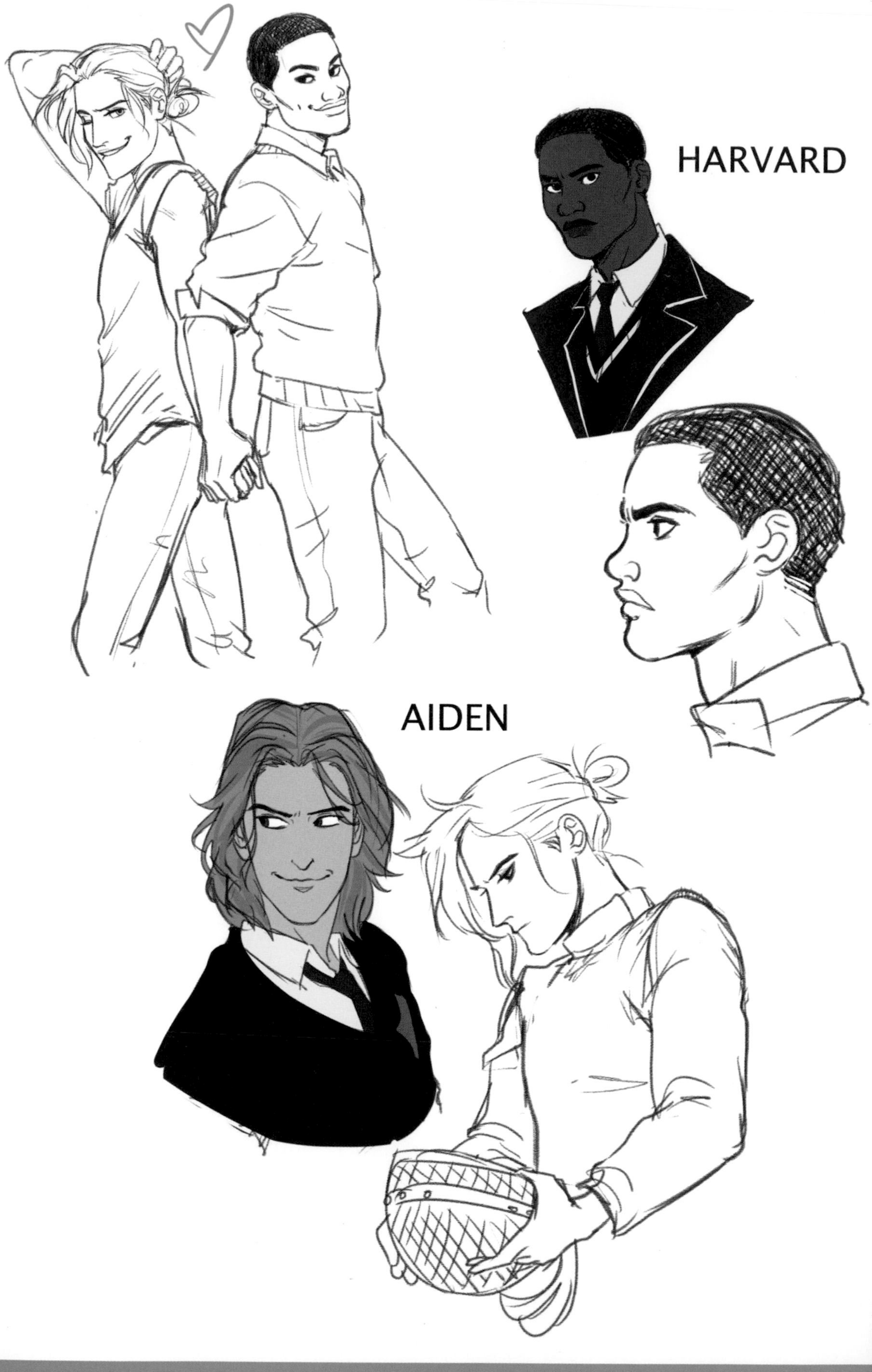
HARVARD
AIDEN

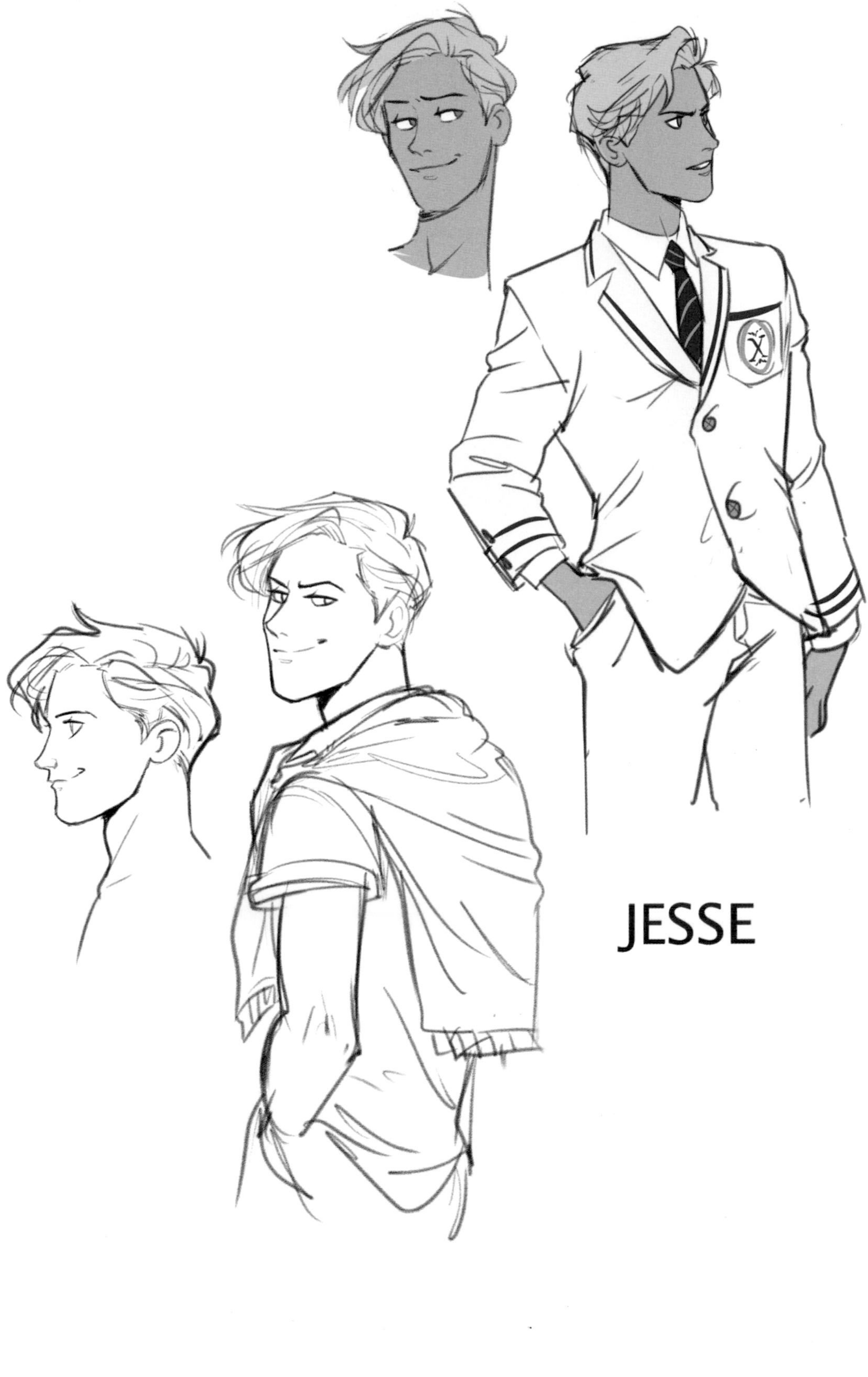

JESSE

HARTLEY

FEDOR

ARUNE

CHARACTER DESIGNS BY **JOHANNA THE MAD**

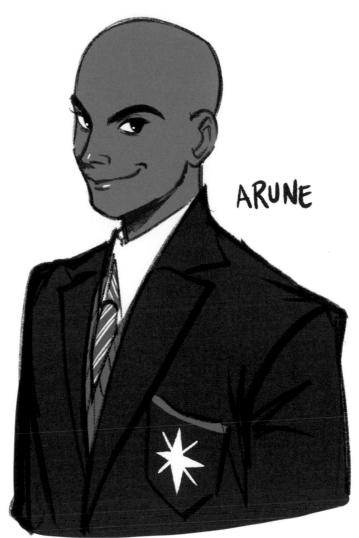

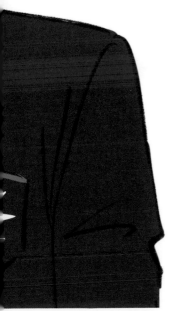

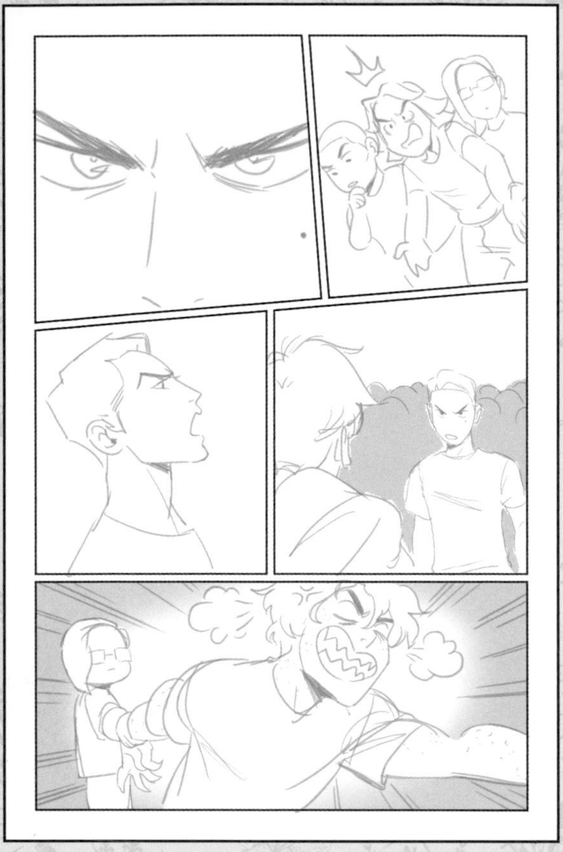
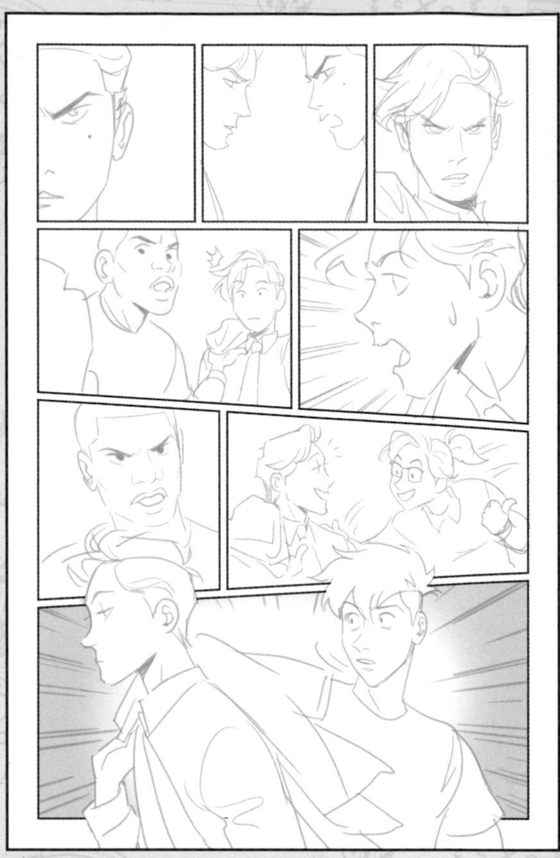
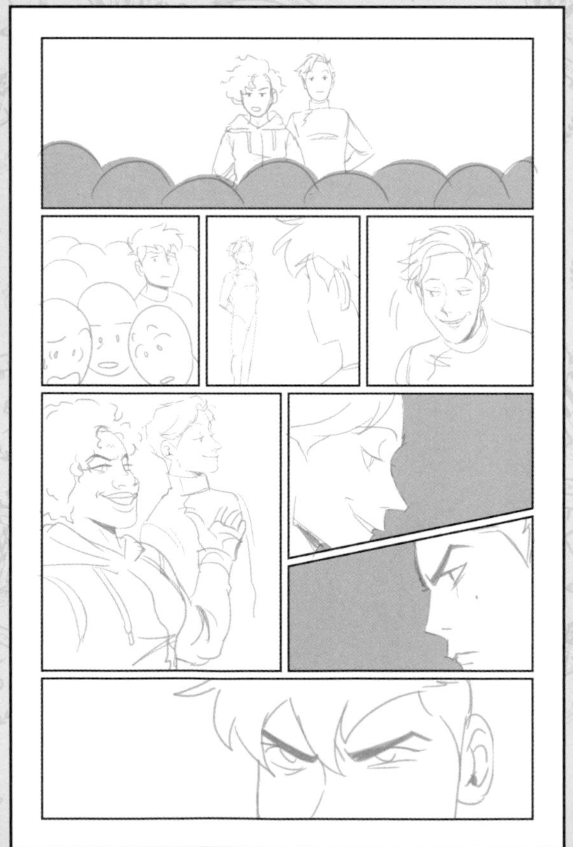
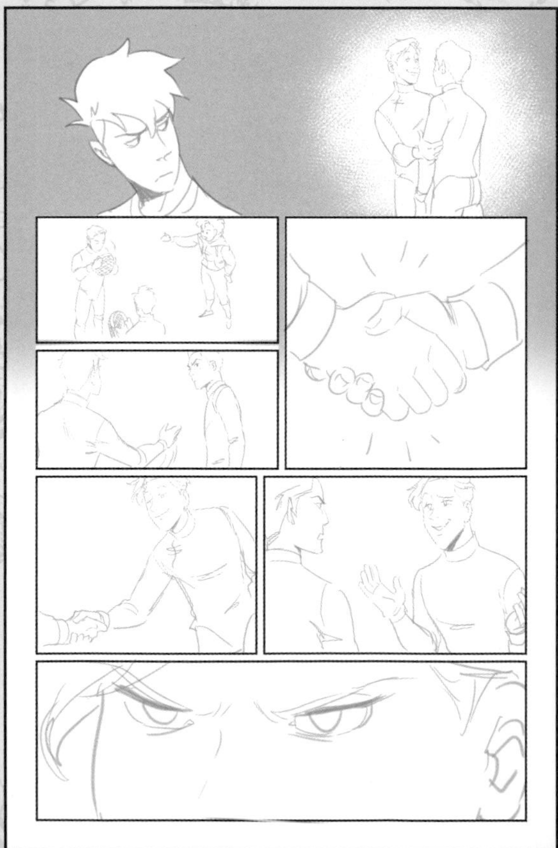

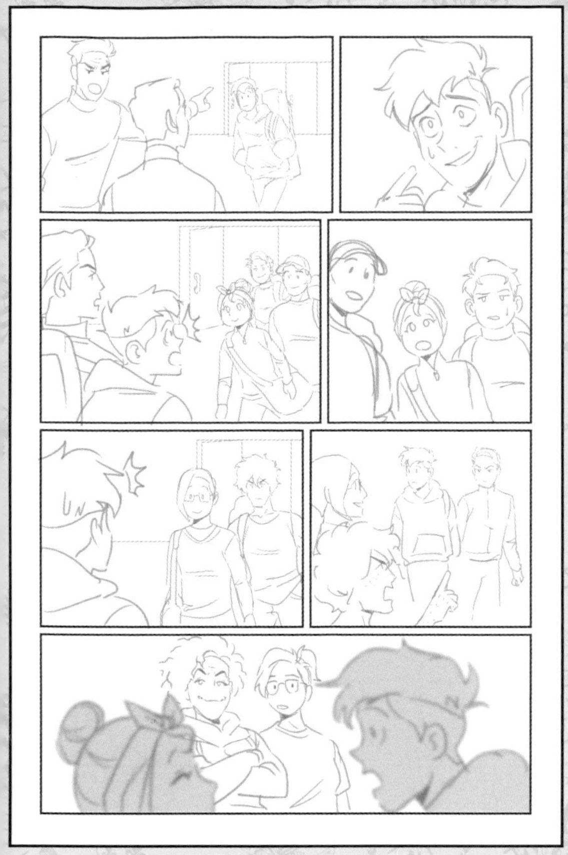

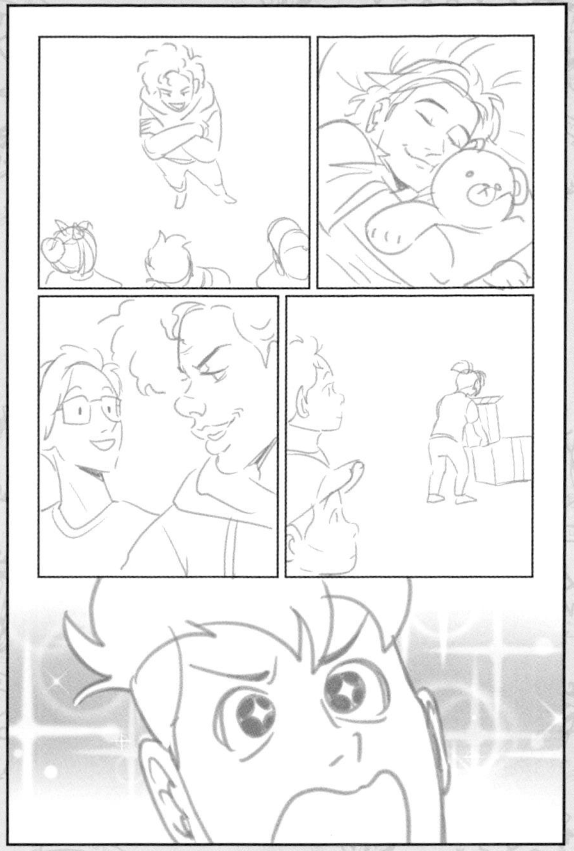

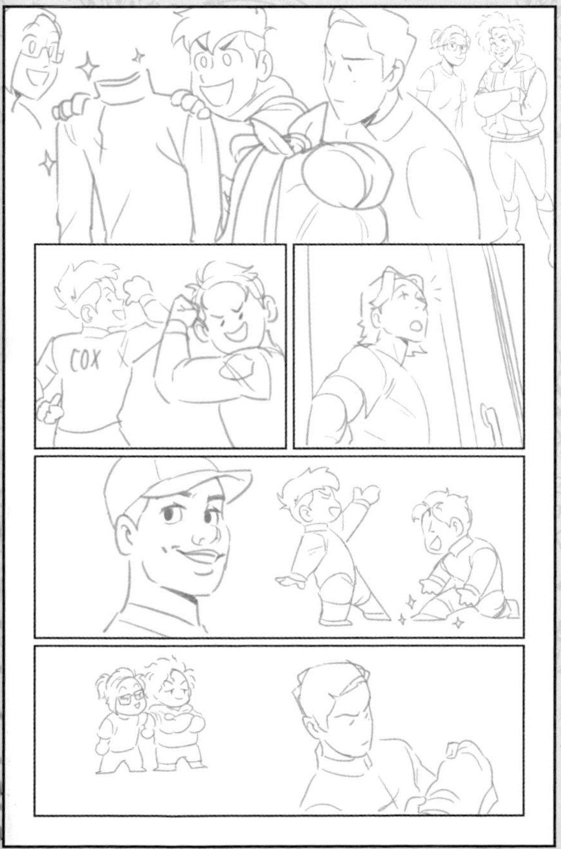
COX

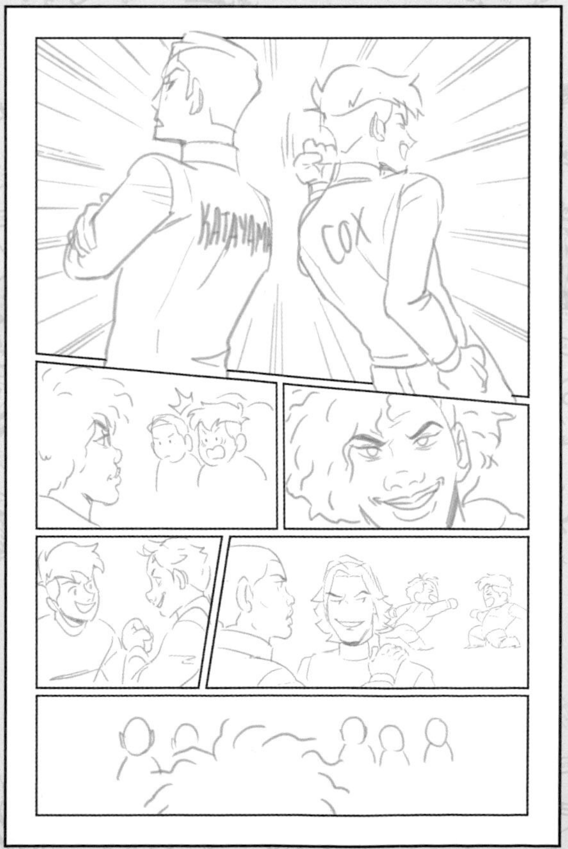
KATAYAMA
COX

PENCILS BY **JOHANNA THE MAD**

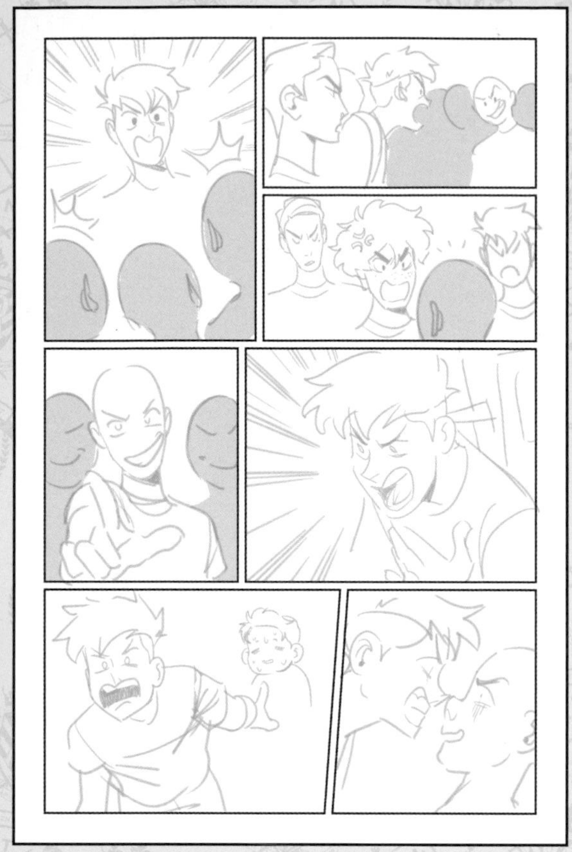

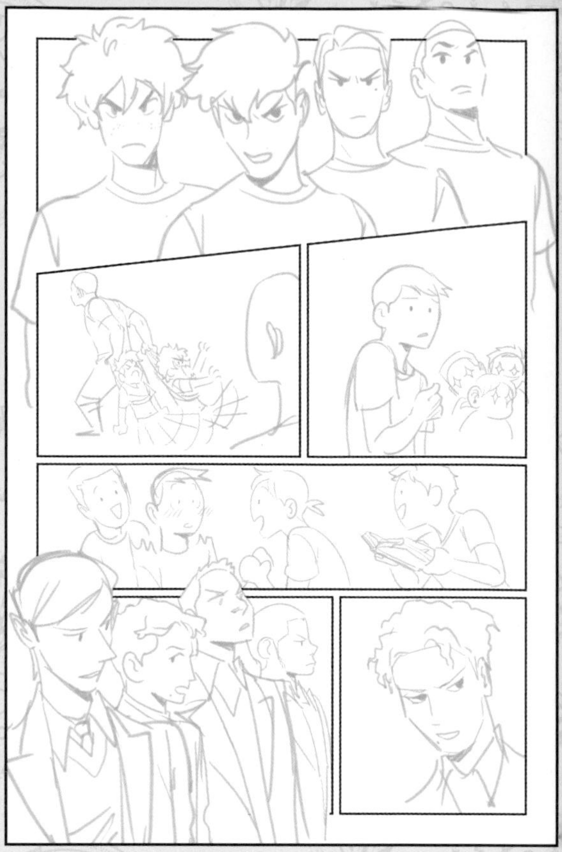

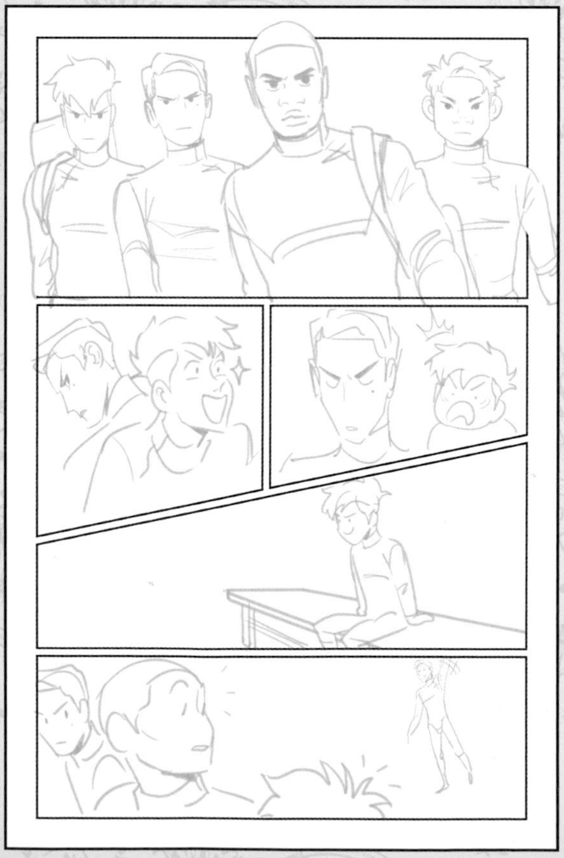

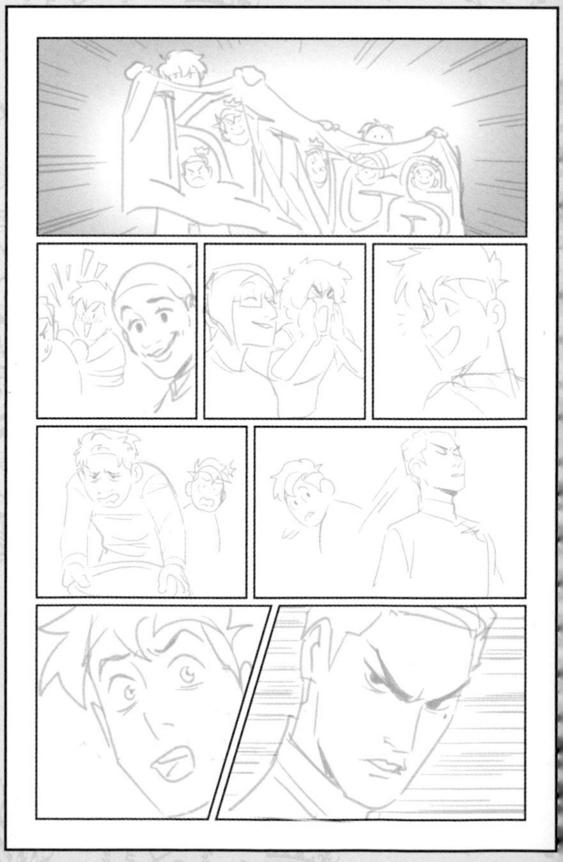
KINGS

FAKE DATING.
REAL SWORDS.

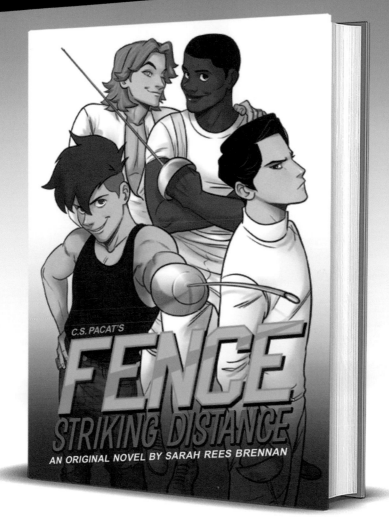

An original novel based on the C.S. Pacat series

Bestselling author Sarah Rees Brennan
brings the boys of Kings Row to life
in the first-ever Fence novel,
featuring art by Johanna The Mad

 thenovl.com/fence

DISCOVER
ALL THE HITS

STEVENSON • ELLIS • WATTERS • ALLEN
LUMBERJANES
BEWARE THE KITTEN HOLY
NEW YORK TIMES
BESTSELLING SERIES

Allison + Treiman + Cogar
GIANT
DAYS
VOLUME ONE

From a writer of Disney's Moana
RIBON • FISH • PEER
SLAM!
VOLUME ONE

Hope Larson • Brittney Williams • Sarah Stern
GOLDIE VANCE
"Scoot over Nancy Drew..."
—Los Angeles Times
Volume One

JAMES TYNION IV • RIAN SYGH • WALTER BAIAMONTE
THE BACKSTAGERS

TYSON HESSE'S
DIESEL
IGNITION

BOOM! BOX™

AVAILABLE AT YOUR LOCAL COMICS SHOP AND BOOKSTORE

To find a comics shop in your area, visit www.comicshoplocator.com

WWW.**BOOM-STUDIOS**.COM

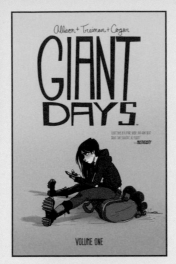

Lumberjanes
Noelle Stevenson, Shannon Watters, Grace Ellis, Brooklyn Allen, and Others
Volume 1: Beware the Kitten Holy
ISBN: 978-1-60886-687-8 | $14.99 US
Volume 2: Friendship to the Max
ISBN: 978-1-60886-737-0 | $14.99 US
Volume 3: A Terrible Plan
ISBN: 978-1-60886-803-2 | $14.99 US
Volume 4: Out of Time
ISBN: 978-1-60886-860-5 | $14.99 US
Volume 5: Band Together
ISBN: 978-1-60886-919-0 | $14.99 US

Giant Days
John Allison, Lissa Treiman, Max Sarin
Volume 1
ISBN: 978-1-60886-789-9 | $9.99 US
Volume 2
ISBN: 978-1-60886-804-9 | $14.99 US
Volume 3
ISBN: 978-1-60886-851-3 | $14.99 US

Jonesy
Sam Humphries, Caitlin Rose Boyle
Volume 1
ISBN: 978-1-60886-883-4 | $9.99 US
Volume 2
ISBN: 978-1-60886-999-2 | $14.99 US

Slam!
Pamela Ribon, Veronica Fish, Brittany Peer
Volume 1
ISBN: 978-1-68415-004-5 | $14.99 US

Goldie Vance
Hope Larson, Brittney Williams
Volume 1
ISBN: 978-1-60886-898-8 | $9.99 US
Volume 2
ISBN: 978-1-60886-974-9 | $14.99 U

The Backstagers
James Tynion IV, Rian Sygh
Volume 1
ISBN: 978-1-60886-993-0 | $14.99

Tyson Hesse's Diesel: Ignition
Tyson Hesse
ISBN: 978-1-60886-907-7 | $14

Coady & The Creepies
Liz Prince, Amanda Kirk, Hannah Fisher
ISBN: 978-1-68415-029-8 | $1